Excel Tables: A Complete Guide for Creating, Using and Automating Lists and Tables

by

Zack Barresse and Kevin Jones

Holy Macro! Books

PO Box 82 Uniontown, OH 44685

Excel Tables: A Complete Guide for Creating, Using and Automating Lists and Tables

Author: Zack Barresse and Kevin Jones

Editor: Kitty Wilson

Layout: Tyler Nash

Published by: Holy Macro! Books, PO Box 82 Uniontown, OH 44685, USA

Printed in USA

First printing: July 2014.

Cover Design: Emily Jones

Indexing: Nellie J. Liwam

ISBN 978-1-61547-028-0 (Print), 978-1-61547-219-2(PDF), 978-1-61547-340-3 (ePub), 978-1-61547-119-5 (Mobi)

Contents

Foreword

Zack and Kevin met for the first time at a Microsoft MVP Summit in 2006. With their mutual respect for each other's skills and talents in place after watching each other post solutions on Experts Exchange, they became friends and eventually started working on projects together. About a year ago Zack approached Kevin with the idea of writing a book about Excel Tables. Kevin, having assisted with the writing of another book with Bill Jelen, Tom Urtis, and Tyler Nash, was eager to work on another, especially with his buddy Zack. Both had been using Tables for a while on various projects and felt that their value was understated and underappreciated. Thus began their journey to bring the simplistic and easy beauty and function of Excel Tables to the rest of us as well as the Excel pros.

Kevin is all about elegance and simplicity. Having worked for all kinds of big and small companies in several different industries, he knows the value of good spreadsheet design. Once he was hooked on the benefit Tables provided, he never wanted to go back. Zack, has always looked for the most efficient method to getting data to just work and look good while doing it. Together they saw a void in the availability of educational material illustrating the power, depth, and value of Excel Tables.

In 2009, Zack was hired by Microsoft to build many of those fancy templates that you see when you click File, New in Excel 2010 and 2013. He was directed by Microsoft to use Tables in each template. So he found himself using Tables a lot over the course of working with hundreds of templates. What he quickly discovered is that Tables really rock! They are brilliant, dynamic, and easy to create and manage.

Why is this book worth it? This book has all the fundamentals for working with Tables effectively and efficiently. Get more work done faster, more efficiently, and have your data looking better than ever before. It's said that less than 1% of all Excel users actually utilize Tables. We've found them to be amazing work horses and have shared that knowledge in this book. Make all your work look like it was implemented by a pro: dominate Excel Tables like a boss! Everyone who picks up this book will learn something, whether you're a beginner in Excel or a seasoned guru. Wherever you stand on the Excel learning curve, this book has something for you!

Here are seven reasons why you will love tables:

- They make formatting your Excel spreadsheets easy and make your data look absolutely amazing. For more on formatting, see section Table Formatting in Chapter 7.
- They automatically grow when you append new data, making them brilliant data sources for PivotTables, charts and dynamic lists. For details, see section Table Behavior in Chapter 2.
- They always have a calculated total row with easy-to-change calculations. For more on the total row, see section Referencing Tables in Chapter 4.
- Sorting and filtering always knows where your data is, so no more asking if you want to expand your sort range, and your data always stays together. For more on sorting and filtering, see section Sorting, Filtering, and Using Slicers in Chapter 6.
- Formulas actually make sense when you read them, Excel Tables creates meaningful names with structured referencing. For more on structured references, see Advantage of Structured References in Chapter 4.
- Tables make data validation and dynamic lists simple and easy. For more on dynamic lists, see section Dynamic Referencing in Chapter 4.
- Most external data sources are brought into Excel as a Table. For more on external data, see section Working with External Data in Chapter 8.

For all the good that tables bring, they also have some major annoyances that will bite you if you are not careful. Here are five major gotchas to watch out for:

1. If you stack one table above one another, the lower table has to be within the same columns or narrower than the first. For details, see Table Behavior in Chapter 2.
2. Entering duplicate column header names will automatically change headers without warning. For more on column header names, see section Table Anatomy in Chapter 2.
3. Using absolute standard cell referencing in a Table won't update formulas properly. For more on absolute cell referencing, see section Calculating a Running Total in Chapter 4.
4. Sorting a Table on a protected sheet doesn't always work. For more on sorting a protected Table, see section Sorting in Chapter 6.
5. Converting imported data from a text file into a Table breaks the connection. For more on imported text data, see Working with Data from Text Files in Chapter 8.

Introduction

About This Book

Inspired by the millions of Excel users who often underestimate the power of Tables, this book aims to increase the knowledge and skill levels of everyday Excel heroes, junkies, and anyone else who uses Excel to make their work and personal life more productive. It will help you become more proficient with Excel Tables in their current form. It will also help you learn the strengths and weaknesses of Excel Tables and how you can leverage their functionality to empower a more rich and productive overall experience. This book is written for all skill levels; anyone can benefit from it, from a novice who doesn't know what a Table is to an expert who has experience with formulas and automation using VBA.

At this writing, Office 2013 and Service Pack 1 (SP1) have been released, and the next version of Excel is in development. Excel 2013 is used as the basis for all discussions, images, and examples in this book. Any differences in functionality between Excel 2013 and earlier versions are mentioned where relevant.

Special Elements

In addition to providing information in as short and concise a manner as possible, this book includes many additional tidbits of helpful information. They are presented in highlighted areas labeled NOTE, CAUTION, and TIP.

> ***NOTE***
>
> A note is an interesting side topic that might be of interest but is not pertinent to the current discussion.

> ***CAUTION***
>
> A caution is something you might run into or with which you might have trouble—a caveat or warning about a possible pitfall.

> ***TIP***
>
> A tip calls out a technique or fact that can add to the quality and value of the current discussion but that is not necessary to realize the results being presented.

We captured most images for this book using Excel 2013 on Windows 7, using TechSmith's SnagIt image capturing utility.

Control References

When it introduced Excel 2007, Microsoft also introduced a new menu system called the ribbon. In this book, references to ribbon controls are presented using this syntax:

{CONTEXTUAL TAB} TAB | Group Name | Control | Subcontrol

In this case, *{CONTEXTUAL TAB}* is an optional reference to a contextual ribbon tab that appears when specific objects are selected. For example, when we talk about the *Insert Slicer* button in the *Tools* group on the *DESIGN* tab in the *TABLE TOOLS* contextual tab, we write:

{TABLE TOOLS} DESIGN | Tools | Insert Slicer

These tabs are discussed further in Chapter 2.

Also note that any reference to a control (for example, a menu, submenu, check box, button, radio button, text edit box, gallery) is italicized.

This book references shortcuts and access keys in the following fashion:

ALT+D, F, F

The plus sign (+) indicates a key combination you press at the same time. A comma (,) indicates a separate keypress that follows the preceding combination. So, for example, in the example above, you hold down the ALT key while pressing the D key, release both keys, then press and release the F key, and then press and release the F key to complete the key sequence. (This particular key combination toggles AutoFilter.)

When you're entering shortcuts, Excel displays the available shortcut keys over their respective controls on the ribbon. The next figure illustrates this behavior.

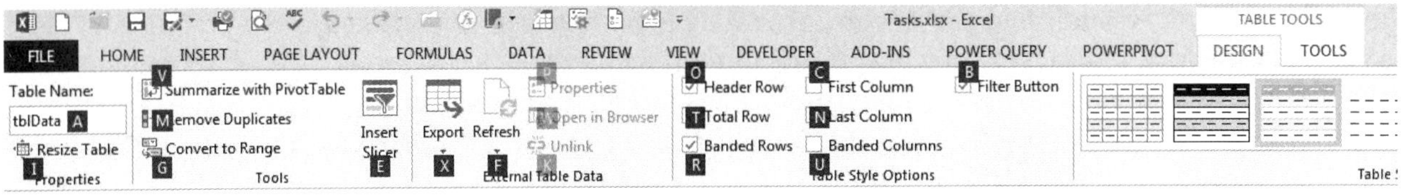

Keyboard shortcuts on the {TABLE TOOLS} DESIGN *tab.*

Occasionally, you'll see two letters displayed over one control. Even though Excel shows these letters together, you press these keys separately. Here's how this book represents such a shortcut:

ALT, JT, A

You enter this keyboard shortcut by pressing and releasing the ALT key, pressing and releasing the J key, pressing and releasing the T key, and pressing and releasing the A key. This shortcut activates the *Table Name* text box control (which you can also access by selecting *{TABLE TOOLS} DESIGN | Properties | Table Name*) and selects the table name text.

> ***TIP***
>
> Any time you're entering a keyboard shortcut sequence, you can press the ESC key to cancel the last keypress. If there are no more keypresses to cancel, ESC cancels the entire sequence and hides the pop-up key codes from view on the ribbon.

The ribbon is dynamic and changes form as its width changes. Therefore, you may occasionally need additional keypresses to complete an action. In such cases, we enclose these optional sequences in curly brackets, like this:

ALT, JT, {ZP}, A

The above sequence will, as in the last example, activate the *Table Name* text box control, but the {ZP} keypresses are needed only if the ribbon is in a collapsed mode and the *Properties* group is displayed as a menu, as shown in the next figure.

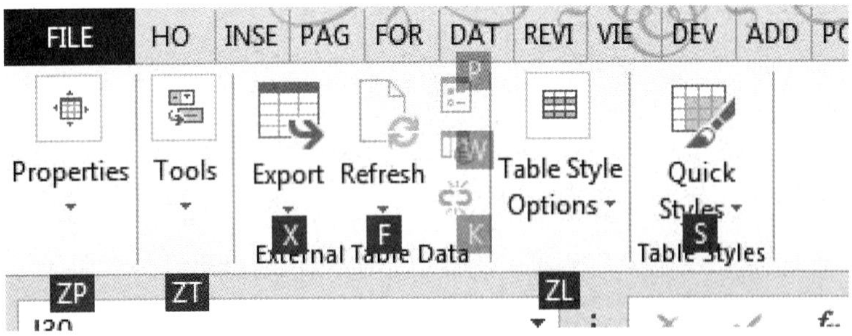

Keyboard shortcuts shown for accessing the Properties group of the {TABLE TOOLS} DESIGN *tab.*

What This Book Does Not Cover

This book is not about Data Tables, which are different from Excel Tables. Data Tables are part of the What-If Analysis functions in Excel, found in *DATA | Data Tools | What-If Analysis | Data Table*. You use them to show how changing one or two variables in a set of related formulas will affect the downstream outcome. The classic example of using Data Tables is to determine possible monthly payment amounts for a loan by varying the interest rate and loan term, among other variables. Other What-If Analysis options are Scenarios and Goal Seek.

Give Us Your Feedback

Knowledge is a shared collection of information. In this book, we've written about what we have learned from Microsoft, our peers, and our customers about Excel Tables. We recognize that there are almost always better, more efficient ways of doing things. We'd like you to provide feedback regarding facts and examples presented in this book and to let us know about new ideas and techniques you feel will be of interest to our audience. Send us an email, at feedback@exceltables.com. We want to hear from you!

In addition to creating this book, we have also created a website that complements the book with tips and tricks, pitfalls and bugs, and tools available for download. Visit www.exceltables.com and ask a question about Tables or Excel in general.

Acknowledgements

Zack Barresse

This book would not have been possible if it weren't for the musings and pushing of some important people in my life. Most important of all, my beautiful wife Skye, for being my sounding board, voice of reason, and best friend. All of my family and friends who had faith in me, and kept my drive. You know who you are, and I humbly say thank you for being you.

Bill Jelen, for being a mad man and taking this on, but I undoubtedly appreciate it and the tireless and persistent work of him and the rest of his team. Without them, this book would never have materialized.

I would be remiss if I didn't thank Kevin Jones, my co-author, who has always been a sane sounding board, brilliant Excel pro, and talented writer. This book surely would have been subpar without him.

Kevin Jones

I acknowledge Zack for inviting me to join him on this journey. Co-authoring is, like most other synergistic experiences, a rewarding and fulfilling process. Bill Jelen for letting us into his club of Excel authors and wizards. A final thank you to Chris "Smitty" Smith for letting me have Zack for the time it took to write this book.

Thank You

The following people supported our effort by letting us use their sample data, link to their websites, reference their books, and use their methodologies:

- Jon Acampora
- Dan Battagin
- Debra Dalgleish
- Rob Collie
- Bob Umlas
- Max Wikstr

About the Authors

Zack Barresse

Zack started using Excel in December 2003, and he quickly fell in love and had a strong desire to learn more. He has contributing to the online community since 2004, and he has been awarded the Microsoft

MVP award every year since his first one in October 2005. For 15 years he served in emergency services, holding positions of volunteer and career firefighter, as well as working in EMS and HazMat and as a vehicle/machinery rescue technician.

Zack is a full-time consultant, focusing on Excel and related technologies, where he can make people's lives easier and more automated—ranging from custom templates created for Microsoft, to custom-built solutions for mom-and-pop outfits, or solutions for some of the world's largest corporations. He has been a technical editor for *The Missing Manual* series of Excel books (O'Reilly Publishing) for the 2007, 2010, and 2013 editions.

In any downtime, Zack can usually be found playing Xbox, fulfilling his love of movies on the big screen, or helping people on various help forums. He lives in Oregon with his family.

Kevin Jones

Kevin is an accomplished user interface and software architecture designer with over 30 years of experience in the technology industry. He has been instrumental in the development of a variety of successful software applications on many different platforms and environments. Kevin has a broad range of skills ideally suited to an entrepreneurial environment, including the ability to both understand and work with information technology while communicating and collaborating with marketing and senior management on product strategies and plans. His ability to work both internally across functional areas and externally with customers and investors has proven invaluable in establishing leadership positions in the marketplace.

Over the past 12 years, Kevin has been working in a consulting capacity with early-stage companies focused on building software and Internet applications that provide productive and satisfying user experiences in the information services, insurance, healthcare, investment, and personal information management marketplaces. He also consults with larger companies such as Chevron and Gap, helping them build information technology solutions for collecting, analyzing, and reporting data for mission-critical tasks such as planning, forecasting, performance evaluations, and inventory optimization.

In 1996 Kevin helped found Husdwag Communications, Inc., and, as vice president of engineering, designed and developed E-RegCard, a successful electronic registration application and service used by more than 100 companies, including Intel, Disney, Block Financial, Broderbund, Activision, Electronic Arts, Interplay, and The Learning Company. In 2000 the company was sold to NBCi for $8.5 million.

Kevin earned a master's in business administration from the Sloan School at MIT in 1983, with a focus in information systems and graphical user interfaces. He studied computer science at California Polytechnic State University in San Luis Obispo, and he received a bachelor of science degree in computer science in 1979. He has spent time at Apple Computer, Power Up Software, and Air Communications managing, designing, and building successful applications that incorporate innovative and practical user interface designs. Early in his career, Kevin developed a major online banking application that incorporated an innovative state processing methodology to model the movement of paper in a complex office environment. At its peak, the application and its derivatives generated more than half a billion dollars of annual revenue for American Management Systems, a major U.S. consulting company.

1 What Are Tables?

Microsoft Excel is a versatile application that millions use to solve many different kinds of problems and perform everyday tasks. We've seen it used to calculate math problems, evaluate complex choices, and analyze data. It's been used to create grocery lists and manage checkbooks. Some use it to create and manage business plans, generate forecasts, and present performance reports.

One of the most common uses of Excel is to create, maintain, and analyze a simple two-dimensional list—anything from a list of financial transactions to the standings and statistics of the sports teams in a league. You typically create, manage, and analyze data by using a database such as Access or FileMaker, but Excel makes it much easier to handle these tasks. Unlike more database-oriented applications, Excel exposes functionality to analyze a list's data by using sorting, filtering, graphing, and other tools in a more intuitive and flexible fashion, thus making your experience more dynamic and, ultimately, more productive with less effort.

If you have a list of data that has a header row and one or more data rows, you can turn that data into an Excel Table that has additional functionality and rules that help you better manage and analyze the data in the Table. When you identify a list of data as an Excel Table, Excel provides tools to, among other things, format, sort, and filter the rows of data more easily than if the list of data were not identified as a Table.

> ***NOTE***
>
> It is important to note here that the only real difference between a simple list of data and an Excel Table is the designation of that list as being an Excel Table versus not being an Excel Table. Designating a list of data as a Table makes additional Table functionality available. You can convert a list of data into an Excel Table and back to a simple list of data without any loss of data. A simple list and an Excel Table are essentially synonymous from a data values perspective.

Who Uses Tables?

Any list of data that has multiple columns, a header row, and an optional total row at the bottom is an excellent candidate for Excel Table designation. Excel Tables are versatile and useful to anyone using spreadsheets to maintain lists of data. Identifying a list of data on a worksheet as an Excel Table instantly adds both additional functionality for maintenance and analysis as well as rules to help keep the data organized and clean. The fact that you can convert a list of data into an Excel Table and back into a simple list of data without any loss of data makes trying out Tables a very easy proposition.

If you're importing data from an external source such as an online analytical processing (OLAP) cube, the default destination is an Excel Table. If you're using one of the newer business intelligence (BI) tools like Power Query, the results of queries are placed in Excel Tables. In essence, Microsoft realizes the universal appeal of a robust table function and is leveraging Excel Tables as much as possible and wherever that kind of functionality makes sense.

Why Use Tables?

Tables don't overwrite existing data or create new data. An Excel Table encapsulates data, extends functionality and visual appearance, and enables faster implementation of solutions. Some of the advantages include:

- Data is structured in rows and columns, without spaces.
- New rows inserted into the Table are automatically formatted the same as the other rows.
- Changes to formulas and formatting in a cell are automatically applied to the entire column.

- An optional total row can be displayed, and each column's "total" value can be any of a number of different aggregate functions.
- Special Table formatting styles instantly format an entire Table with banded rows and/or columns.

These dynamic features and many others are readily available with Excel Tables and are covered in this book.

History of Tables

Excel 2003 introduced the concept of "Lists," which had limited functionality. With Lists, even though a lot of the currently available Excel Tables functionality was available in one form or another (sorting, filtering, formatting), it was not presented as part of the List itself and therefore was rather elusive for the average Excel user.

Excel 2007 redefined Lists as Excel Tables. Microsoft rethought how Tables could be most effectively used and put significant effort into this redesign. Not only did Tables become more user friendly, they became much more prominent in Excel's user experience model: They became the default downstream presentation form for OLAP cube queries and Power Query.

Microsoft continues to provide new functionality and refinements in Tables. Excel 2013 includes a number of changes and additions to Tables, as described in this book. Tables have become a mainstay in many versions of Excel, from the desktop version to Excel Online (the browser-based, free version of Excel). Excel Tables are here for the long term.

2 Table Behavior and Anatomy

In this chapter we discuss Table anatomy and behavior—the cornerstones in working with Tables and the rules every Table adheres to. This chapter also covers naming conventions and compatibility issues. Not all versions of Excel are the same, so this chapter explains things you should be aware of in the various versions.

Table Anatomy

There are three main parts to an Excel Table: the header row, the data body range, and the total row. Together they represent the entire Table. The following sections discuss these three parts. The following sections also cover calculated columns and the sizing handle.

The Header Row

The header row is the topmost row of a Table. You can optionally hide it from view, but the default is for the header row to be visible. The value in the header row for a column defines that column's name, which is also called the **field name**. To maintain consistency and allow advanced formula references (structured references), all header row values must be constants and not formulas. If a header can be changed in the course of working with that Table, you can use a validation list to present the user with a list of possible header values. When a header is changed, all formula references to that column are automatically adjusted.

In addition to defining the column or field names, the header row is used to display a **filter button** (a downward-pointing black triangle) over each column. When you click the filter button, Excel opens a dialog that presents many options for filtering and sorting the Table using that column. The next figure highlights the header row and filter buttons in a Table.

OrderDate	Region	Rep	Item	Units	Cost	Total
1/6/2012	East	Jones	Pencil	95	1.99	189.05
1/23/2012	Central	Kivell	Binder	50	19.99	999.5
2/9/2012	Central	Jardine	Pencil	36	4.99	179.64
2/26/2012	Central	Gill	Pen	27	19.99	539.73
9/27/2013	West	Sorvino	Pen	76	1.99	151.24
10/14/2013	West	Thompson	Binder	57	19.99	1,139.43
10/31/2013	Central	Andrews	Pencil	14	1.29	18.06
11/17/2013	Central	Jardine	Binder	11	4.99	54.89
12/4/2013	Central	Jardine	Binder	94	19.99	1,879.06
12/21/2013	Central	Andrews	Binder	28	4.99	139.72
Total						**5290.32**

The header row of a Table.

Table header values must be unique within a Table. When you enter a header value that is the same as another header in the same Table, Excel appends a number to the end of the rightmost header value to make it unique. For example, if there is a column with the header "ID", if you enter "ID" into another column to the left of the existing value, the rightmost header value, the original "ID", changes to "ID2". If instead you enter the new "ID" to the right of the existing "ID" header, Excel changes the new header to "ID2".

> ***TIP***
>
> Formulas aren't allowed in the header row. However, you can get around this limitation. To use formulas in place of a Table's header row, you hide the header row and then enter the formulas in the empty row above the Table. Note that you can't display the filter and sort drop-downs without making the Table's header row visible, so this isn't a very practical solution for Tables you're using for analysis that involves heavy sorting and filtering.

The Data Body Range

The data body range is the area of a Table between the header row and the total row, where data is displayed, entered, and maintained. If there is no data, the Table displays one empty row for entering data. The number of rows in a Table's data body range is limited only by the number of rows in a worksheet. The next figure highlights the data body range in a Table.

OrderDate	Region	Rep	Item	Units	Cost	Total
1/6/2012	East	Jones	Pencil	95	1.99	189.05
1/23/2012	Central	Kivell	Binder	50	19.99	999.5
2/9/2012	Central	Jardine	Pencil	36	4.99	179.64
2/26/2012	Central	Gill	Pen	27	19.99	539.73
9/27/2013	West	Sorvino	Pen	76	1.99	151.24
10/14/2013	West	Thompson	Binder	57	19.99	1,139.43
10/31/2013	Central	Andrews	Pencil	14	1.29	18.06
11/17/2013	Central	Jardine	Binder	11	4.99	54.89
12/4/2013	Central	Jardine	Binder	94	19.99	1,879.06
12/21/2013	Central	Andrews	Binder	28	4.99	139.72
Total						**5290.32**

The data body range of a Table.

The Total Row

The total row is the bottom row of a Table. You can optionally show this row, but the default is to hide the total row. When you select a cell in the total row, a drop-down menu control appears; you can click this drop-down to see a list of possible built-in aggregate functions. The functions aggregate only the visible cells in the column directly above the total row. In addition to using the built-in functions, you can enter into any total row cell custom functions that reference any cells inside or outside the Table. The next figure highlights the total row in a Table.

OrderDate	Region	Rep	Item	Units	Cost	Total
1/6/2012	East	Jones	Pencil	95	1.99	189.05
1/23/2012	Central	Kivell	Binder	50	19.99	999.5
2/9/2012	Central	Jardine	Pencil	36	4.99	179.64
2/26/2012	Central	Gill	Pen	27	19.99	539.73
9/27/2013	West	Sorvino	Pen	76	1.99	151.24
10/14/2013	West	Thompson	Binder	57	19.99	1,139.43
10/31/2013	Central	Andrews	Pencil	14	1.29	18.06
11/17/2013	Central	Jardine	Binder	11	4.99	54.89
12/4/2013	Central	Jardine	Binder	94	19.99	1,879.06
12/21/2013	Central	Andrews	Binder	28	4.99	139.72
Total						**5290.32**

The total row in a Table.

> ***NOTE***
>
> You aggregate visible cells by using the SUBTOTAL function, which can aggregate all cells in a range or only the visible cells in a range. This feature is useful when you're filtering rows and want to see the aggregation of only the rows that match the filter criteria. Chapter 4 discusses this feature in more detail.

Calculated Columns

A calculated column is a column that contains a single formula applied to the entire data area part of that column. A column that contains different formulas in different cells is not a calculated column.

In a calculated column, any formula entered is automatically assumed to be the new default formula and is applied to all cells in the data area range of the column. In a column that contains formulas or values but is not a calculated column, entering a formula in any cell changes only that cell's formula. An *AutoCorrect Options* button appears in the bottom-right corner of the cell, with an option to apply the formula to the entire column; you can select this option to enable the calculated column and overwrite everything in the column with the formula you enter.

Excel maintains the formulas in calculated columns and uses them in new rows.

> ***TIP***
>
> There is no easy way to determine whether a column is a true calculated column. The only way we currently know to make this determination is to change a formula in the column and see if Excel presents the *AutoCorrect Options* button. If you change a formula and then see an option to apply the formula to the entire column, select that choice, and the column is then a calculated column.
>
> Excel is smart enough to know whether a formula has actually been changed and when it has just been reentered, so, for the purposes of this tip, you have to change the formula, not just re-enter it.

The Sizing Handle

In the bottom-right corner of a Table is a small icon called the **sizing handle**. This icon both shows where the Table ends and allows you to increase or decrease the Table's range: Just drag the handle.

The sizing handle of a Table. Click and drag it to resize a Table.

> **NOTE**
>
> You can also resize Tables from the ribbon by clicking *{TABLE TOOLS} DESIGN | Properties | Resize Table*. The *Resize Table* dialog appears, and in it you can enter a revised range for the Table.

> **CAUTION**
>
> You can resize Tables only if the worksheet is unprotected.

Table Behavior

Before you create a Table, it is important to understand what works with a Table and what does not. Several limitations affect how Tables appear and how they function. These limitations are in place to support the functionality that Excel's Table functions provide. For example, Excel does not allow you to give two Tables in a workbook the same name, as doing so would prevent you from referencing the Tables within formulas.

Table Limitations

When a list of data is defined as an Excel Table, Excel does not allow that Table to:

- Have headers in more than one row
- Have totals in more than one row
- Include duplicate column header values
- Include multiple-cell array formulas (but single-cell entered array formulas are allowed)
- Have any cells overlap any other Table
- Be named the same as any other Table in the workbook

Excel also does not allow you to save a workbook with any Tables as a shared workbook. However, you can share an Excel Table by using SharePoint.

As long as you follow these rules, Tables behave as any normal range, with a few subtle exceptions that are discussed in this book.

Basic Table Behavior

A Table is basically just a list of data that has been designated as an Excel Table. With that designation you get some additional functionality designed to make working with the list of data easier and more productive. The following are some examples of the differences between a list of data and an Excel Table:

Feature	List of Data	Excel Table
Header row	You have to manually insert header rows above the data. You can use more than one row as headers, and they are not required to be unique.	Excel creates one header row automatically. Each column header must be unique in the Table. You can hide or show the header row by clicking a check box in the ribbon.
Data rows	You insert and delete data rows by selecting a range and performing the action. Excel blindly follows instructions, regardless of the list's boundaries, so undesirable changes to the worksheet's layout could occur.	You insert and delete data rows by using Table-aware commands. Excel performs the actions while constraining the effects to the Table region and ensuring that entire rows are affected rather than just partial rows. Excel goes to great lengths to ensure that formulas remain consistent throughout a Table.
Total row	You must manually add total rows below the data. You can use more than one row for totals. You must manually enter any aggregation formulas.	Excel creates one total row automatically. You can hide or show the total by clicking a check box in the ribbon. Excel provides a set of possible aggregate functions via a drop-down menu for each column.
Sorting and filtering	Sorting and filtering are effectively the same with lists as with Excel Tables. Excel may prompt you to expand a selection if it can't figure out your data structure.	Sorting and filtering are effectively the same with Tables as with simple lists of data. Excel doesn't prompt you to expand a selection because it knows the Table's boundaries.
Formatting	You must do all formatting manually, and Excel generally propagates that formatting to new rows only one row at a time.	Excel provides automatic formatting, including banding and other options. Excel maintains formatting with all Table rows and columns with Table styles. (Chapter 7 discusses Table styles.)
Formulas	All formulas use standard range references and, for the most part, have to be manually maintained.	Formulas use structured references that refer to a Table's parts, providing more robust referencing. Excel automatically keeps formulas consistent down an entire column.

How Tables Interact with Other Worksheet Objects

Unlike with a list of data, Excel confines actions taken with a Table to that Table's range. Cells outside the Table's range are left intact as much as possible. Excel never overwrites existing data when inserting new rows and columns, nor does Excel resize a Table to overlap other cells that contain values or formulas. When new rows are inserted into a Table, Excel shifts down only cells in the Table (below the row[s] being inserted) and cells below the Table. When you add a new row to the bottom of a Table (by pressing TAB while the last cell of the last row is selected), Excel adds the new row without shifting anything below unless there is no room, in which case it shifts down everything below by one row.

> **NOTE**
>
> There is a distinction between inserting rows in a Table and appending rows in a Table. **Inserting** rows means selecting one or more cells and using Excel's *Insert* function, via the ribbon or the contextual right-click pop-up menu. **Appending** rows means adding a row to the bottom of a Table. You can append in two different ways:
>
> 1. Select only the last cell in the Table (the bottom-right cell) and press the TAB key.
>
> 2. Enter a value in any cell in the first empty row below the Table.
>
> Subsequent sections have more to say about how Excel handles inserting and appending.

> **CAUTION**
>
> When you stack Tables vertically, each Table must use fewer columns or the same number of columns as the Tables above. Say that no more rows can be appended to a Table that has fewer columns than any Tables below the one you're editing; Excel displays an error when you attempt to insert rows into that Table.

The next figure shows three Tables stacked vertically. These Tables are separated by two blank rows. If you append a new row to the bottom of the topmost Table by using the TAB key, Excel increases the Table size by a single row, without shifting the Tables below. The topmost Table takes up one of the rows below it that was originally blank, increasing the Table size by one row. It can do that one more time because there is another blank row below the Table. Then, when there are no more empty cells for appending rows to the Table, the selection moves to the next row in the first column, but the Table is not resized and extended down any more rows.

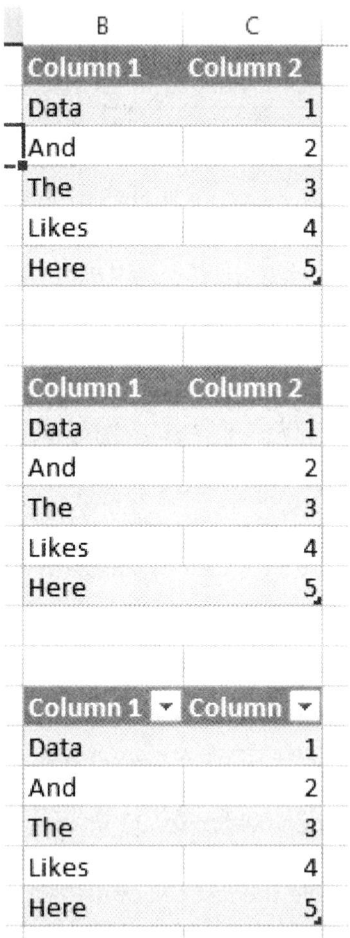

Multiple Tables stacked vertically.

> **TIP**
>
> To prevent empty rows below a Table from being consumed when you append rows by using TAB or inserting Table rows, you can merge two or more cells in the first empty row below the Table; the merged cells cannot extend beyond the Table's columns. When merged cells are present and you append rows by using TAB, Excel always inserts rows rather than appending them. Note that you cannot append rows by entering values below the Table (entering a value, pasting, or filling down) when you have merged cells in the first blank row below a Table.

Excel manages Table header and total rows in a similar manner. When a Table's header row is turned on, Excel shifts down cells only if there is no room for the header row. When the header row is turned off, Excel does not shift any cells, and a row of empty cells remains in its place. When the total row is turned on, Excel always shifts the following cells down one row. When the total row is turned off, Excel always shifts the following cells up one row.

Awareness and Visibility

Sometimes it may be difficult to tell whether a range of cells or a single cell is part of a Table. Selecting any cell within a Table results in the display of the contextual *{TABLE TOOLS} DESIGN* tab. If this tab is present on the ribbon, the active cell resides in a Table.

> **NOTE**
>
> Excel displays a contextual tab when you select an object to which that tab is relevant. A single group heading with one or more related tabs below it is displayed in the ribbon. For example, when you select a PivotChart, Excel displays three tabs—*ANALYZE*, *DESIGN*, and *FORMAT*—under the common header *PIVOTCHART TOOLS*. This book uses the convention *{CONTEXTUAL TAB} TAB* to refer to such tabs—for example, *{PIVOTCHART TOOLS} ANALYZE*.
>
> Other contextual ribbon tab groups are *CHART TOOLS*, *PIVOTTABLE TOOLS*, *SLICER TOOLS*, *TIMELINE TOOLS*, *SPARKLINE TOOLS*, *DRAWING TOOLS*, *PICTURE TOOLS*, *SMARTART TOOLS*, *INK TOOLS*, *HEADER & FOOTER TOOLS*, and *EQUATION TOOLS*.
>
> You might have noticed that the names of ribbon tabs and tab groups are now all uppercase. Microsoft introduced this convention in Office 2013 as part of its user experience that includes Office Online applications.

Determining Column Names

Excel Tables can become very large. When you're working with a large Table, you may have trouble identifying columns when the Table's header row is not visible. One way to solve this issue is to freeze the Table's header row (by selecting *VIEW | Window | Freeze Panes | Freeze Panes*) so that it doesn't scroll. If the worksheet's *Freeze Panes* option is **not** enabled, Excel displays the Table's headers in the worksheet header row (where normally it displays the column letters A, B, C, etc.) as long as the active cell is inside that Table, as shown in the next figure.

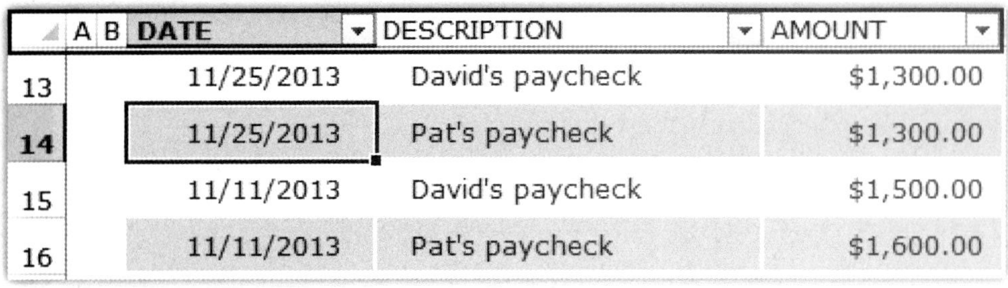

With Freeze Panes disabled, Table headers are visible while scrolling through a large Table.

When the Table's headers are displayed this way, the filter buttons are available.

> **CAUTION**
>
> You can toggle the *Filter Buttons* option (*{TABLE TOOLS} DESIGN | Table Style Options | Filter Buttons*) to show and hide the filter buttons. However, if the Table's header row is displayed in the worksheet header, the filter buttons do not immediately reflect the new setting. You must scroll the worksheet to make the Table's header row visible in order to reset the visibility of the filter buttons to match the option's setting.

Accessibility

For users who have accessibility needs and tools, such as screen readers, many Excel objects support alternative text to help those users understand the content. You edit a Table's alternative text by right-clicking any cell in the Table and selecting *Table | Alternative Text*.

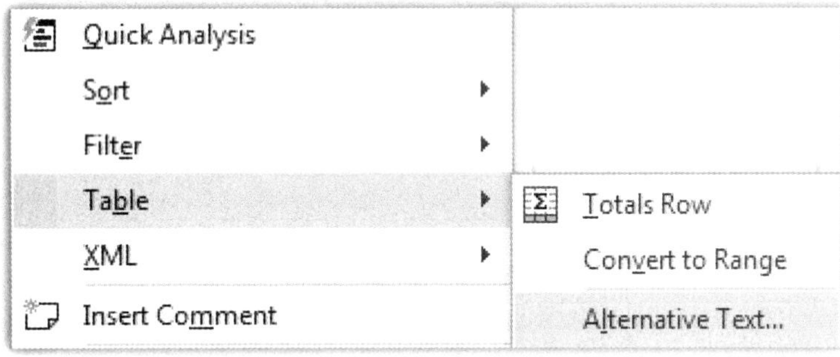

Accessing the Alternative Text *option by right-clicking a cell.*

You may also want to use alternative text when publishing content to a web page or DAISY-formatted file. When a user hovers the mouse over an object that has alternative text, that text displays.

Table Names

Every Table has a name. As you already know, within a workbook, every Table name must be unique. Excel automatically assigns the name "Table" with a number appended for each new Table—for example, "Table1", "Table2", etc. When you copy a Table to another location, Excel uses the name of the original Table with another number appended to ensure that the name is unique within the scope of the workbook; for example, Excel might change "Table2" to "Table21". When you import data from an external database such as SQL Server or Access, Table names default to "Table_QueryName"—for example, "Table_Employees".

Changing Table Names

You can change a Table's name at any time. Besides being unique within the scope of the workbook, a Table name must:

- Not contain special characters other than an underscore

- Not contain spaces
- Always start with a letter or an underscore

You change a Table's name by editing the name displayed in the *{TABLE TOOLS} DESIGN | Properties | Table Name* text box, as illustrated in the next figure.

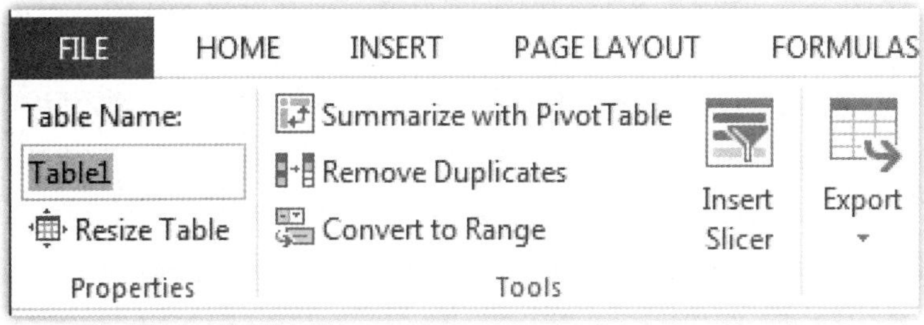

Editing a Table name in the Properties *ribbon group.*

As shown in the next figure, Excel displays an error message if the name you enter is not unique or does not follow one or more of these rules.

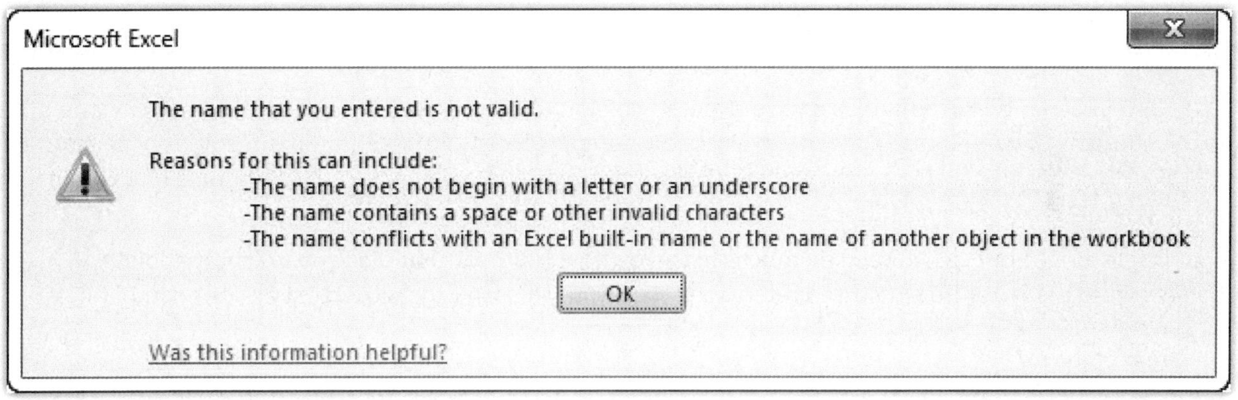

An error message for an invalid name.

When you change the name of a Table generated as the result of a query, the name does not revert back to its default name when you refresh the query. However, if you delete the Table and reconnect the query, the new Table gets the default name.

When you change the name of a Table, Excel automatically applies the change to any and all formulas that reference the Table by name.

> **CAUTION**
>
> Be careful when deleting a Table generated as the result of a query. When you do, Excel converts the references in any formulas referring to that Table to #REF!, and you can't undo this without manually editing every affected formula.

Naming Conventions

A traditional naming convention is called **Hungarian notation**. Hungarian notation uses the first few letters of a name to identify the type of object (called the **type prefix**). These letters are set in lowercase. They are usually a shortened form of the object type, such as "wkb" for workbook or "wks" for worksheet. For Tables, it's generally accepted to use either "tbl" (for **Table**) or "lo" (for **List object**). Programmers and Excel users have used type prefixes for many years. Although most modern standards no longer use them, they can make object names more intuitive.

However, you really don't need to use a type prefix for Table names , and doing so can be confusing. Meaningful names such as "Data", "Assets", "Expenditures", etc. can be just as helpful or more so to those using and maintaining workbooks that contain Tables. We recommend using meaningful names over prefixed or Hungarian notation.

Keep in mind two things when naming Tables:

- With formulas using structured references that reference a Table but are located outside that Table, you need to use Table names.
- You can and should use Table names for referencing Tables when automating Tables using VBA, as discussed in Chapter 9.

Forward and Backward Compatibility

Microsoft works very hard to ensure that files will be forward compatible—that is, that files created in older versions of Excel still work with newer versions. Microsoft also tries for backward compatibility—that is, ensuring that files created in newer versions work with older versions. With backward compatibility, for example, a file created in Excel 2013, using the full feature set and tools that may not be available in previous versions, will still be able to open, without errors, in previous versions of Excel. Although some of the newer features aren't available in previous versions of the application, the file won't break or become corrupted when it's opened in the older version. In this section we describe how Microsoft has worked to ensure backward and forward compatibility with Excel Tables.

Formulas

When Excel 2007 introduced Tables as a reinvented version of lists, one of the major additions was the introduction of *structured references*. A structured reference accomplishes the same result as a traditional R1C1 or A1 reference: It references a range of one or more cells. However, it uses the names of the Table parts to create the reference. (Chapter 4 covers structured references in detail.)

What is relevant about structured references in the context of forward and backward compatibility? Changes were made to the structured reference syntax and rules in Excel 2010 that are not compatible with Excel 2007.

Consider this simple formula in Excel 2010 or 2013:

```
=[@Col1]+1
```

This formula references a Table column within square brackets, and the @ character instructs Excel to use the current row for that reference. In Excel 2007, you would need to construct this formula differently:

```
=Table1[[#This Row],[Col1]]+1
```

Note that the Table name is prepended to the reference and the text `[@Col1]` *is changed to* `[[#This Row],[Col1]]`.

In Excel 2010 and 2013, you can enter formulas using either the old or new syntax. Excel automatically converts the old syntax to the new syntax. Also, when you open workbooks with the new syntax in Excel 2007, Excel converts the new syntax to the old syntax so the formulas still work. However, when you're using Excel 2007, you can enter only the old syntax.

> ***NOTE***
>
> How does Excel 2007 accommodate the new syntax introduced in Excel 2010? The answer is both simple and clever: It doesn't. Excel 2010 and 2013 do not store formulas using the new syntax in the workbook; rather, they store the formulas using the old syntax but display them using the new syntax. This means Excel 2007 can open an Excel 2010 or 2013 workbook and calculate the formulas. The only limitation is that you can't enter the new syntax in Excel 2007.

> **NOTE**
>
> Excel 2007 and later workbook files (with the XLSX, XLSM, or XLAM extension) are XML-formatted files. With very little effort, you can compress (zip) such a file and then unzip the workbook file, find the XML representing the Table, and inspect it for various Table properties, such as the calculated column formulas. Visit www.exceltables.com for more information and instructions on how to unzip and inspect XLSX, XLSM, and XLAM workbook files.

Objects

Excel 2010 introduced a new filtering tool called the **Slicer**, which is a visual filter for PivotTables and PivotCharts. Excel 2013 also supports the use of Slicers in Tables. (Chapter 6 covers Slicers as they apply to Tables.)

If you add a Slicer to a Table in Excel 2013 and then open that workbook in Excel 2010, the Slicer stays in the same location, but you cannot use or edit it. Any attempt to change the Slicer's properties renders the Slicer invalid. Instead of getting an error message, users see a shape where the Slicer was, with a message like the one shown in the next figure.

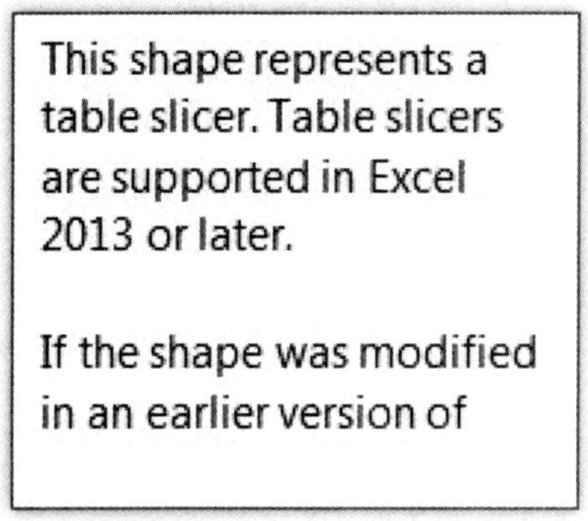

A Table Slicer opened in Excel 2010.

The message in the shape isn't as useful as it could be: It doesn't explain is that if you move the Slicer, Excel converts that Slicer into a functionless shape that will no longer function when that workbook is opened in Excel 2013.

Excel 2013 includes an enhancement to Slicers called **Timelines**. Timelines are Slicers that handle date such as time data in a more intuitive manner. The next figure illustrates what a Timeline slicer looks like when a workbook is opened in a version of Excel earlier than Excel 2013.

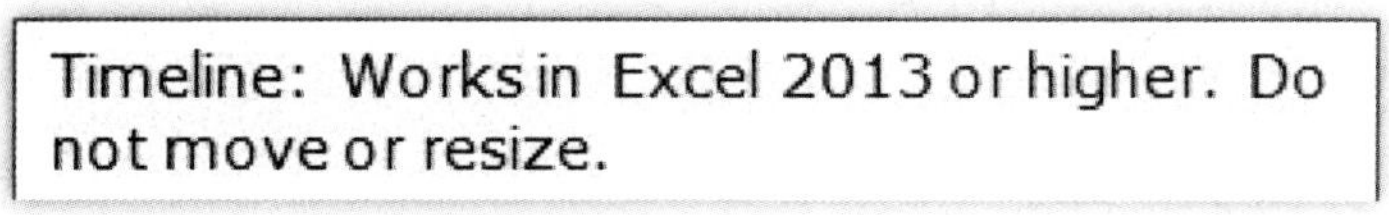

A Timeline opened in Excel 2010.

3 Working with Tables

In this chapter we discuss different methods for working with Tables, including creating tables, resizing them, inserting and deleting rows and columns, moving columns, and exporting data from Tables. These are some of the essential operations you need to become fluent with when working with Tables.

Creating Tables

You can create a Table with or without existing data. When you create a Table, Excel prompts for the location of the data and whether there are headers. The next figure illustrates this prompt. If there are no headers, uncheck the box *My table has headers*, and Excel creates default headers. Excel names the first column "Column 1", the second "Column 2", the third "Column 3", etc.

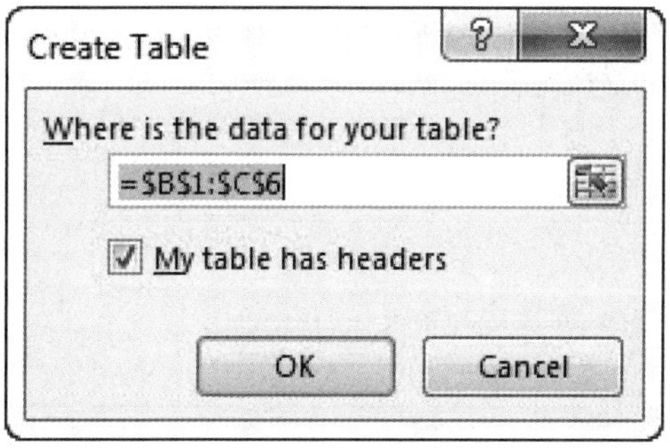

Create Table *dialog box.*

Creating a Table from the Ribbon

There are multiple ways to create a Table from the ribbon. One way is to click *HOME | Styles | Format as Table*. Then you select any Table format from the menu shown in the next figure. Excel then inserts a Table.

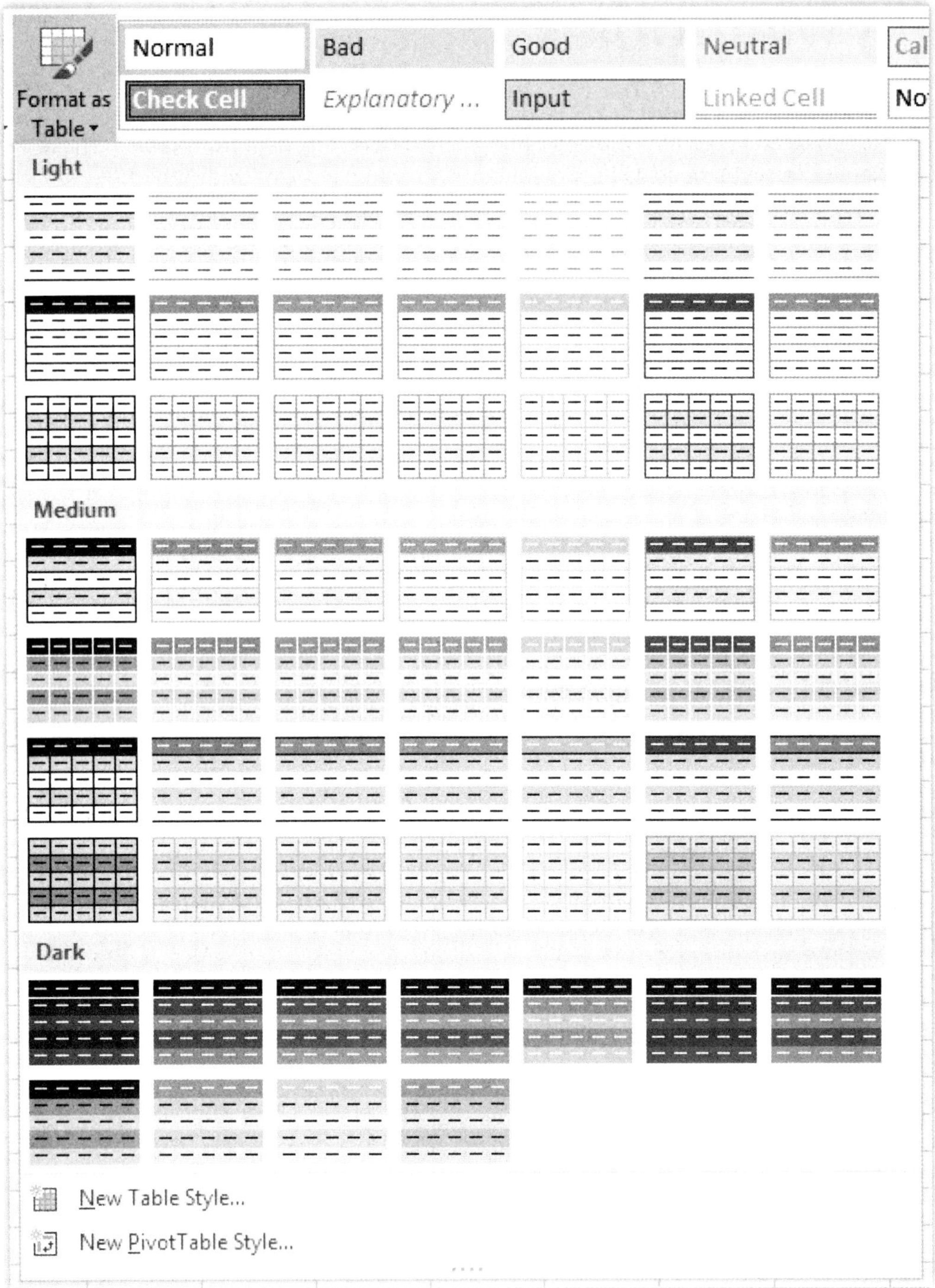

Creating a Table from the HOME *tab.*

Alternatively, you can select *INSERT | Tables | Table* to insert a Table.

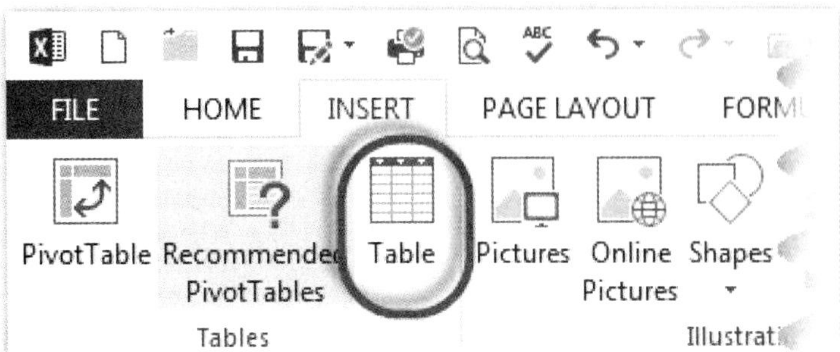

Creating a Table from the INSERT *tab.*

Excel Online has a similar *INSERT* ribbon tab.

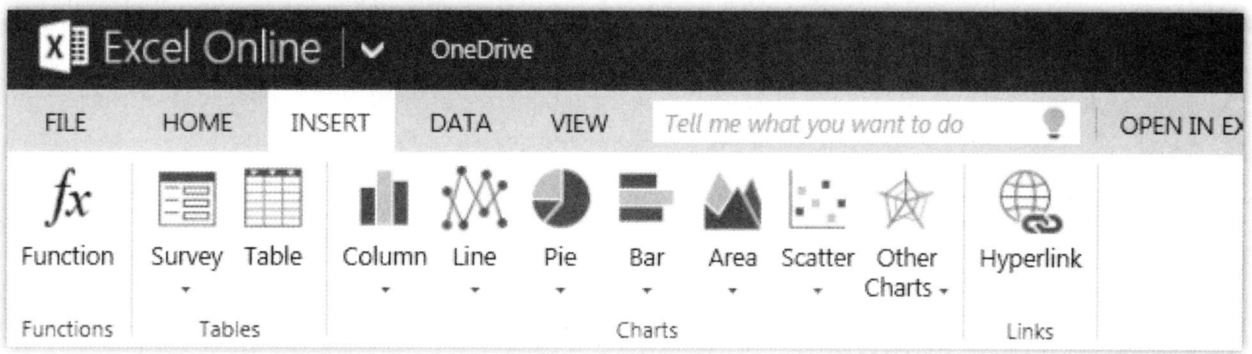

Excel Online INSERT *ribbon tab.*

Creating a Table from the Keyboard

Two access keys instruct Excel to insert a Table: CTRL+T and CTRL+L. To insert a Table using keyboard shortcuts, from the *HOME* tab press ALT, H, T and then use the keyboard arrows to navigate to the desired Table. You can then press the Enter key to insert a Table that has the selected style. To insert a Table from the *INSERT* tab, press ALT, N, T.

> ***NOTE***
>
> Why CTRL+L for creating a Table? The letter L doesn't seem like a logical choice with Tables. When Microsoft introduced the ribbon in Excel 2007, it removed command bars but allowed the keyboard shortcuts from Excel 2003 to continue to work in 2007 and beyond. (These keystrokes are now called **access keys**.) Remember that Excel 2003 had Lists rather than Tables. In it, the keyboard shortcut for creating a List was CTRL+L, and Microsoft has maintained that association.
>
> In versions of Excel other than the US English version, CTRL+L is the only keyboard shortcut to use for creating Tables. CTRL+T does not always work because it is sometimes repurposed for other commands in languages other than English.

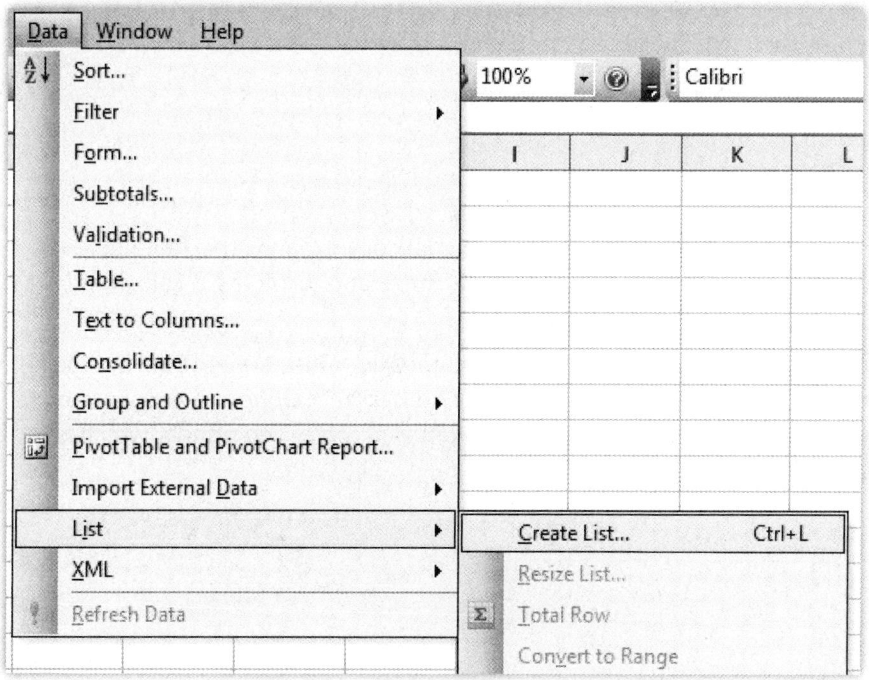

Excel 2003 command bar for creating a List.

Once a Table is created, a new ribbon tab appears, titled *{TABLE TOOLS} DESIGN*. It is a **contextual tab**, which means it's visible when the active cell is within a Table. If the active cell is not part of a Table, then the *{TABLE TOOLS} DESIGN* ribbon tab is not displayed.

Many types of objects have contextual tabs, including PivotTables, Slicers, pictures, charts, etc. We discuss some of these in more detail in subsequent chapters.

Resizing Tables

You can resize a table either manually or automatically. In addition, you can use a workaround for maintaining blank rows below a Table.

Resizing a Table Manually

There are two ways to manually resize a Table:

- **Using the sizing handle**—The sizing handle is a small black icon located at the bottom-right corner of a Table. By clicking and dragging the sizing handle, you can resize a Table to include additional or fewer rows or to include additional or fewer columns—but you can't do both at the same time. To change the number of rows **and** columns, you use the sizing handle twice in two separate gestures, or you can use the *Resize Table* control, as described below.
- **Using the *Resize Table* control on the ribbon**—If you click *{TABLE TOOLS} DESIGN | Properties | Resize Table*, Excel displays a dialog box with a single RefEdit control, as shown in the next figure. Enter the desired range or select the desired range on the worksheet and click *OK*. You can select any range, as long as at least one header cell and one body cell are selected. The new range **must** overlap the current Table range.

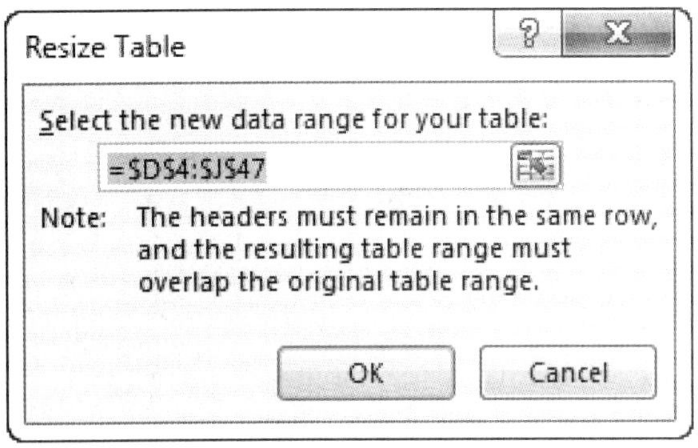

Resize Table *dialog box.*

Resizing a Table Automatically

When you enter data in the first empty row below a Table, Excel automatically expands the Table to include that new row of data. The new row is initialized with all the formats and formulas in calculated columns.

You can tell Excel whether to automatically include new rows and columns as values are entered into cells adjacent to the Table. To do so, you select *FILE | Options | Proofing | AutoCorrect Options | AutoFormat As You Type* and then either check or uncheck *Include new rows and columns in table*. The option, which is an application-level option, is enabled by default.

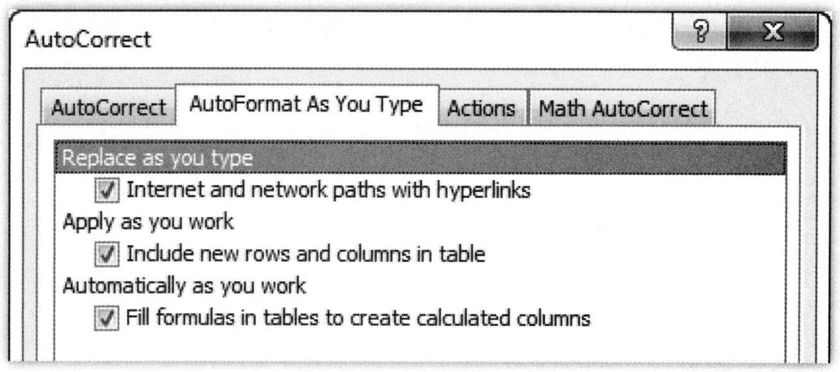

AutoCorrect options for Tables, both to include new rows and columns in Tables and to fill in formulas for calculated columns.

By selecting the bottom-right cell in the data body range (not the total row, if displayed) and pressing the TAB key, you can append a new row. The *Include new rows and columns in table* option discussed above does not affect this behavior.

> **CAUTION**
>
> If a worksheet is protected, regardless of the *Insert Rows* parameter setting, you cannot insert a new row.

Maintaining Blank Rows Below a Table

Placing data below a Table or stacking more than one Table vertically on a worksheet is generally not recommended, although there may be times when the workbook design dictates that you use one of these methods. As a Table grows with new rows of data, it consumes the empty rows below. If there is any data (values, formulas, or another Table) below the Table, Excel starts shifting those cells downward to make room for the new rows once the empty rows are consumed.

Problems start occurring if the data below a Table is aligned with data in those same rows that is not under the Table. Excel pushes down the data directly below the Table, but it doesn't push down the other data, thus causing the data in those rows to become misaligned. If one or more Tables are present below the Table being expanded, and those Tables extend beyond the left or right edges of the Table being expanded, Excel does not sift anything downward under any circumstances.

That said, if data or one or more Tables are placed under a Table, you might want to maintain some empty rows between the bottom of the expanding Table and the first row of the other data below the expanding Table. In this case, you can merge one or more cells in the row immediately below the last row of the expanding Table. As long as the merged cells do not extend beyond the left or right edge of the Table, Excel shifts down the merged cells, along with every cell below and within the left and right Table boundaries when inserting or appending new rows. As a result, the empty rows are not consumed because the merged cells are above them, and they cannot be consumed.

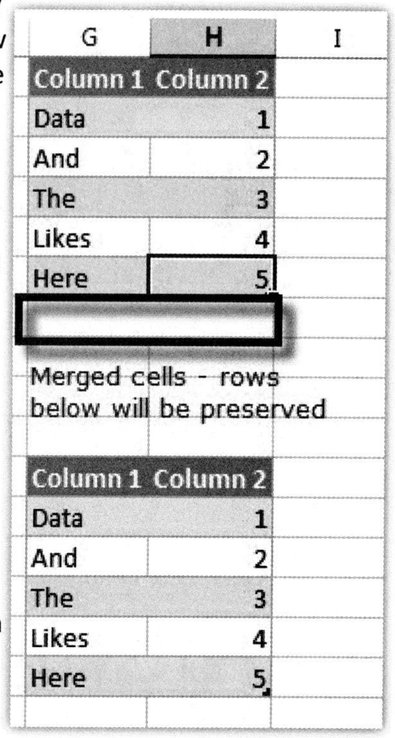

Merged cells below a Table.

If merged cells extend beyond the left or right edge of the Table above, Excel gives you the warning message shown in the next figure.

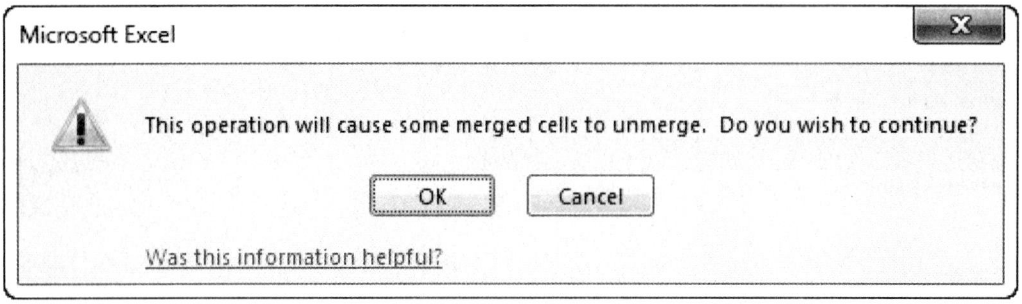

Insert row error caused by merged cells.

Moving Columns

To rearrange columns in a Table, you select an entire column, including the header and total rows, if they are visible. Then you hover the cursor over any edge of the selection and click and drag the column left or right, into the desired position. A bold green vertical line appears at the closest insertion point to the mouse, as shown in the next figure.

OrderDate	Region	Rep	Item	Units	Cost	Total
1/6/2012	East	Jones	Pencil	95	1.99	189.05
1/23/2012	Central	Kivell	Binder	50	19.99	999.5
2/9/2012	Central	Jardine	Pencil	36	4.99	179.64
2/26/2012	Central	Gill	Pen	27	19.99	539.73
3/15/2012	West	Sorvino	Pencil	56	2.99	167.44
4/1/2012	East	Jones	Binder	60	4.99	299.4
4/18/2012	Central	Andrews	Pencil	75	1.99	149.25
5/5/2012	Central	Jardine	Pencil	90	4.99	449.1
5/22/2012	West	Thompson	Pencil	32	1.99	63.68
6/8/2012	East	Jones	Binder	60	8.99	539.4

Moving the column "Cost" between the columns "Item" and "Units".

When the move is complete, Excel adjusts any Table references in formulas. If a column contains formulas that reference a range of columns and that column is moved to a location within that range, Excel gives you the circular reference warning shown in the next figure.

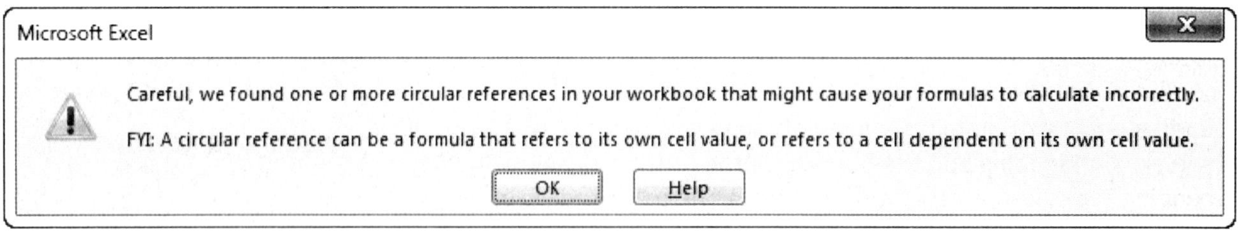

Circular reference warning.

Inserting Rows and Columns

There is no option to insert rows or columns from the *{TABLE TOOLS} DESIGN* ribbon tab. Instead, you insert rows and columns by clicking *HOME | Cells | Insert* and then choosing an option from the menu shown in the next figure.

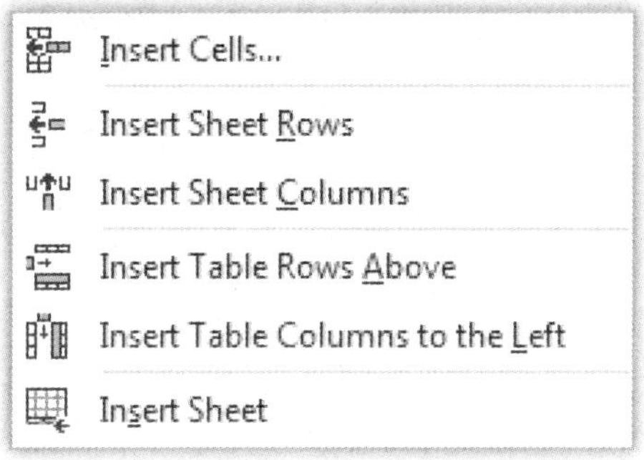

Inserting a column or row from the HOME *tab.*

Another way to insert rows and columns is to right-click the desired insertion location within a Table to display the context menu and select *Table Columns to the Left* or *Table Rows Above*, as shown in the next figure.

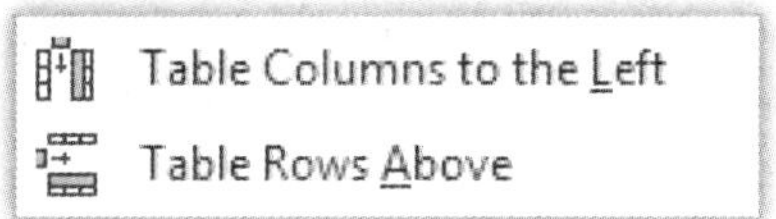

Inserting a column or row from the right-click context menu.

When you insert rows or columns in a Table, Excel constrains the new rows or columns to within the Table boundaries, as long as the current selection is within the Table's boundaries. (Excel uses the current selection to determine where to insert the new rows or columns.) If entire rows or columns are selected, Excel shifts entire rows or columns to make room for the new rows or columns.

When you insert rows, Excel assumes that the number of new rows desired is the number of rows selected, regardless of how many columns are selected. When you insert columns, Excel assumes that the number of new columns desired is the number of columns selected, regardless of how many rows are selected.

To append a new row at the end of a Table, select the bottom-right cell in the data range area and press the TAB key.

> **CAUTION**
>
> Excel does not allow you to insert new rows or columns on a protected sheet.

When you insert rows, if there are merged cells anywhere below the Table that extend beyond the left or right edges of the Table, Excel displays a warning, as shown in the next figure, that the action will cause cells to unmerge.

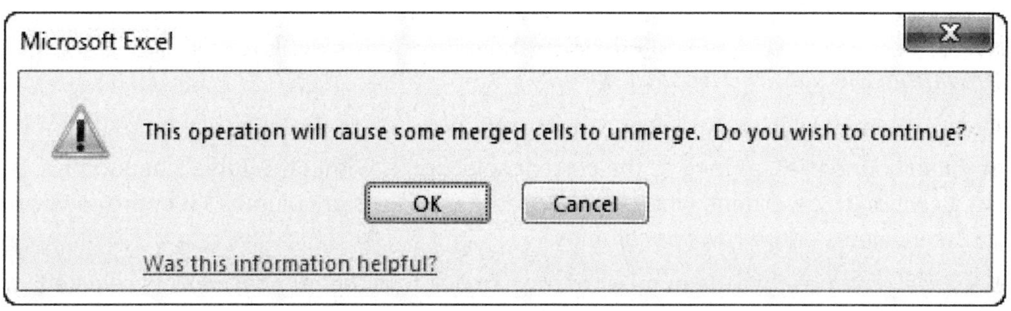

Inserting rows causes merged cells outside the Table dimensions to unmerge.

If Excel cannot insert rows or columns due to structural designs (for example, one or more Tables below extend beyond the expanding Table's left or right edges), Excel cancels the action and displays the message shown in the next figure.

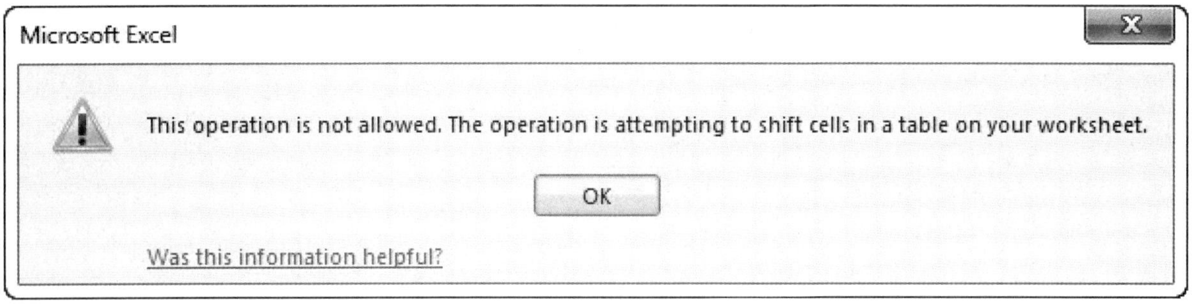

Message displayed if an insertion cannot be completed due to structure conflicts.

> **NOTE**
>
> When you insert columns with the *Filter Button* disabled (*{TABLE TOOLS} DESIGN | Table Style Options | Filter Button*), new columns display the AutoFilter drop-down control anyway.

Deleting Rows and Columns

There is no option to delete rows or columns from the *{TABLE TOOLS} DESIGN* ribbon tab. Instead, you delete rows and columns by clicking *HOME | Cells | Delete* and then choosing an option from the menu shown in the following figure.

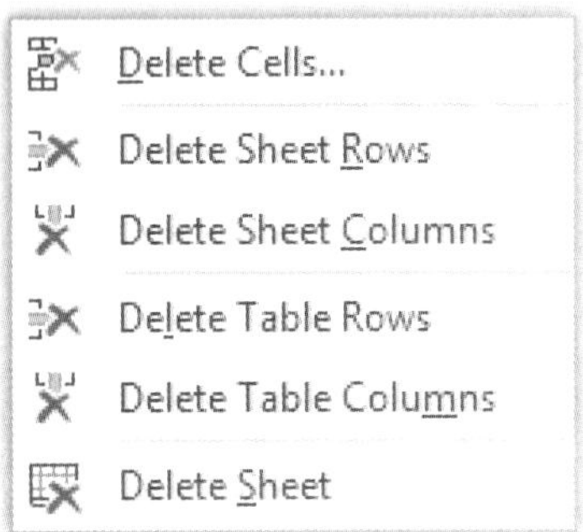

Deleting a column or row from the HOME tab.

Another way to delete rows or columns is to right-click the desired deletion location within the Table to display the context menu and select *Table Columns* or *Table Rows*, as shown in the next figure.

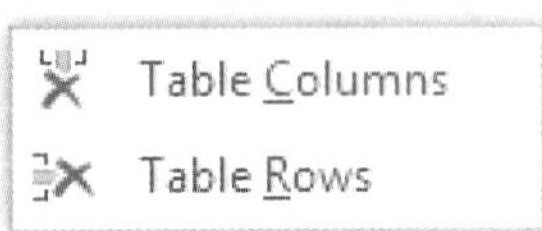

Deleting a column or row from the right-click context menu.

As with inserting, when you delete rows or columns in a Table, Excel constrains the deleted rows or columns to within the Table boundaries, as long as the current selection is within the Table's boundaries. (Excel uses the current selection to determine where to delete the new rows or columns.) If entire rows or columns are selected, Excel deletes entire rows or columns.

When you delete rows, Excel assumes that the number of rows to delete is the number of rows selected, regardless of how many columns are selected. When you delete columns, Excel assumes that the number of columns to delete is the number of columns selected, regardless of how many rows are selected.

If Excel cannot delete rows or columns due to the structural design (for example, one or more Tables below that extend beyond the expanding Table's left or right edges), Excel cancels the action and displays the message shown in the next figure.

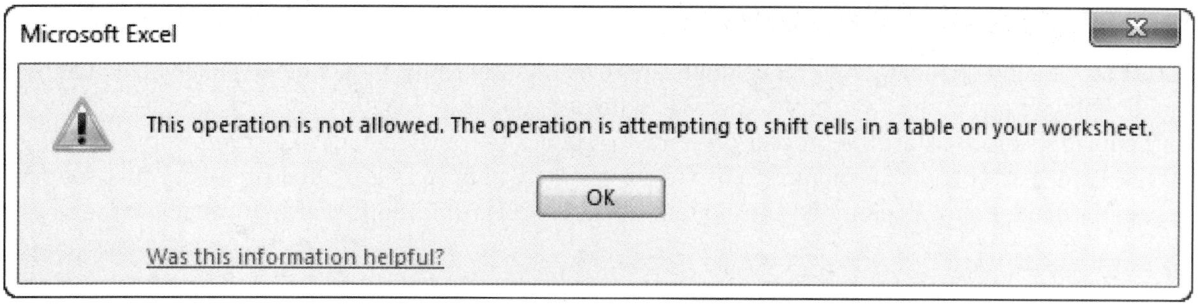

Message displayed if a deletion cannot be completed due to structure conflicts.

Converting a Table to a Range

Limitations with Tables sometimes prevent certain activities, so converting a Table to a range may be advantageous. For example, duplicate header values are not allowed in a Table, but you can use them if you convert a Table to a range.

There are repercussions when you convert a Table to a static range. All structured references to the Table or any of the Table parts in any formulas or names inside and outside the Table are converted to standard (absolute) cell references. No references break.

For example, this formula with structured references:

```
=[@Units]*[@Cost]
```

Is converted to this:

```
=Sheet1!$H5*Sheet1!$I5
```

The only exceptions are external and static (text) references, such as when you use the `INDIRECT` function. Excel doesn't see these references at conversion time and leaves them as-is.

> **CAUTION**
>
> Once a Table is converted to a range, the structured references that are converted to standard references are not converted back to structured references if the range is converted back into a Table. There is no workaround for this.

Before you convert a Table to a range, consider that there may be an alternative solution. For example, you can create two headers that appear to be identical by following one of them with a space character.

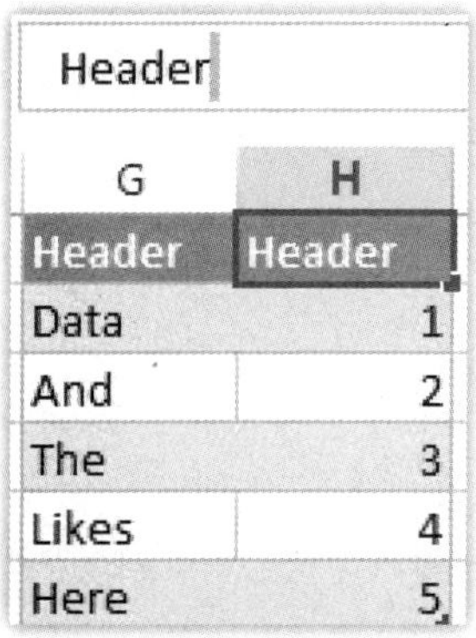

Two seemingly identical column headers, but the second one has a space character at the end, shown selected in the formula bar.

Removing Duplicate Rows

Excel 2007 introduced the ability to remove duplicate rows of data from a worksheet. While you can apply this functionality to any data, it's easiest to do when the data is in a Table because Excel knows exactly where the headers are. To start the process of removing duplicate rows, select *DATA | Data Tools | Remove Duplicates*. Excel asks you which columns to use to determine when a row is a duplicate of another row. It keeps the first unique row, deletes all subsequent duplicate rows, and shifts up the rows below the deletion.

Exporting Table Data

There are two methods for exporting data from a Table: Export to SharePoint as a List or export to Visio as a PivotDiagram. For both of these options, you must have the respective application. For example, you must have Visio in order to export a Table to a PivotDiagram.

Exporting to SharePoint

SharePoint is the default standard sharing service used with Office 365 and Power BI. To share a Table using SharePoint, you select a range in the Table and select *{TABLE TOOLS} DESIGN | External Table Data | Export*. Then you select *Export Table to SharePoint List* to begin the export process.

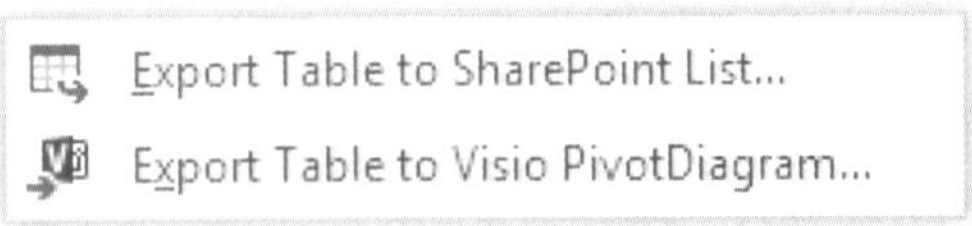

Exporting data to a SharePoint list.

Excel displays a wizard that takes you through a two-step process. First, you enter the SharePoint URL—for example, http://user.sharepoint.com/TableTools/. Then you specify whether the SharePoint list is read-only and enter a display name and description.

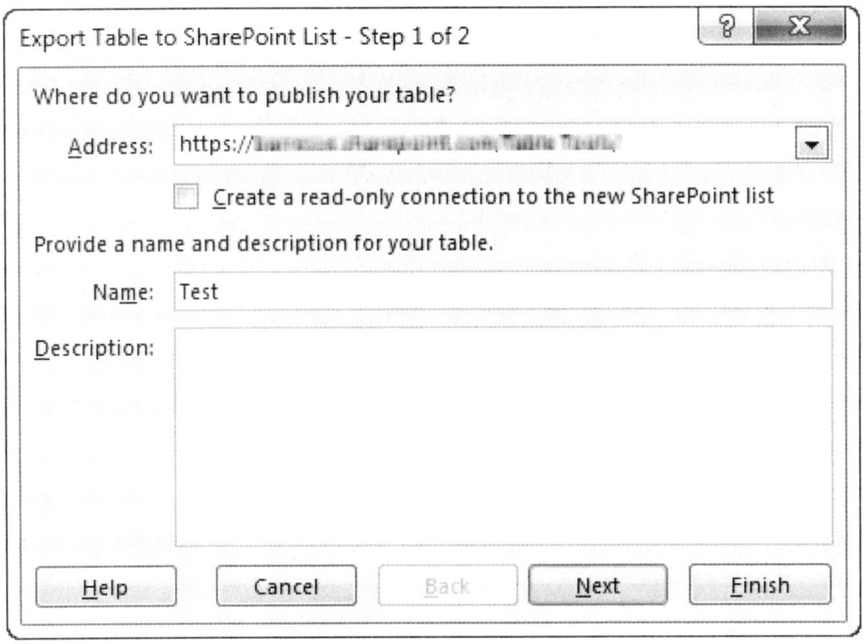

Exporting to a SharePoint list, step 1.

To use this feature, you must log on to the SharePoint site by providing your email address and password.

> **TIP**
>
> If you're using Office 365, you should sign in to Excel 2013 using the same account you use to access your SharePoint site.

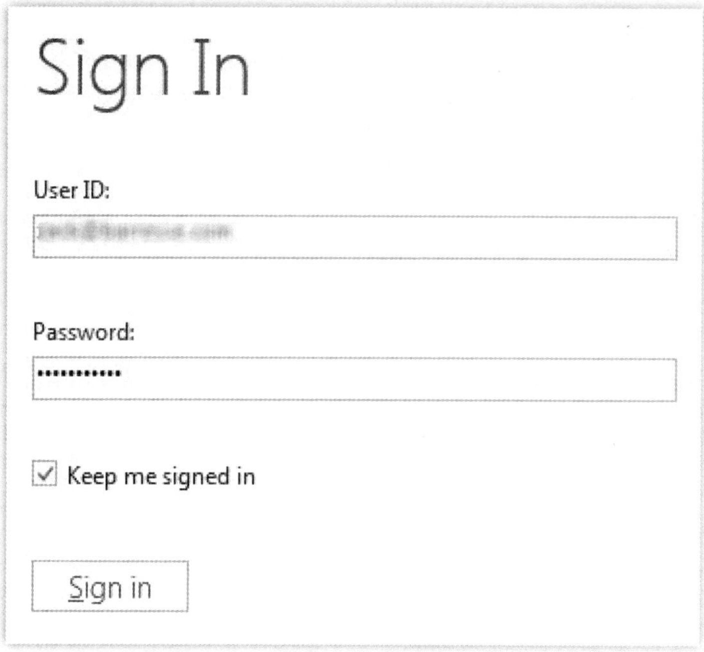

Authentication in exporting to a SharePoint list.

Once you are authenticated, the second step of the wizard verifies the data. Excel asks you to confirm the data type of each column. If any issues require adjustment, you must cancel the process and make the changes before starting the export again.

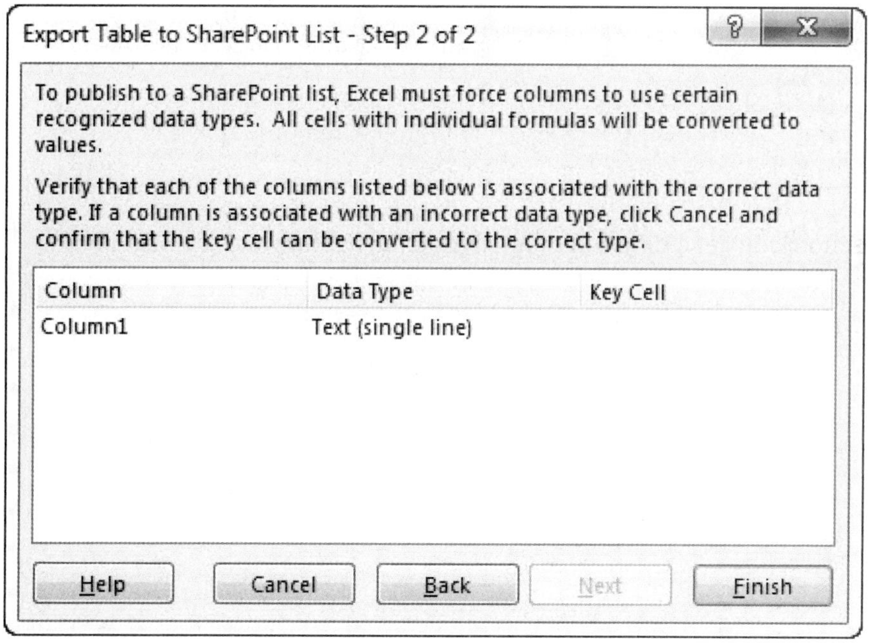

Exporting to a SharePoint list, step 2.

Excel displays one of the messages shown in the next two figures, indicating whether the action was successful.

Successful export to a SharePoint list.

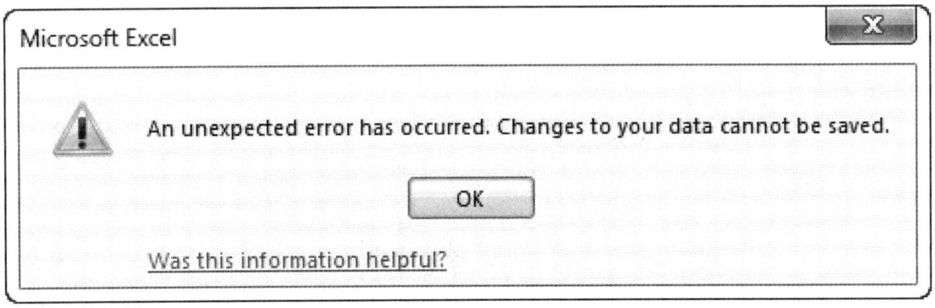

Unsuccessful export to a SharePoint list.

The connection is an OLEDB connection that you can view by selecting *{TABLE TOOLS} DESIGN | External Table Data | Properties*. A connection string looks something like this example:

```
Provider=Microsoft.Office.List.OLEDB.2.0;Data
Source="";ApplicationName=Excel;Version=12.0.0.0
```

> **CAUTION**
>
> Once a Table has been exported to a SharePoint list, you cannot change the data in the Table. If you make any changes, they will be lost (without warning) when the Table is refreshed.

For a Table with an external connection, you get a different right-click menu, as shown in the next figure.

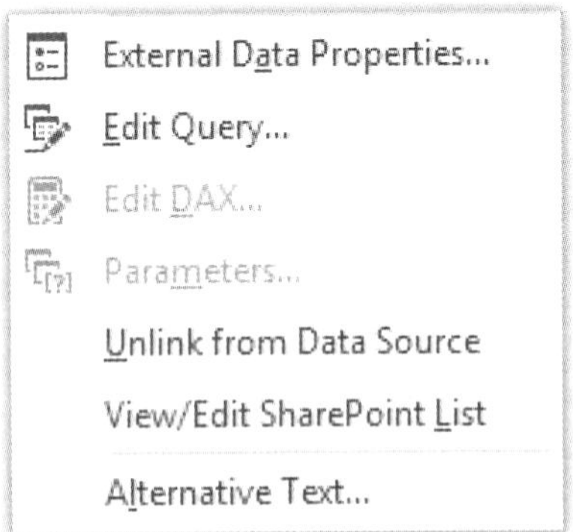

Right-click menu for a Table with an external connection.

Depending on the type of connection, some controls may be disabled. For instance, the control *Edit DAX* is disabled for a SharePoint list but is enabled for a Table linked to a SQL Server query or another OLAP data source.

Exporting to Visio

You can export a Table to a Visio PivotDiagram. A **PivotDiagram** is a collection of shapes in a hierarchical tree structure. Each node in the tree is broken down into subnodes, based on the Table data. PivotDiagrams are similar to Excel PivotTables in that they allow you to view the data from different angles in a visual arrangement. You can highlight certain areas, as with conditional formatting in Excel. You must have Visio installed in order to use this function.

To export a Table to a Visio PivotDiagram, select *{TABLE TOOLS} DESIGN | External Table Data | Export | Export Table to Visio PivotDiagram*. (If Visio is not installed, this selection is disabled.) You must save the workbook before you can export an Excel Table to Visio.

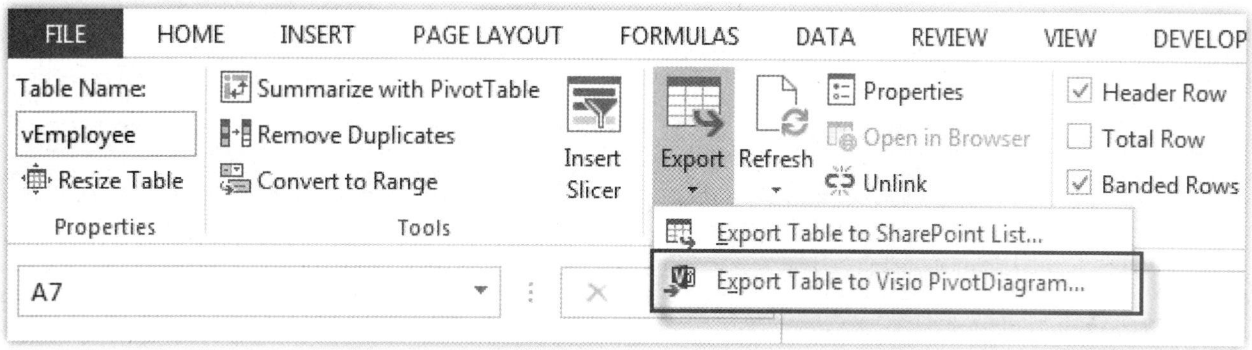

The Export Table to Visio PivotDiagram ribbon command.

Once the Table is exported to Visio in a PivotDiagram, you get a task pane, as shown in the next figure, with the Table columns as categories or totals.

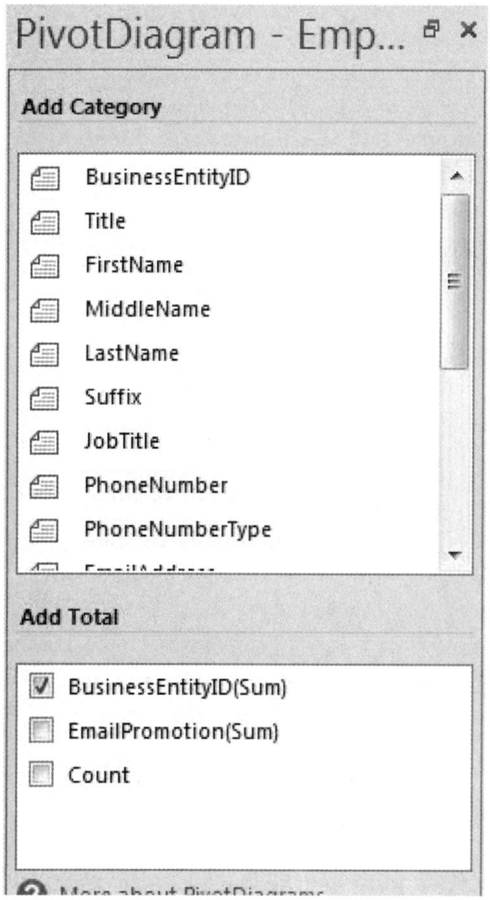

Visio's PivotDiagram task pane of an exported Excel Table.

You can use other data sources for PivotDiagrams, including:

- An Access database
- A SharePoint list
- A SQL Server database
- SQL Server Analysis Services
- OLEDB or ODBC data sources

If you try to export a Table to a Visio PivotDiagram, and the workbook is not saved, Excel gives you the warning shown in the next figure. To get around this, just save the workbook before attempting to export to Visio.

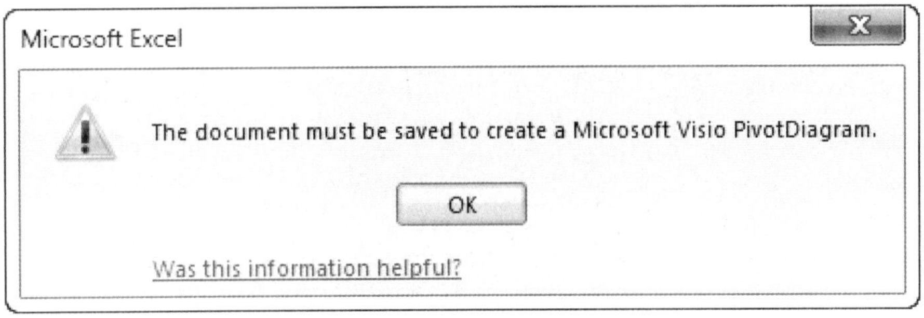

An unsaved workbook does not export to Visio.

You can manipulate a Visio PivotDiagram in many ways that are beyond the scope of this book, such as visually summarizing data.

Table Options

This section discusses some options that are especially important to understand when dealing with Tables. Referencing the header and total rows can be difficult if you're not familiar with how the *Header Row* and *Total Row* options work. Learning about these special Table designations—as well as *First Column* and *Last Column*—will help you understand the information in this book. In addition, *Filter Button* is unlike any other control in Excel and has functionality that cannot be replicated anywhere else.

Header Row

You use the *Header Row* option to show or hide the header row. If this option is checked, you can reference the header row in formulas; otherwise, if you try to reference the header row, the formula returns an error message. You'll learn more about this in Chapter 4.

Total Row

You use the *Total Row* option to show or hide the total row. If this option is checked, you can reference the total row in formulas; otherwise, if you try to reference the total row, the formula returns an error message. You'll learn more about this in Chapter 4.

First Column/Last Column

The *First Column* and *Last Column* options enable you to use custom formats on the first and last columns. You'll learn more about this in Chapter 7.

OrderDate	Region	Rep	Item	Units	Cost	Total
1/6/2012	East	Jones	Pencil	95	1.99	**189.05**
1/23/2012	Central	Kivell	Binder	50	19.99	**999.5**
2/9/2012	Central	Jardine	Pencil	36	4.99	**179.64**
2/26/2012	Central	Gill	Pen	27	19.99	**539.73**
3/15/2012	West	Sorvino	Pencil	56	2.99	**167.44**
4/1/2012	East	Jones	Binder	60	4.99	**299.4**
4/18/2012	Central	Andrews	Pencil	75	1.99	**149.25**

First and last columns of a Table.

Filter Button

Filter Button is a new control in Excel 2013. It is completely different from the AutoFilter functionality, which you could use in previous versions of Excel by using access keys. Tables were revamped in Excel 2007, and since then, you've had the ability to set an AutoFilter for the worksheet and also set an AutoFilter for each Table. It is therefore not typically a good idea to have multiple Tables structured horizontally, since filtering one Table will hide the entire sheet row. There may be times when structuring multiple Tables horizontally is beneficial, but you should do this with caution.

> **CAUTION**
>
> When you structure multiple Tables horizontally, if a filter is applied to one of the Tables, it filters the entire sheet row, so it affects the other Tables aligned horizontally with it.
>
> Likewise, when you structure multiple Tables vertically, you should also use caution. Although you'll avoid the filter issue in this case, you may come up against other obstacles, such as row insertion errors.

Filter Button provides functionality that you can't get any other way:

- It removes the AutoFilter drop-down controls from the Table.
- It causes the AutoFilter applied to the Table to remain in effect.

This could be beneficial when you're creating workbooks or reports for others to consume and you want them to use only the slicer functionality you've created. Or perhaps you want to leave a filter applied and not allow someone to change it. The keyboard shortcut for this is ALT, JT, {ZL}, B.

The functionality just discussed for *Filter Button* is different from the traditional functionality you get by toggling the *Filter* command. If you select *HOME | Editing | Sort & Filter | Filter*, you can turn the AutoFilter on or off. If you apply a filter, Excel makes your Table unfiltered and removes the AutoFilter drop-down controls. You can accomplish the same thing by using the access key ALT+D, F, F.

> **CAUTION**
>
> Using the access key ALT+D, F, F toggles (that is, enables/disables) *Filter Button*. People often think of this as a bug. When you're turning off filtering for a Table with this action, there are no AutoFilter drop-down controls to hide, which makes this control useless, hence the control being disabled.
>
> Excel 2013 provides no access key for the *Filter Button* functionality (that is, taking away the drop-down controls but leaving the current filter applied). You can access this functionality only via keyboard shortcuts, through the ribbon, or by using VBA, which is covered in Chapter 9.

4 Table Formulas

This chapter covers referencing Tables in formulas, both internal (within the Table) and external (outside the Table). It also covers some methods for dynamically referencing Table ranges.

Referencing Tables

Structured referencing is only as good as the naming conventions used to name a Table and the columns in the Table. It makes range references more readable—as long as both the Table names and Table column names are meaningful. If a Table is named "Table1" and the columns are named "Column 1", "Column 2", etc., then a structured reference using those names will not be much better than traditional A1 or R1C1 referencing. The best names are meaningful and of a reasonable length—not too short and not too long. Name length is a matter of preference, and your preference will develop as you learn more about the syntax of structured referencing.

Understanding how structured references work starts with understanding their syntax, which is shown in the next figure.

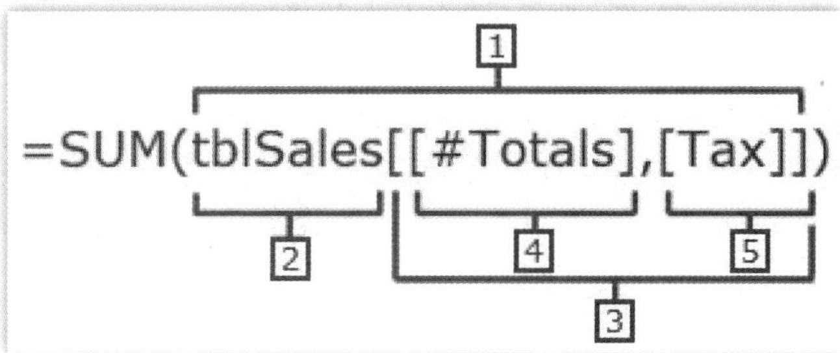

Structured reference syntax.

The following descriptions correspond to the numbers in the figure:

1. This is a single **structured reference**, representing a range of cells.
2. This is the **Table name**. If the structured reference is in a cell inside the Table, then the Table name is not required. If you don't enter the Table name when specifying multiple columns, Excel adds it automatically when you enter the structured reference. The Table name references the entire data body range, excluding header and total rows.
3. The **Table reference** specifies the range in the Table by specifying the column name(s) and, optionally, a special identifier that modifies the column name reference.
4. The **special identifier** modifies the column name(s) reference to refer to specific predefined areas of the Table:

   `[#All]` refers to the entire Table, including the header and total rows, if they're enabled.

   `[#Headers]` refers to the header row, if it's enabled.

   `[#Data]` refers to the data body range if any data rows exist.

   `[#Totals]` refers to the total row, if it's enabled.

   `[#This Row]` refers to the same row in which the structured reference is entered. In Excel 2010, this special identifier was deprecated and the @ symbol used instead. (This is discussed in more detail later in this chapter.)

5. The **column name** refers to a specific Table column or a range of columns.

Implicit Intersections

When working with Tables and structured references, understanding **implicit intersections** is an important part of understanding how structured references function. Sometimes referred to as **relative intersections**, implicit intersections have been a feature of Excel for many years.

An implicit intersection occurs when a reference in a cell refers to a single column of cells in another column, with the cell containing the reference in a row that intersects the referenced column of cells. With an implicit intersection, Excel resolves the reference to the single cell in the referenced column of cells that is in the same row as the cell containing the reference.

Excel does not resolve the reference down to a single cell if the cell containing the reference to the column of cells is not in a row that intersects the referenced column of cells. It also does not resolve the reference if the reference is being passed to a function that expects an array of cells. In the former case, Excel returns a `#VALUE!` error.

The next figure illustrates an implicit intersection with a reference to a column in a Table that uses structured referencing.

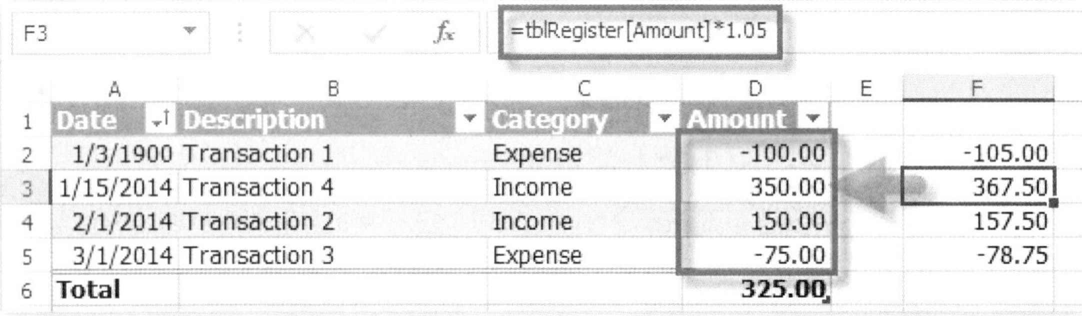

An example of an implicit intersection.

The advantage with implicit intersections is that the same formula is used in multiple cells, but the formula takes the value from a single cell in the same row where it intersects the referenced column of cells.

Advantage of Structured References

Besides encouraging the use of implicit intersections, which eases formula maintenance, structured references have the distinct advantage of being easier to read. Before structured references, Excel users relied on named ranges to make formulas easier to read and understand. With Tables, Excel is more diligent about encouraging the use of names versus column letters and row numbers. Consider this formula using regular referencing:

```
=A2-B2
```

The strings A2 and B2 don't tell you what the formula really refers to, and you need to look further to understand the purpose of the formula. When structured references are used with reasonably well-named Tables and Table columns, the purpose of the formula is clearer, without additional discovery. For example, these more meaningful names make the formula easier to understand and maintain:

```
=[@Income]-[@Expenses]
```

> ### NOTE
>
> When you're using a structured reference, if a Table column name includes manual line breaks (ALT+ENTER) and other special characters, you must include those special characters in the structured reference. (Use of special characters in column names is covered later in this chapter.) When you change column headers, Excel automatically ensures that all structured references that refer to those column names are also changed.

Creating Formulas

Clicking on cells when entering formulas is an easy way to get Excel to enter cell references instead of typing them. You can also do this with Tables, and Excel creates the structured reference for you. If Excel cannot represent the selected cells with a structured reference, it enters a standard reference. For example, in the next figure, the referenced cell is one row below the cell into which the formula is being entered.

BusinessEntityID	CreditCardID	ModifiedDate		
3268	14196	12/19/2006		=C6
7710	11522	3/23/2008		
3638	13622	1/5/2008		

Referencing a Table cell that cannot be represented as a structured reference.

In contrast, if the referenced cell is in the same row as the cell in which the formula is being entered, Excel creates a structured reference, as shown in the next figure.

BusinessEntityID	CreditCardID	ModifiedDate		
3268	14196	12/19/2006		=Table_PersonCreditCard[@ModifiedDate]
7710	11522	3/23/2008		
3638	13622	1/5/2008		

Referencing a Table cell that can be represented as a structured reference.

> **CAUTION**
>
> When you enter a formula with multiple cells selected, Excel inserts standard references instead of structured references. The workaround is to enter a formula with only one cell selected.

> **CAUTION**
>
> If the SUBTOTAL function is used in a calculated column, each time the Table is filtered, additional rows are excluded from the filter for no reason, even though they are included in the filter criteria. This is a confirmed bug in Excel 2013. The workaround is to not use the SUBTOTAL function in a calculated column.

Referencing Header Rows

You reference a header row by using the `[#Headers]` special identifier. For example, this reference resolves to the header cell in the column "Category":

```
=tblRegister[[#Headers],[Category]]
```

When you reference the header row in formulas, the header row must be enabled, or the formula will return `#REF!`. This might not seem obvious at first because a Table *always* has headers, even when the header row is disabled. But when the header row is disabled, there is no range to reference, and thus Excel resolves any reference to it as a reference error.

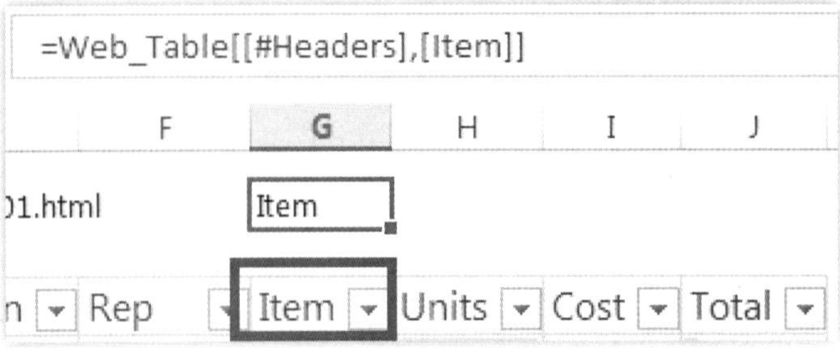

A formula referencing a visible Table header in the Table named "Web_Table".

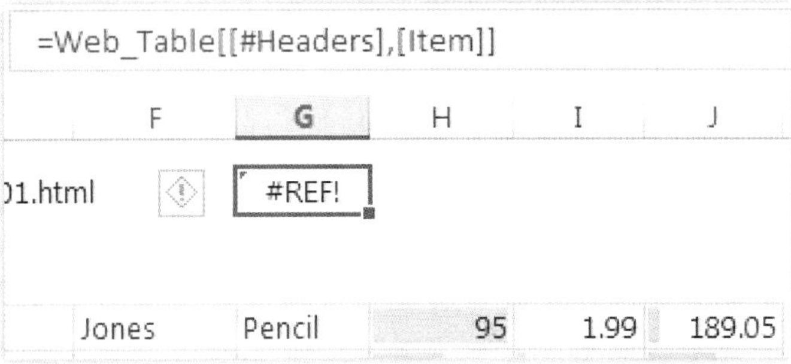

A formula referencing a disabled Table header in the Table named "Web_Table".

Referencing Total Rows

You reference the total row in a Table by using the `[#Totals]` special identifier. For example, this reference resolves to the total cell in the column "Category":

```
=tblRegister[[#Totals],[Category]]
```

When you reference the total row in a formula, the total row must be enabled, or the formula will return `#REF!`.

Unlike a header row, a total row can contain functions. Excel provides some built-in functions that work well with Tables and take into consideration rows hidden with the Table filter function. In addition to using these built-in functions, you can enter any formula or constant into a total row cell, and it can reference any Table part or, for that matter, any cell outside the Table.

> ***NOTE***
>
> You cannot use data validation in a total row.

Excel shows a list of built-in functions if you select a total row cell and click the drop-down menu button. These built-in functions utilize the SUBTOTAL function. When you select one of these aggregation functions, Excel places the SUBTOTAL function in the total row cell with the appropriate parameters to produce the desired result. The table below lists the available aggregation functions and their respective SUBTOTAL function numbers.

Total Row Function	SUBTOTAL **Function Number**
None	**Clears the cell**
`Average`	`101`
`Count`	`103`
`Count Numbers`	`102`
`Max`	`104`
`Min`	`105`

Total Row Function	SUBTOTAL Function Number
None	**Clears the Cell**
`Sum`	`109`
`StdDev`	`107`
`Var`	`110`
More Functions...	Brings up the *Function Wizard* dialog

The SUBTOTAL function is not specific to Tables, but because you will see it used in the total row by default to calculate all the aggregation functions, we include a description below. The following is the syntax for the SUBTOTAL function:

```
SUBTOTAL(function_num,ref1,[ref2]…)
```

These are the various parts of the syntax:

- **function_num**—A required number in the range 1 to 9 or 101 to 109. If you use 1 to 9, SUBTOTAL ignores filtered rows but not manually hidden rows. If you use 101 to 109, the SUBTOTAL function ignores filtered rows and manually hidden rows.
- **ref1**—A required range or reference you want to subtotal.
- **ref2**—An optional range or reference you want to subtotal. You can add up to 254 additional references.

In addition:

- Other SUBTOTAL functions in the range(s) calculated are ignored to avoid double-calculating figures.
- Subsequent ranges do not need to be sized identically.
- You are not limited to a single column reference.

Referencing Columns

Each column reference is enclosed in square brackets:

```
tblRegister[Category]
```

The default behavior of this reference is to use **implicit intersections** to resolve the reference. When you pass it to a function that expects an array, Excel resolves it to the Table's column.

When you reference multiple columns, you use a second set of square brackets, with a colon separating the two column references, just as you do with regular references:

```
tblRegister[[Description]:[Category]]
```

This reference is always resolved to entire data area columns. To constrain the reference to just a row, you use an @ symbol in front of the first reference:

```
tblRegister[@[Description]:[Category]]
```

When you AutoFill formulas across columns, Excel treats structured references as relative references and shifts them across columns. However, it does not treat multiple-column references as relative references; it treats them as absolute references. Therefore, to prevent Excel from shifting single-column references, you can construct a single-column structured reference as if it were a multiple-column reference:

```
tblRegister[[Category]:[Category]]
```

We cover absolute referencing in structured formulas in more detail later in this chapter.

The `[#This Row]` or @ Special Identifier

In Excel 2007, to constrain a column reference to the row in which the reference resides, you precede that column reference with `[#This Row]`:

```
tblRegister[[#This Row][Description]]
```

Excel 2010 replaced `[#This Row]` with @:

```
tblRegister[@[Description]]
```

In the context of implicit intersections, the @ symbol is taking away some of the implicit nature of the syntax and stating explicitly "use the value from the column in this row."

Using IntelliSense

IntelliSense ("intelligent sense") is a helpful feature that makes formula entry easier. When you enter text in the formula bar, Excel presents a pop-up list of possible objects or functions you might want to use. You can select an object or function from this pop-up list to insert it into the formula. If you're using the keyboard rather than the mouse to enter a formula, you can use arrow keys to select the desired object or function and then press the TAB key to enter the selection into the formula.

When you enter a formula into a Table's cell, IntelliSense presents all the Table parts that are legal, given the syntax entered to that point.

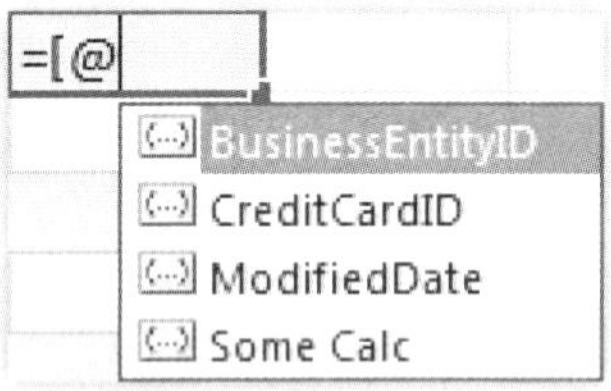

Structured reference IntelliSense.

Using Absolute Structured Referencing

Absolute referencing and relative referencing are concepts that describe how Excel modifies references to cells as a reference is moved to other locations on a worksheet. With an absolute reference, the target does not move as the reference is moved. With a relative reference, the target moves in the same way the reference moves.

For example, with traditional A1 referencing, placing a dollar sign ($) in front of both of the column letter and the row number establishes that reference as an absolute reference (for example, `$A$1`). No matter where the reference is moved, the reference will always refer to A1. Without the $ signs, the target shifts with the reference.

A reference can be a mixed reference, with a $ sign in front of the column but not the row, in which case the column is not changed, and the row shifts. If the $ sign is in front of the row but not the column, the row is not changed, but the column shifts.

Structured references are naturally relative references, and there is no obvious way to make them absolute references. With regard to rows, structured references—and Tables in general—do not support the notion of specific rows, nor are they of much concern because, most of the time, formulas are concerned only about other cells in the same row. How Excel manipulates these references when you move or copy formulas depends on the method used. You can move or copy formulas from one column to another by using four different methods:

- **Copy/paste**—Structured references do not change when they are moved to other columns.
- **Fill handle**—Structured references do change when they are moved to other columns.
- **Fill**—Structured references do not change when they are moved to other columns.
- **Array formulas**—Structured references do not change when they are moved to other columns.

Not only does Excel shift a structured reference's target in some cases, when it shifts a target, it does so in a way that is not always useful. Excel doesn't always shift the target in the same direction as the reference; when it reaches the edge of the Table, it moves to the other edge and then continues across the Table again, like a loop. Remembering the circumstances under which references' targets are shifted and how they are shifted can be confusing.

Excel does not provide an obvious way to make a structured reference an absolute reference in order to avoid shifting reference targets. However, you can use a couple tricks to force a structured reference to be an absolute reference so that Excel does not move the target when the reference is moved. One trick is to use `OFFSET` or `INDIRECT`, but there are some drawbacks to using these functions. There is a way to create absolute structured references without additional formulas.

To create an absolute structured reference, you can use a multiple-column structured reference that targets a single column:

```
Table1[[Column1]:[Column1]]
```

This reference's target ("Column1") will not move, regardless of how the formula is copied. It is equivalent to the traditional A1 reference with absolute column referencing:

```
$A1
```

Unlike with standard cell referencing, you cannot toggle the absolute/relative syntax by using the F4 key.

The following figure shows a Table named "tblData" that is used in the following examples.

Product	Color	Region	Q1 Units	Q2 Units	Q3 Units	Q4 Units
Shirt A	Blue	East	1	2	3	4
Shirt A	Green	East	1	2	3	4
Shirt A	Red	East	1	2	3	4
Shirt A	Blue	West	1	2	3	4
Shirt A	Green	West	1	2	3	4
Shirt A	Red	West	1	2	3	4
Shirt B	Blue	East	1	2	3	4
Shirt B	Green	East	1	2	3	4
Shirt B	Red	East	1	2	3	4
Shirt B	Blue	West	1	2	3	4
Shirt B	Green	West	1	2	3	4
Shirt B	Red	West	1	2	3	4

Sample data and method provided courtesy of Jon Acampora, of www.excelcampus.com.

This example shows how to accomplish a simple summary of a Table by using formulas. It demonstrates why absolute referencing is advantageous when you're developing and copying formulas using structured referencing to reference data in a Table.

In this case, you want to summarize all units by quarter and color, using the layout shown in the next figure, for the Table named "tblSum".

	A	B	C	D	E
1	Color	Q1 Units	Q2 Units	Q3 Units	Q4 Units
2	Blue				
3	Green				
4	Red				

Formula destination range: B2:E4.

You want to build a formula that can be copied from column to column without some of the targets changing so that you won't have to build multiple formulas. Using the `SUMIF` function, the formula is:

```
=SUMIF(tblData[[Color]:[Color]],tblSum[[Color]:[Color]],tblData[Q1 Units])
```

> **NOTE**
>
> The SUMIF formula's syntax is:
>
> `SUMIF(range, criteria, [sum_range])`
>
> where `range` is the range of cells to compare against the criteria, `criteria` is the criteria to use to select which cells to sum, and `sum_range` is the range of cells (optional) to sum if the criteria are satisfied in that row.

You use these references in the formula:

- **tblData[[Color]:[Color]]**—This is the range to compare against the criteria. Because it is a multiple-column reference (even though only one column is referenced), it will not shift as the formula is copied from column to column. Because the SUMIF function expects a range for this parameter, the entire column is used.
- **tblSum[[Color]:[Color]]**—This is the cell that contains the criteria used to compare against the first range. It is a multiple-column reference and will not shift. Because the function expects a single value for this parameter, only the cell's value in the same row that contains the formula is used.
- **tblData[Q1 Units]**—This is the range to sum if the criteria are satisfied in that row. It is a single-column reference and therefore will shift as the formula is copied.

Placing the formula in cell B2 in the "tblSum" Table and using the fill handle to copy it across to the other three columns yields these formulas:

```
=SUMIF(tblData[[Color]:[Color]],tblSum[[Color]:[Color]],tblData[Q1 Units])
=SUMIF(tblData[[Color]:[Color]],tblSum[[Color]:[Color]],tblData[Q2 Units])
=SUMIF(tblData[[Color]:[Color]],tblSum[[Color]:[Color]],tblData[Q3 Units])
=SUMIF(tblData[[Color]:[Color]],tblSum[[Color]:[Color]],tblData[Q4 Units])
```

Note that the first two references did not shift but the last reference, `sum_range`, did shift one column to the right for each column to the right the formula was copied.

> **NOTE**
>
> The technique described here requires the use of the fill handle to copy the formulas across columns. Using copy and paste will not shift the last parameter's target.

Disabling Structured Referencing

To avoid structured references altogether, you can select *FILE | Options | Formulas | Use Table names in formulas* and turn off the *Use table names in formulas* option.

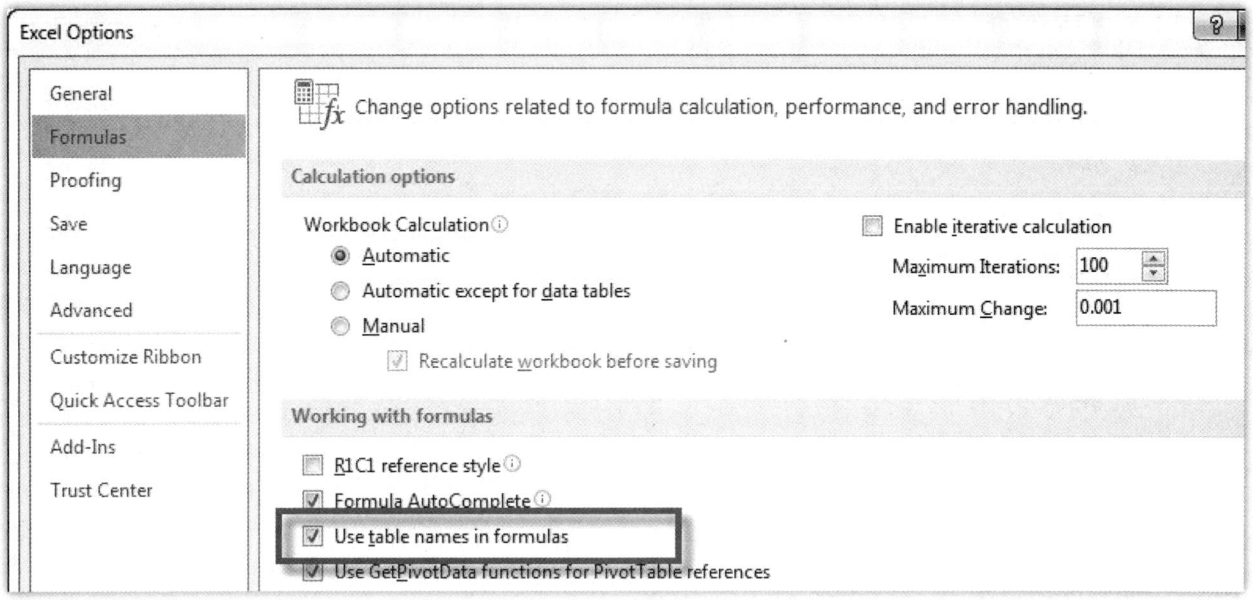

Disabling structured references by turning off the Use table names in formulas *option.*

Structured Reference Operators

As with standard cell referencing, several operators work identically with structured references:

- **Colon** (:)—This is the range operator, which joins everything between and including the two references.
- **Comma** (,)—This is the union operator, which joins everything specified in the two references.
- **Space** (   )—This is the intersection operator, which joins everything overlapping between the two references.

The following table provides some examples using the three different reference operators and the equivalent standard reference. The Table name is "Table1", the Table header is in row 1, and the data body range starts in row 2 and ends in row 20. Columns are in this order, beginning in column A: "OrderDate", "Region", "Rep", "Item", "Cost".

Reference	Refers to	Type
`=Table1[[OrderDate]:[Rep]]`	A2:C20	Range
`=Table1[Region],Table1[Item]`	B2:B20,D2:D20	Union
`=Table1[[Rep]:[Units]] Table1[[Item]:[Cost]]`	D2:E20	Intersection

Special Characters Used in Structured References

When a column name contains any of the following special characters, the name must be enclosed in an extra set of square brackets:

- Space (   )
- Line feed
- Carriage return
- Comma (,)
- Colon (:)
- Period (.)
- Left bracket ([ ) †
- Right bracket ( ]) †

- Pound sign (#) †
- Single quotation mark (apostrophe) (') †
- Quotation mark (   )
- Left curly bracket (brace) ({)
- Right curly bracket (brace) (})
- Dollar sign ($)
- Caret (^)
- Ampersand (&)
- Asterisk (*)
- Plus sign (+)
- Minus sign (-)
- Equal sign (=)
- Greater than (>)
- Less than (<)
- Division (/)

The characters marked in this list with a † have special meaning and so require an escape character in order to be properly recognized. The escape character is an apostrophe ('):

```
[Order '#]
```

When a column name contains any of the special characters listed above and the @ symbol is used to keep the target of the reference on the same row as the reference, an added layer of square brackets surrounding the text is required, as shown below with the column name "$ Amount":

```
[@[$ Amount]]
```

Dynamic Referencing

You use dynamic referencing to create named ranges that are **dynamic** (that is, change depending on conditions) and that can be used in conditional formatting and validation lists. Here are some examples:

- Creating a validation list using a column of values in a Table
- Creating conditional formatting rules based on looking up a cell's value in a Table to get a value in another column (VLOOKUP) and comparing the result to a specific value
- Summing a specific month's sales figures in a Table, where multiple columns contain sales data, and each column contains a single month's sales figures

Named ranges, which are also called **named formulas**, are useful even when they're not dynamic because Excel does not allow structured referencing in conditional formatting rules or validation lists. The following example demonstrates the steps for creating a simple named dynamic range that is used in a validation list, based on a column in a Table:

1. Create a new Table and name it "tblValues". Name one of the columns "Value" and enter two or more unique values in the column.
2. Select the data area range portion of the "Value" column. If the header or total rows are showing, do not select them; select just the data body range of the column.

> ### TIP
> You can move the mouse over the top edge of the Table's column header (not the worksheet header) to turn the cursor into a bold down arrow. You can click there to select the entire Table data area range column (excluding the header and total rows). You can click again to select the Table's column, including the header row and total row. Subsequent clicks toggle between these two selections.

3. Select *FORMULAS | Defined Names, Name Manager* (or use the keyboard shortcut CTRL+F3) to open the *Name Manager* dialog box.

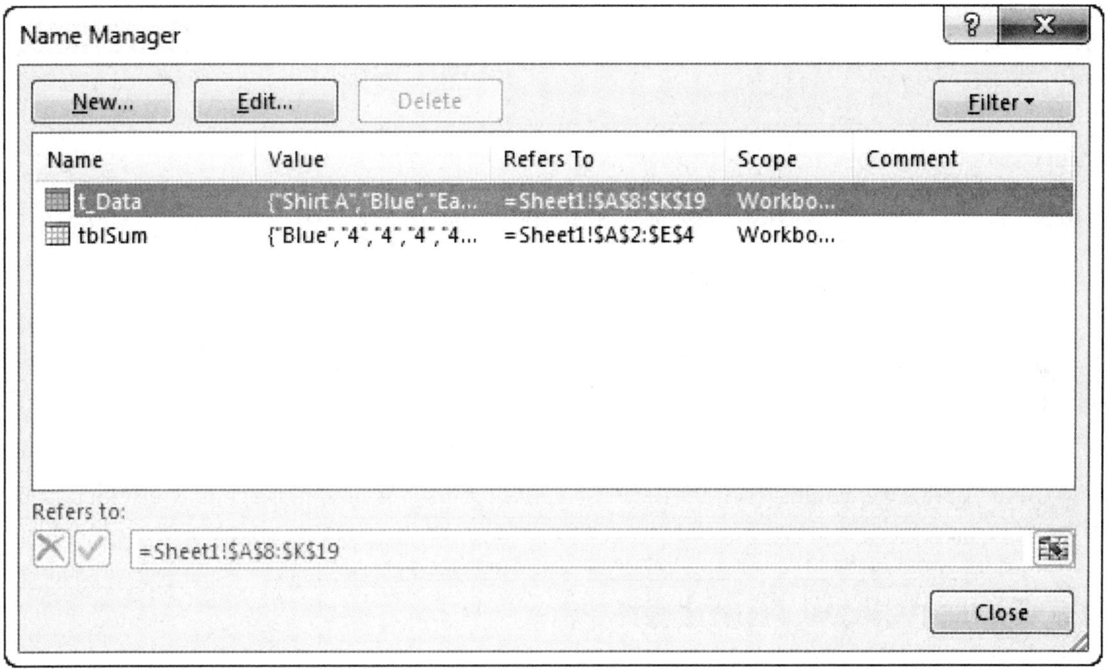

Name Manager *dialog box.*

4. Click the *New* button to open the *New Name* dialog box.

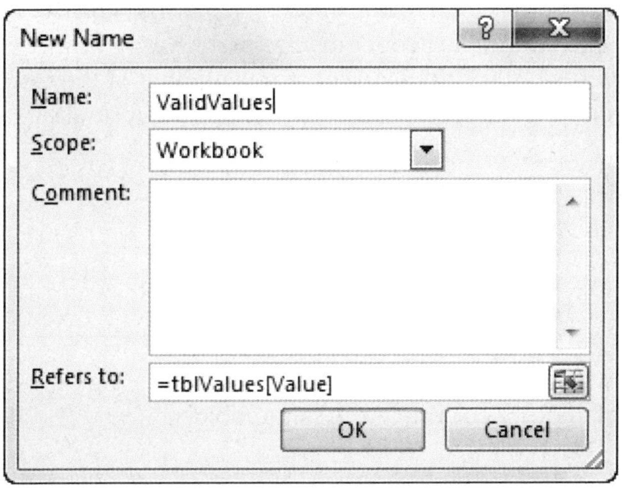

New Name *dialog box.*

5. Enter "ValidValues" in the Name text box. Note that the structured reference to the Table's "Value" column is already entered into the Refers to text box. Click OK.

6. Select the cell to which the validation list is to be applied and select *DATA | Data Tools | Data Validation | Data Validation*. Select "List" from the *Allow* combo box, enter "=ValidValues" in the *Source* text box, and click *OK*.

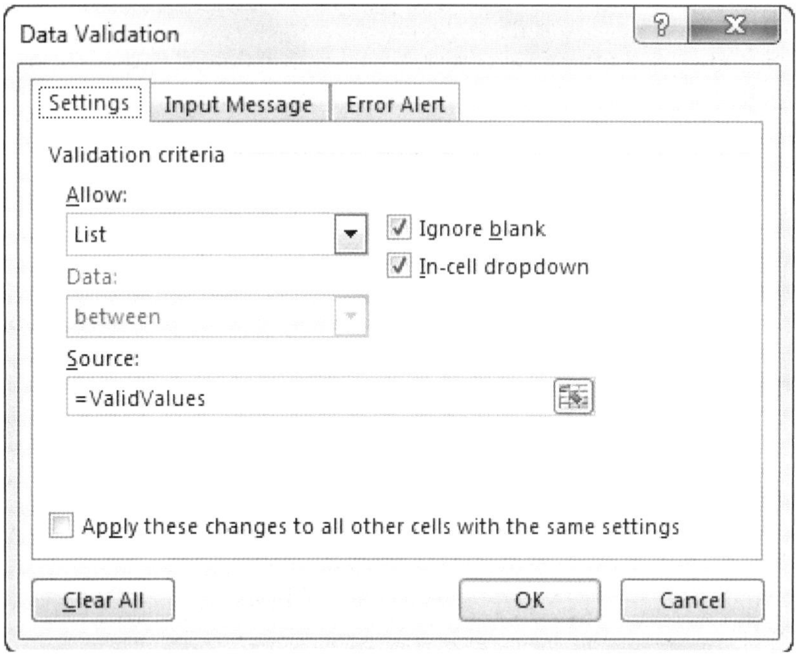

Creating a validation list using a named dynamic reference.

A validation list that contains the values from the Table's "Value" column is now in place in the selected cell.

Using the Current Row Number

The following formula displays the row number in a Table where the row number is relative to the first row in the Table and not the worksheet's row number:

```
=ROW()-ROW(Table1[[#Headers],[Column1]])
```

The row number can also be useful when you're referencing the same row in another Table. The formula works by subtracting the worksheet's row number in which the Table header resides from the worksheet's row number in which the formula resides. The ROW formula returns the worksheet row number of the first row of the range reference passed to it, or the worksheet row number of the row in which the formula resides if no range reference is passed to it.

If the first data row is always in a specific worksheet row, a more direct approach is to use a constant instead of passing the Table's header row to the ROW function:

```
=ROW()-1
```

Calculating a Running Total

The following formula displays a simple running total of another column in the same Table:

```
=SUM(tblRegister[[#Headers],[Amount]]:[@Amount])
```

This formula assumes that the header row is enabled; the SUM function ignores the text value in the header. If the header row of the referenced column is not enabled, the above example returns #REF!. To avoid this, reference the first cell of the Table column by using the INDEX function:

```
=SUM(INDEX([Amount],1):[@Amount])
```

> **CAUTION**
>
> You can implement this example by using standard referencing as =SUM(D$2:D2), assuming that Amount is in column D. You use absolute row referencing to keep the first part of the range absolute, while the second part shifts as the formula is copied down rows. However, there is a known issue when using absolute standard row referencing (A$1) in a Table: When new rows are added, Excel mangles the reference and the column formatting, rendering the formula in the new row and preceding rows in error. The workaround is to find an alternative approach that avoids absolute standard row referencing, as demonstrated in the preceding example.

If the amounts used to calculate the running total are in two columns, one for debits and one for credits, then the formula is:

```
=SUM(INDEX([Credit],1):[@Credit])-SUM(INDEX([Debit],1):[@Debit])
```

Using structured references can have a negative impact on calculation performance on large data sets, as in the example above. In the context of these examples, a large data set is anything over around 100,000 rows of Table data on most modern computers. The problem lies in how structured references are used: Each row sums all the rows above, including the same row, to get the running total for that row.

The next formula example utilizes standard cell referencing to improve calculation performance by working with only three cells in the row above and in the same row; this avoids repeated summing of thousands of rows. From the previous formula, it is assumed that Credit is in column C, Debit is in column D, the running total calculation is in column E, and the headers are in row 1. The formula in cell E2 (the running total in the first data row) is:

```
=N(E1)+C2-D2
```

When copied down the length of the column, the formula takes the running total from the previous row, adds the credit, and subtracts the debit on the same row to get a new running total for that row. This assumes that debits are entered as positive values, as they are on an accounting ledger.

Why use the N function? In the first row, the formula uses the header value in a numeric calculation; if the header is a text value, the formula produces a #VALUE! error. The N function solves this problem by taking the parameter passed to it and returning the same value if the parameter is numeric or zero if the parameter is text.

Another way to solve this problem is to use the SUM function, which ignores text values (effectively treating them as zero values):

```
=SUM(E1,C2,-D2)
```

5 Pivoting with Tables

Tables make great data sources. They must adhere to specific rules, such as single-row headers and unique header values, that ensure good data structuring. Tables are therefore ideal for use as data sources for PivotTables or other reporting methods. In this chapter we explain why.

Creating PivotTables

Because Tables can expand and contract with data, they make excellent data sources for PivotTables. For example, when you type into a blank row directly beneath a Table, the Table expands to include the new row. As the Table expands and contracts, Excel maintains the Table's name and related range references. This feature makes it convenient to reference the Table from external locations, such as a PivotTable.

> **CAUTION**
>
> Excel does not allow a Table to expand or contract on a protected worksheet, and it produces no error if you try to make such a change.

Creating a PivotTable

To create a PivotTable using a Table's data, select any part of the Table and then select *{TABLE TOOLS} DESIGN | Tools | Summarize with PivotTable.*

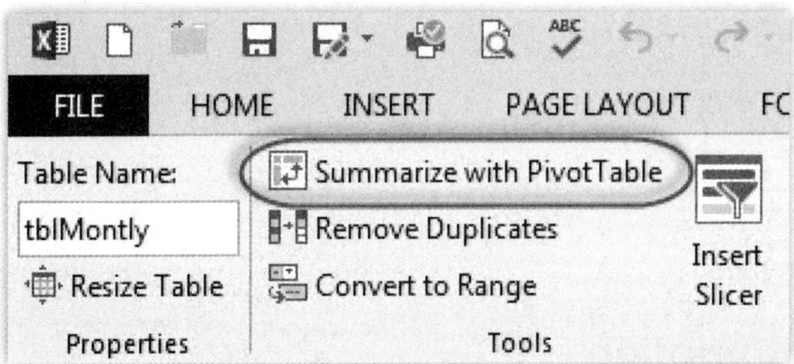

Create a PivotTable by selecting {TABLE TOOLS} DESIGN | Tools | Summarize *with PivotTable.*

The *Create PivotTable* dialog box appears. By default, the Table's name is entered as the source, and the destination is directed to a new worksheet.

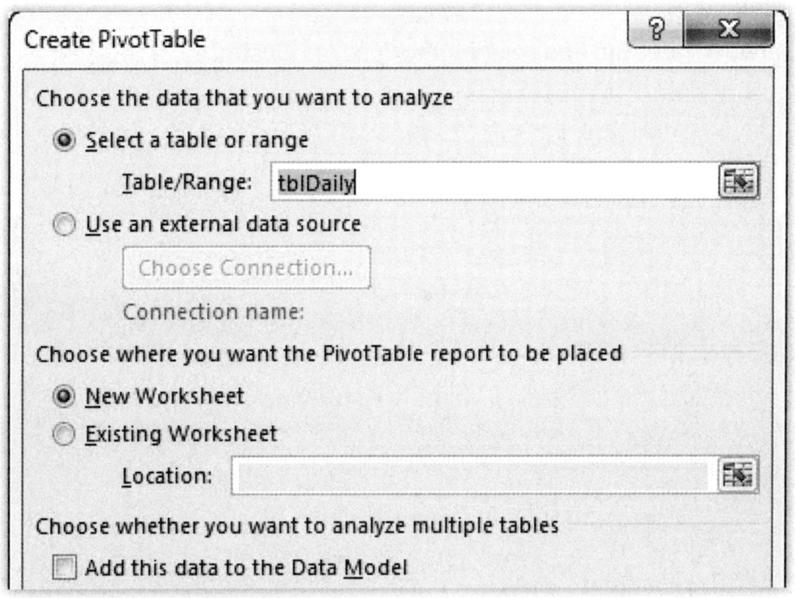

Create PivotTable *dialog box.*

Refreshing Manually

Excel does not automatically refresh PivotTables; you have to refresh them manually. To refresh a PivotTable, select any cell in the PivotTable and select *{PIVOTTABLE TOOLS} ANALYZE | Data | Refresh* or right-click any cell in the PivotTable and select *Refresh*.

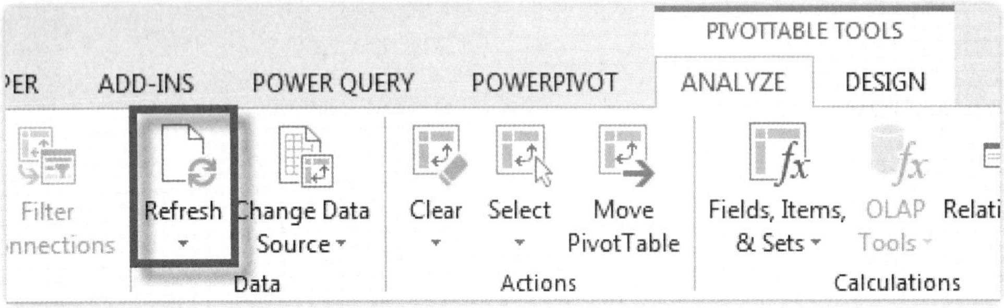

PivotTable Refresh *button on the ribbon.*

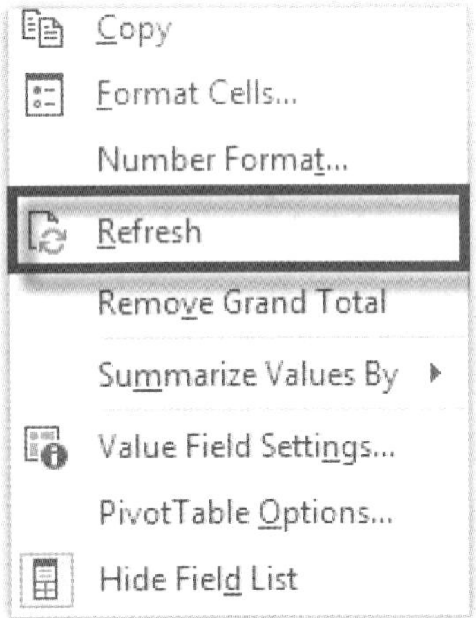

PivotTable Refresh *option on the right-click context menu.*

Refreshing Automatically, Using Automation

Using VBA (Visual Basic for Applications) for automation is a powerful way to expand Excel's functionality. Chapter 9 extensively discusses automating Tables using VBA. This section explains how to use VBA to trigger an automatic PivotTable refresh. Implementing this solution does not require any knowledge of VBA, programming, or the Excel Object Model.

To implement this solution, right-click the worksheet tab and select *View Code*, as illustrated in the next figure.

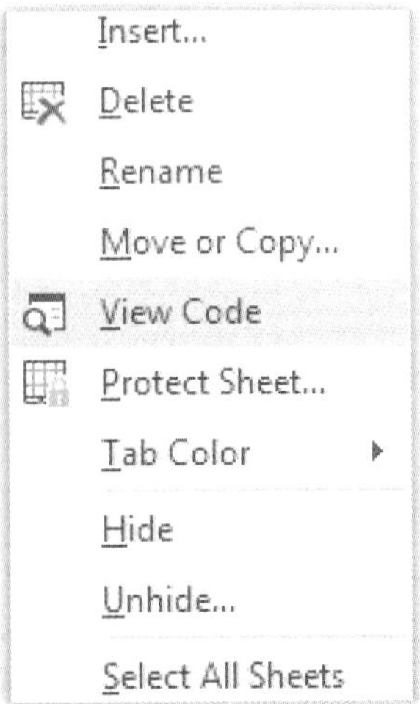

Worksheet right-click menu.

Copy and paste this code into the code window that appears:

```
Private Sub Worksheet_Activate()
    Dim PT As PivotTable
    For Each PT In Me.PivotTables
        PT.PivotCache.Refresh
    Next PT
End Sub
```

Press CTRL+F11 to return to Excel.

The code runs when the worksheet is activated. It refreshes all PivotTables on the worksheet.

> **CAUTION**
>
> If the worksheet that contains the PivotTable is protected, the VBA code produces an error. A workaround is to set the `UserInterfaceOnly` parameter of the `Protect` method to `True` when protecting the worksheet.

> **NOTE**
>
> *VBA code is not allowed in the XLSX file format. As soon as VBA code is added to a workbook, the workbook must be saved in the XLSM format. Other formats allow VBA code, but that topic is beyond the scope of this book.*

Power BI

Power BI (Business Intelligence) is a new offering (currently in preview at this writing) for Office 365 ProPlus and SharePoint subscriptions. Through Excel and the power of the cloud, Power BI provides powerful, large-scale BI analysis services to many more users. Its publishing features give Excel users more robust and varied distribution paths and venues to share the results of their analytical efforts.

Beginning with Power Pivot, which was initially released for Excel 2010, Microsoft has introduced several "Power" projects, all of which are components of Power BI: Power Query, Power Map, Power Pivot, Power View, and Power BI Sites. For more information, visit http://office.microsoft.com/en-us/excel/power-bi-FX104080667.aspx.

> **NOTE**
>
> This book covers Power Pivot and Power Query only as they relate to Tables.

Power Pivot

Understanding how Tables work with Power Pivot requires a basic understanding of what Power Pivot is and how it's used. Introduced for Excel 2010 as an add-in, Power Pivot consumes data from any number of connections to data sources without having to adhere to Excel's row limitations. The data consumed is maintained in the Power Pivot Data Model and delivered to consumers such as PivotTables and PivotCharts via extremely fast queries. In essence, Power Pivot gives Excel users access to very large data sets from multiple sources while providing powerful and fast transformation and query functions to create Excel-friendly tables and charts for analysis and presentation.

> **NOTE**
>
> Beginning with Excel 2007, Excel's row limit is 1,048,576. If you open a pre-2007 Excel file (XLS), it will retain the old limit (65,536 rows) unless you save it in one of the new file formats, close it, and reopen it.
>
> Prior to Microsoft's announcement of Power BI, Power Pivot was known as PowerPivot (no space). To keep it more in line with the new suite of add-ins (Power Query, Power Map, Power View), Microsoft renamed it Power Pivot. However, the add-in is still named without a space, and it shows up that way on the ribbon.

Microsoft made significant improvements to the Power Pivot add-in with the release of Excel 2013. One of the most significant changes was in the in-memory analytics engine known as VertiPaq, or xVelocity, that drives the Data Model. VertiPaq uses compression and optimized access algorithms to load large amounts of data quickly and efficiently and to make the requested data available to data visualization objects such as PivotTables in worksheets.

AMO, ADOMD.NET, and the OLEDB provider all facilitate data access; they are all installed with the add-in and support connections to the Data Model. In addition, the OData format is a data feed provider for importing and refreshing data.

One of the most powerful characteristics of Power Pivot is its ability to simultaneously connect to multiple disparate data sources, including Excel Tables. Excel Tables can also consume data queried from a Data Model using DAX (described later in this chapter).

> **NOTE**
>
> The terms **Power Pivot** and **Power Pivot Data Model** are often interchanged and roughly refer to the same thing. Specifically, Power Pivot is the entire add-in and the user experience exposed to the user, and the Power Pivot Data Model (or just Data Model) is the entire collection of data, relationships, and measures created and maintained by Power Pivot.

> **NOTE**
>
> You cannot use a standard range as a source type for the Data Model. The source must be in Table format.

In Excel 2010, if you're working with a Power Pivot–based workbook, the Power Pivot add-in must be installed. It's a free download for all editions of Excel 2010. To install Power Pivot, you must have administrative privileges, so you may need IT support in a corporate environment. At this writing, there are two versions of Power Pivot available: 10 and 11. We recommend using the latest version, 11, with Excel 2010. The VertiPaq engine is included only in the add-in for Excel 2010 that is required to interact with the Data Model.

Since the VertiPaq engine is built into Excel 2013, the Power Pivot add-in is not required for working with a PivotTable based on a Power Pivot Data Model. However, in order to manage the Data Model, the Power Pivot add-in must be installed.

> **NOTE**
>
> Only certain versions of Excel 2013 support the Power Pivot add-in:
>
> - **Excel 2013 ProPlus**—Available only with an Office 365 subscription
> - **Excel 2013 Professional Plus**—Available only through volume licensing
> - **Excel 2013 standalone**—Available at retail outlets (for example, Amazon.com)
>
> The Power Pivot add-in is not available in any other editions of Excel 2013.

Once the add-in is installed, you get a new *POWERPIVOT* ribbon tab, as shown in the next figure.

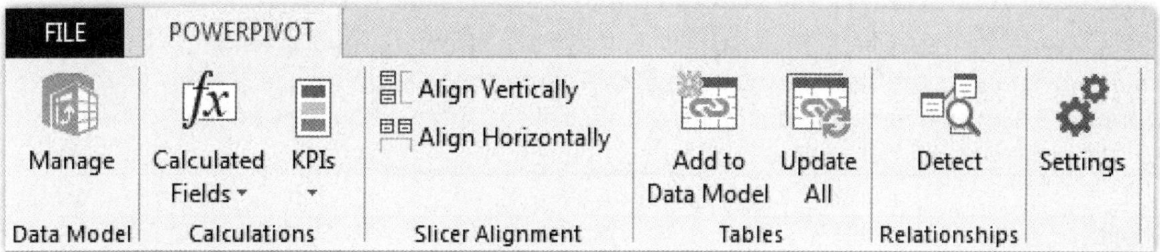

POWERPIVOT *ribbon tab.*

Once a Power Pivot workbook is created, you can publish it to a 2010 SharePoint Server or Power BI Site that has Excel Services and a deployment of SQL Server Power Pivot for SharePoint. You can also open a workbook with Power Pivot objects in Excel 2007, but the user cannot interact with any of the PivotTables or PivotCharts created from the Data Model. During any client-side data refresh or Data Model import, all access to external sources goes through the xVelocity engine and runs inside the Excel process. This integrated approach gives the user the ability to create self-service BI solutions from within an Excel session.

> **NOTE**
>
> A 64-bit version of Power Pivot is available and must be used with 64-bit Office. If you're using 32-bit Office, you must use the 32-bit of Power Pivot (referred to as x86).

Adding a Table to the Data Model

You add a Table to the Data Model by selecting *POWERPIVOT | Tables | Add to Data Model.* Once a Table is part of the Data Model, it becomes a Linked Table, and you can use it to create relationships and measures in the same way as any other data source.

While a Table is linked to a Data Model, the *Linked Table* ribbon tab is displayed in the Power Pivot window. The *Linked Table* tab is a contextual tab, so it appears only when the selected Table is a Linked Table. This ribbon tab has the following controls:

- ***Update All***—Updates all linked Tables in the model
- ***Update Selected***—Updates only the selected Table in the model
- ***Excel Table***—Lists all Linked Tables in the workbook so you can click one to jump to it or type in a name
- ***Go to Excel Table***—Goes straight to a Linked Table on the worksheet
- ***Update Mode***—Sets whether Linked Tables update automatically or manually

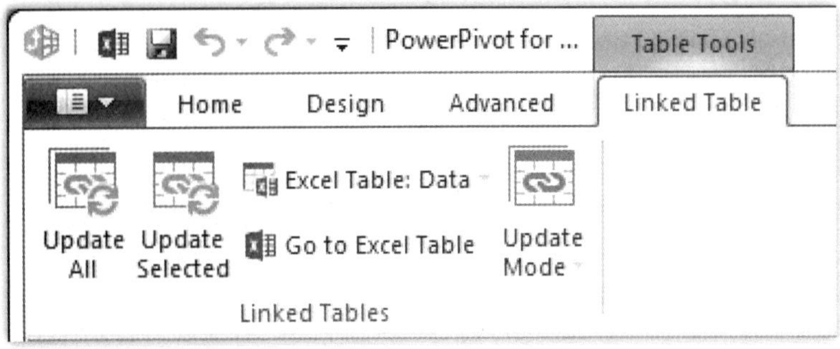

Linked Table *ribbon tab in the Power Pivot window.*

> **CAUTION**
>
> When you query a Data Model that exposes a table loaded from a Linked Table, the default table name is the same as the Linked Table name, but you can change it. You use the Data Model table name, not the upstream Linked Table name, in any queries directed at the Data Model.

> **NOTE**
>
> Windows XP users do not see a ribbon tab. Instead, they see a command bar control menu with all the same controls. For more information, see http://technet.microsoft.com/en-us/library/gg399147.aspx.

Updating Data

By default, all Linked Tables are set to automatically refresh. This does not mean every modification to a Table triggers an update to the Data Model, especially if the Data Model was created in Excel 2013 and distributed to users who do not have the add-in installed. Some kind of interaction with the Data Model triggers an update. The easiest way to trigger an update is by selecting *POWERPIVOT | Tables | Update All*.

Another way to refresh the data in the Data Model is to select *DATA | Connections | Refresh All*. This action refreshes all connections to and from Tables, Data Models, PivotTables, and PivotCharts.

> **NOTE**
>
> A Linked Table is a Table added to a Data Model, and the data flows from the Table to the Data Model; it is not a Table that queries a Data Model.

DAX Table Queries

For years MDX (Multidimensional Expressions) has been the standard query language for extracting data from external databases such as SSAS (SQL Server Analysis Services). DAX (Data Analysis Expressions) replaced MDX when Power Pivot was created. DAX provides much faster access to data and is more tightly integrated into Excel than MDX.

DAX is a query language for Power Pivot and SQL Server Analysis Tabular models. Microsoft designed the DAX language to be easier to use than its predecessor, MDX, by modeling the language after Excel formulas and including dynamic aggregation and relational data functions. It is designed to be easier to understand and learn than other query languages, while leveraging the larger Data Models typically found in Power Pivot Data Models and SSAS. DAX effectively brings powerful data query services to Excels user in a familiar form.

The rest of this section presents an example of using DAX in a Table to query a Power Pivot Data Model and return a set of unique values in a field. This is a common Excel task involved in creating a unique list of data. There are many reasons you might want a unique list of values, such as for summarizing data or for using in-cell drop-down lists with data validation.

> **CAUTION**
>
> You can use DAX queries in a Table only with an OLAP data source (for example, Power Pivot). DAX cannot be used on standalone Excel Tables, text file connections (which can't return to Tables at all), or web connections (unless the web connection is brought into the Data Model first).

The next figure shows an example of a Table returned from a SQL Server data source. Since this Table is connected to a database, refreshing the Table updates it with the latest data in SQL Server.

	A	B	C	D	E	F	
1	BusinessEntityI	Title	FirstName	MiddleName	LastName	Suffix	JobTitle
2	130		Rob	T	Caron		Production Techni
3	131		Baris	F	Cetinok		Production Techni
4	132		Nicole	B	Holliday		Production Techni
5	133		Michael	L	Rothkugel		Production Techni
6	134		Eric		Gubbels		Production Superv
7	135		Ivo	William	Salmre		Production Techni
8	136		Sylvester	A	Valdez		Production Techni
9	137		Anibal	T	Sousa		Production Techni
10	138		Samantha	H	Smith		Production Techni

SQL Server data source in an Excel Table.

> **NOTE**
>
> The sample data used here is from the AdventureWorks2012 database, provided free by Microsoft, at http://msftdbprodsamples.codeplex.com/releases/view/93587.

When you establish a connection to a SQL Server database and define a query, Excel creates a default DAX query, based on how the query was defined—but only if the data is loaded into a Power Pivot Data Model. To load the data into the Data Model, you need to ensure that the check box Add this data to the Data Model is checked, as shown in the next figure, when you define the connection and query.

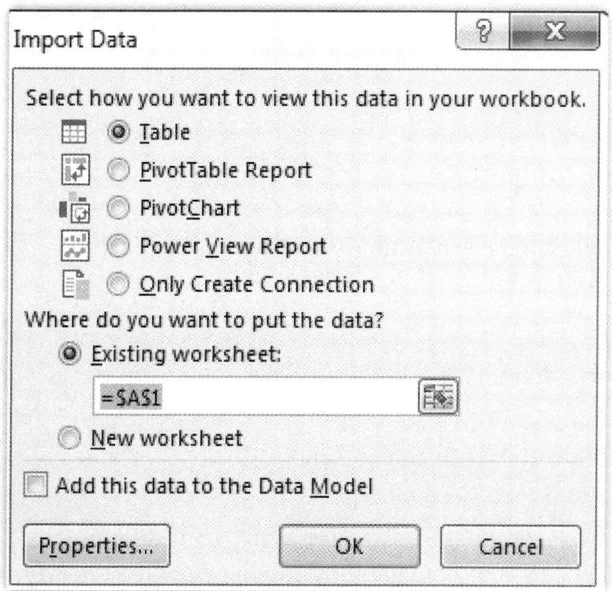

Dialog box for importing data.

> **NOTE**
>
> When you build a query to load a Table, the data must be added to the Data Model (that is, loaded into Power Pivot) in order to enable DAX.

> **TIP**
>
> To get a more in-depth understanding of DAX, see Rob Collie's book *DAX Formulas for PowerPivot: The Excel Pro's Guide to Mastering DAX.*

You edit a DAX formula by right-clicking any cell in the Table and selecting *Table | Edit DAX*, as shown in the next figure.

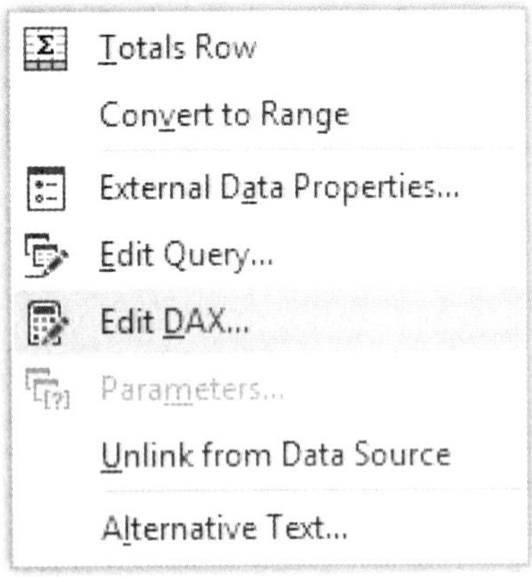

Table right-click submenu on an OLAP data source.

In the *Edit DAX* dialog box that appears, the *Command Type* combo box defaults to "Table". Change this to "DAX" to allow editing of the DAX expression in the text box, as shown in the next figure. Then you can edit and evaluate the DAX statement.

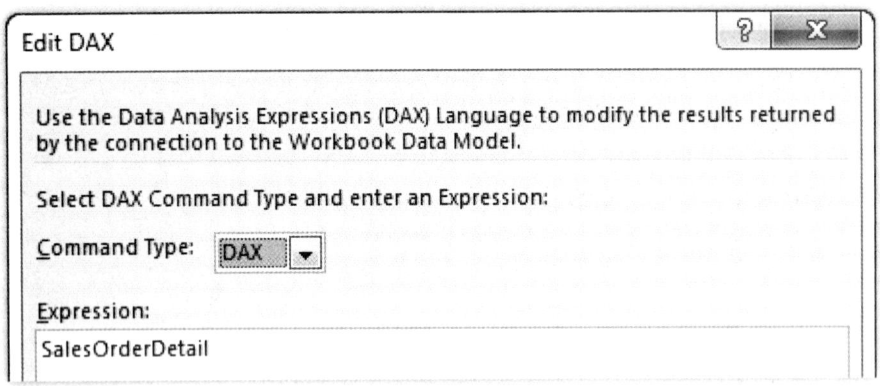

Edit DAX dialog box for editing DAX Table queries.

In this example, your goal is to retrieve all the unique values in the "LastName" field. The DAX query for this example is:

```
Evaluate(Summarize(Person, Person[LastName]))
```

While the open and close parentheses for the `Evaluate` statement aren't necessarily needed, they can make the statement easier to read and maintain.

You can use many different forms of DAX queries to return results into an Excel Table. Power Pivot does not have to be installed to utilize this feature; you just need an OLAP data source.

While this method is very fast, it isn't always user friendly. Error messages, as shown in the next figure, don't give much information and can be cryptic. Currently, this is the most information you get if a query statement is invalid. In the specific case shown here, there is a "z" after the "LastName" field name.

The only way you know if a DAX query is valid is to get no error message and have the query perform as expected in the Table.

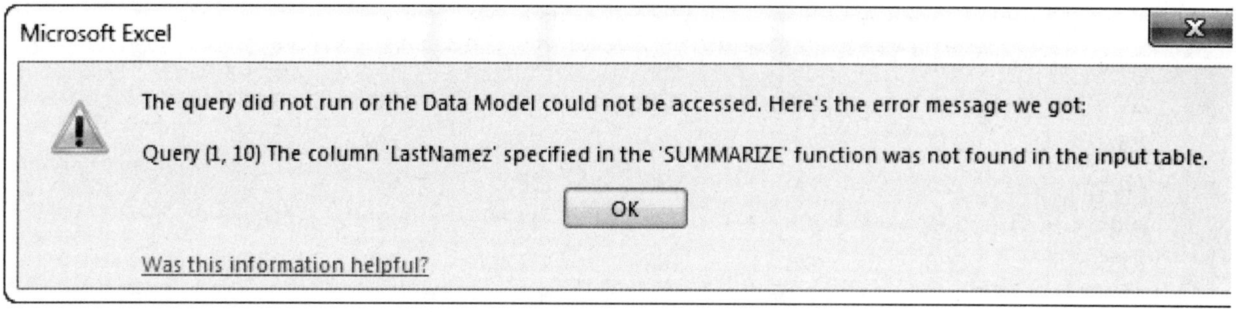

DAX Table query error message.

Power Query

As part of the "Power" suite of tools, Power Query provides the ability to inspect, query, transform, organize, and expose data from many sources. Unlike traditional query editors, it utilizes the **M** language, which runs quickly and returns only the final query results.

> **TIP**
>
> Power Query is a free download from the Microsoft website. It is available for both 32- and 64-bit versions of Office 2010 and 2013. Search for "download power query" to find the current download location.

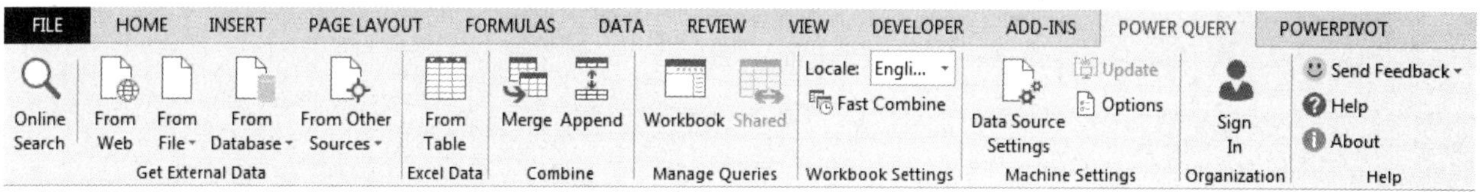

POWER QUERY *ribbon tab.*

Power Query can pull data from many different kinds of data sources, including Tables. When you use a Table as the data source for a query, you see a new *QUERY* ribbon tab in the *TABLE TOOLS* contextual ribbon tab group in addition to the *DESIGN* tab, as shown in the next figure.

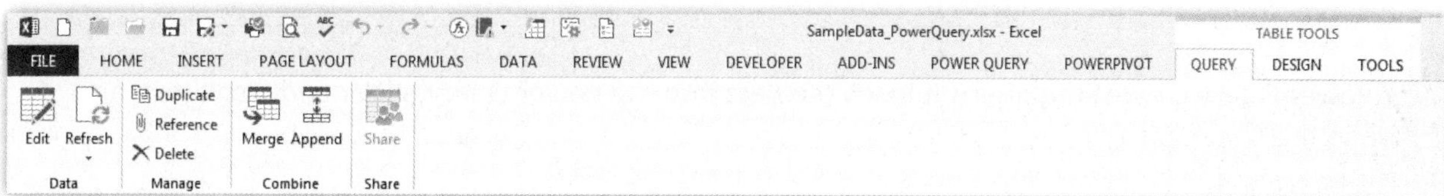

QUERY *ribbon tab in the TABLE TOOLS contextual ribbon tab group when a Table returned from a Power Query is selected.*

> **CAUTION**
>
> Once you use a Table as the data source for a Power Query, you can't convert it to a normal range unless the query is removed from the workbook.

Power Query is exceptionally good at transforming data from forms that are difficult to manage and analyze into forms that are better structured. The following example takes a badly formed report and transforms it into a form more conducive to analysis.

The sample data is in a pivoted format (see the next figure), which means there is relational data extending down rows and to the right over columns. A better structure would be to have both the age range and the year extend down rows. Power Query can accomplish this transformation in a couple steps.

	A	B	C	D	E	F	G	H
1								
2		Year	Ages <18	Ages 18-25	Ages 26-35	Ages 36-45	Ages 46-55	Ages >56
3		2000	446	305	300	402	323	292
4		2001	341	264	379	345	211	340
5		2002	311	275	332	226	247	227
6		2003	226	396	196	386	435	276
7		2004	196	209	271	417	278	163
8		2005	286	423	182	212	369	220

Starting sample data to be transformed into a usable data structure.

To start working with this data in Power Query, select POWER QUERY | Excel Data | From Table. If the source data is not already a Table, Power Query converts it to a Table.

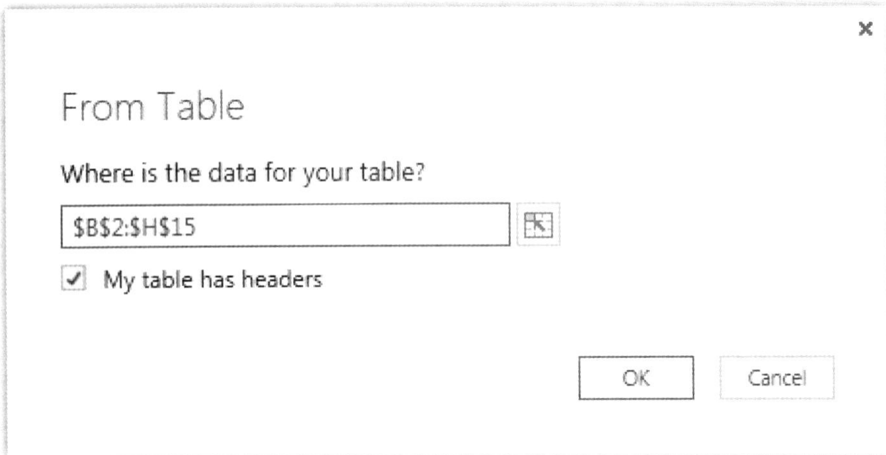

Making a Table from Power Query.

> **NOTE**
>
> Creating a query from Power Query generates a data connection within the workbook to the final query output. The connection type is an OLEDB query, and the provider is listed as "Microsoft.Mashup.OleDb.1".

After Power Query creates the query, it loads the data into the Power Query editor and displays it, as shown in the next figure.

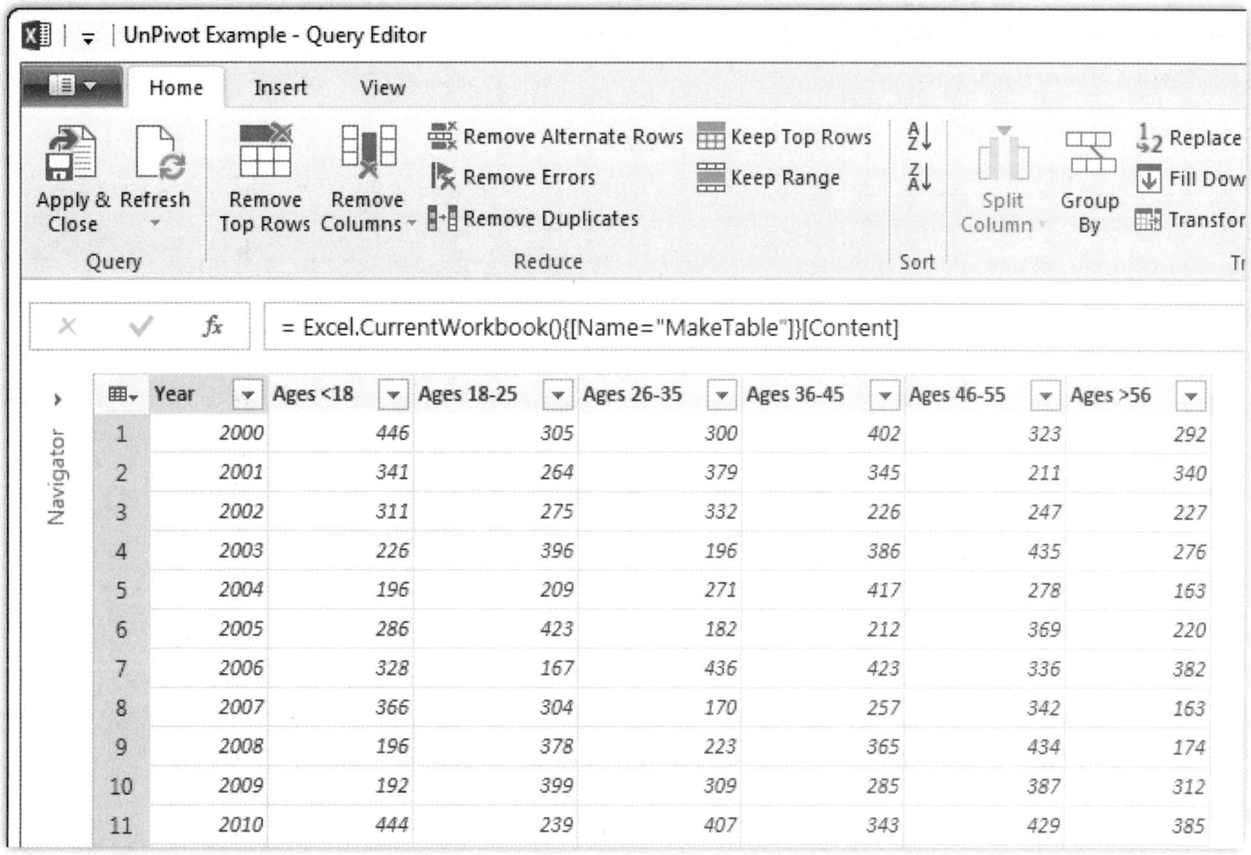

	Year	Ages <18	Ages 18-25	Ages 26-35	Ages 36-45	Ages 46-55	Ages >56
1	2000	446	305	300	402	323	292
2	2001	341	264	379	345	211	340
3	2002	311	275	332	226	247	227
4	2003	226	396	196	386	435	276
5	2004	196	209	271	417	278	163
6	2005	286	423	182	212	369	220
7	2006	328	167	436	423	336	382
8	2007	366	304	170	257	342	163
9	2008	196	378	223	365	434	174
10	2009	192	399	309	285	387	312
11	2010	444	239	407	343	429	385

Power Query Editor *window.*

To transform the data (that is, unpivot it), you need to select all the age columns in the Power Query editor. You can't select multiple columns in this editor, so select the leftmost column to unpivot—in this case the "Ages <18" column. Then, while holding down the SHIFT key, select the rightmost column to unpivot—in this case the "Age >56" column. In the Query Editor window, select *Home | Transform | Unpivot*. The data now appears in three columns, as shown in the next figure.

	Year	Attribute	Value
1	2000	Ages <18	446
2	2000	Ages 18-25	305
3	2000	Ages 26-35	300
4	2000	Ages 36-45	402
5	2000	Ages 46-55	323
6	2000	Ages >56	292
7	2001	Ages <18	341
8	2001	Ages 18-25	264
9	2001	Ages 26-35	379
10	2001	Ages 36-45	345
11	2001	Ages 46-55	211
12	2001	Ages >56	340

Unpivoted data.

Next, you need to rename the age column from "Attribute"—the default name that Power Query assigned—to "Age Range" by right-clicking the header of that column and selecting *Rename*.

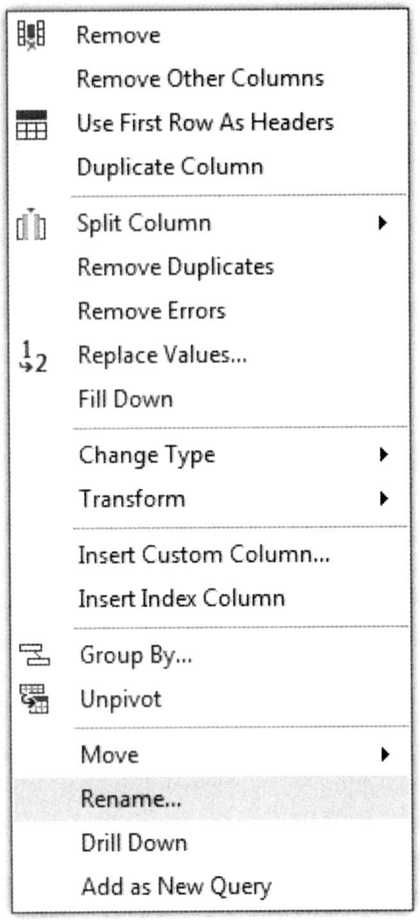

Column right-click context menu in Power Query.

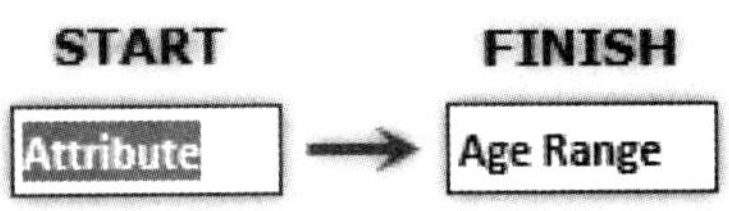

Renaming a column in Power Query.

You select *HOME | Query | Apply & Close* to complete the query. Power Query places the resulting Table in a new worksheet, as shown in the next figure, and closes the editor.

	A	B	C
1	Year	Age	Value
2	2000	Ages <18	446
3	2000	Ages 18-25	305
4	2000	Ages 26-35	300
5	2000	Ages 36-45	402
6	2000	Ages 46-55	323
7	2000	Ages >56	292
8	2001	Ages <18	341
9	2001	Ages 18-25	264
10	2001	Ages 26-35	379
11	2001	Ages 36-45	345
12	2001	Ages 46-55	211
13	2001	Ages >56	340
14	2002	Ages <18	311
15	2002	Ages 18-25	275
16	2002	Ages 26-35	332
17	2002	Ages 36-45	226
18	2002	Ages 46-55	247
19	2002	Ages >56	227
20	2003	Ages <18	226
21	2003	Ages 18-25	396
22	2003	Ages 26-35	196
23	2003	Ages 36-45	386
24	2003	Ages 46-55	435

Final output from the Power Query example, unpivoted and in a Table.

> **CAUTION**
>
> Any changes you make to the Table that contains the query results will be overwritten when the query is refreshed.

> ***NOTE***
>
> When creating a query in the *Query Editor*, the *Load to worksheet* check box is checked (which it is by default), Power Query creates a Table in a new worksheet or updates the existing Table, if already loaded. When the *Load to Data Model* check box is checked (which is not the default), Power Query loads the data into the Data Model for use with Power Pivot. If the query is edited and either check box is changed from checked to not checked, Power Query removes that destination.

In summary, this Power Query example involves three distinct actions to restructure the data into a usable format:

1. Define a Table as the data source for the query.
2. Unpivot the data columns.
3. Rename the "Attribute" column.

The following M code results from performing these three steps:

```
let
    Source = Excel.CurrentWorkbook(){[Name="MakeTable"]}[Content],
    Unpivot = Table.UnpivotOtherColumns(Source,{"Year"},"Attribute","Value"),
    RenamedColumns = Table.RenameColumns(Unpivot,{{"Attribute", "Age Range"}})
in
    RenamedColumns
```

Since this is a Power Query–generated Table, the contextual *QUERY* tab is displayed in the *TABLE TOOLS* ribbon tab group when the Table is selected. You use this ribbon tab to edit the query.

You can also use the *Workbook Queries* task pane to look at or edit a query. To display or hide this task pane, select *POWER QUERY | Manage Queries | Workbook*. The *Workbook Queries* task pane shows all queries in the workbook; from this task pane, you can edit or refresh any of them.

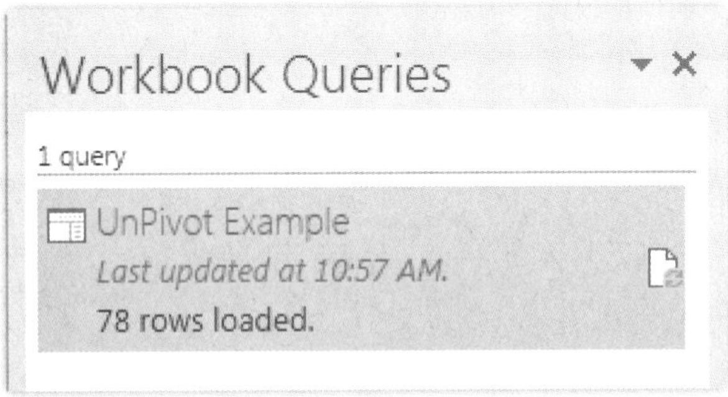

Workbook Queries *task pane, visible when a Table is selected that is created from Power Query.*

When you hover over a query in the task pane, as shown in the next figure, you get a quick analysis pop-up that displays the data (limited to the first 3,000 records), the columns (with a clickable hyperlink to select the sample data above), the last refresh time, and the load settings.

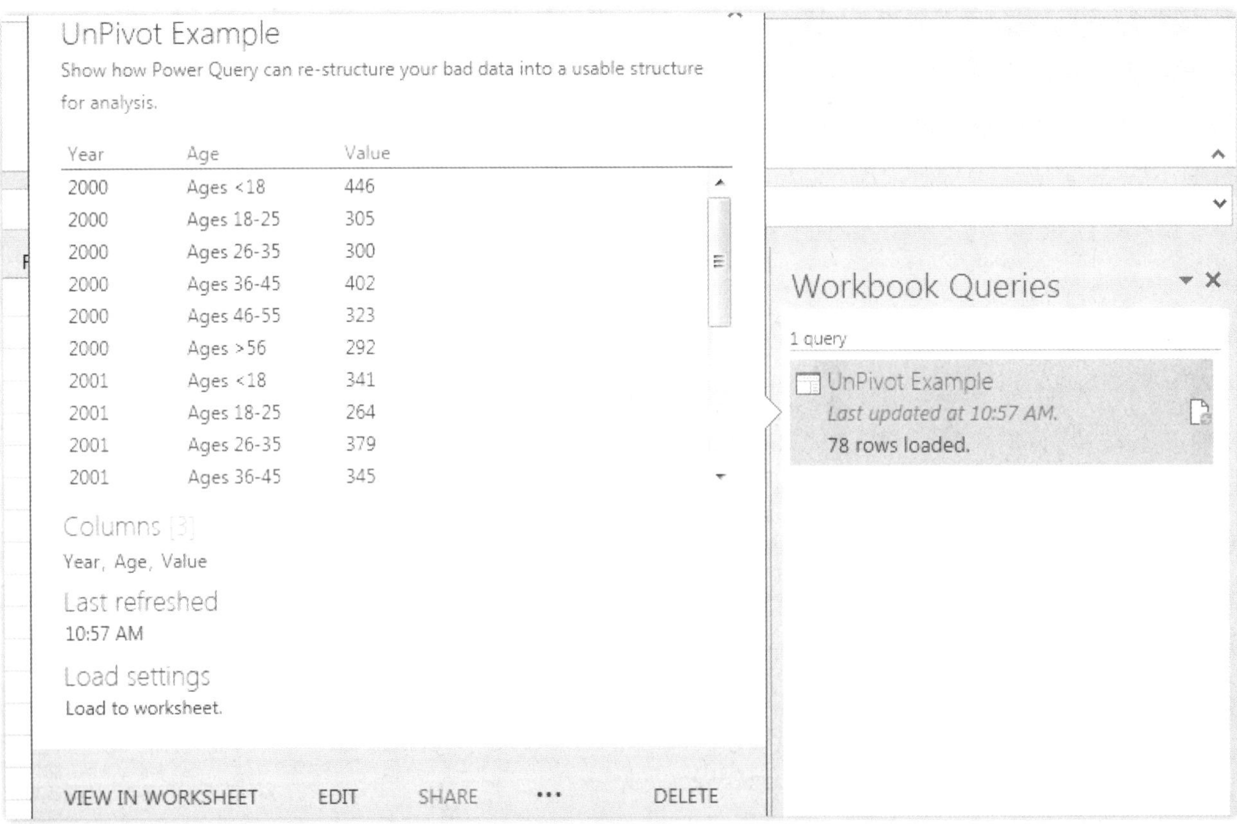

Quick analysis pop-up for the Workbook Queries *task pane.*

At the bottom of this quick analysis pop-up is an ellipsis button that you can click to see four additional commands for working with your query, as shown in the next figure.

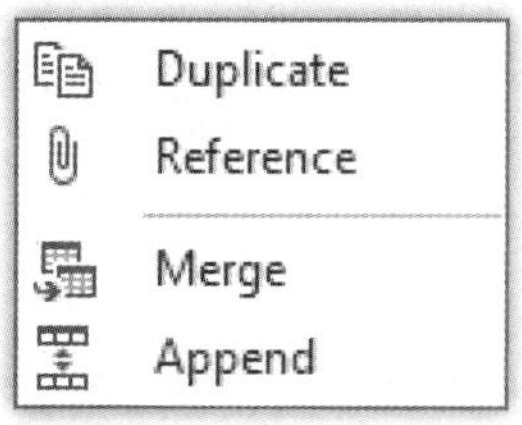

Ellipsis submenu in the quick analysis pop-up.

When Power Query loads the query results to a new worksheet, it adds four additional custom Table styles to the workbook (see the next figure):

- *TableStyleQueryError*
- *TableStyleQueryInfo*
- *TableStyleQueryPreview*
- *TableStyleQueryResult*

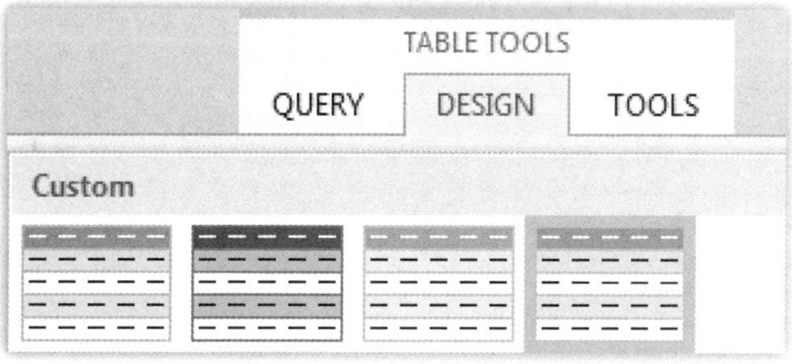

Custom Table styles added with the Power Query.

> **TIP**
>
> If these Table styles were previously created in the workbook, Power Query does not overwrite them. The styles remain unchanged.

When you open a workbook that contains a Power Query–generated Table in Excel 2010 or 2013 without the Power Query add-in installed, you get the error message shown in the next figure.

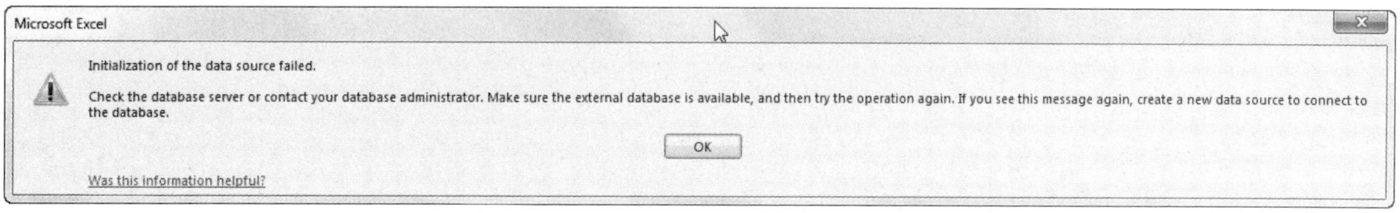

Error when refreshing a Power Query–generated Table without Power Query installed.

When you open a workbook that contains a Power Query–generated Table in Excel 2007 and attempt a refresh, Excel displays a slightly different error message than before, as shown in the next figure.

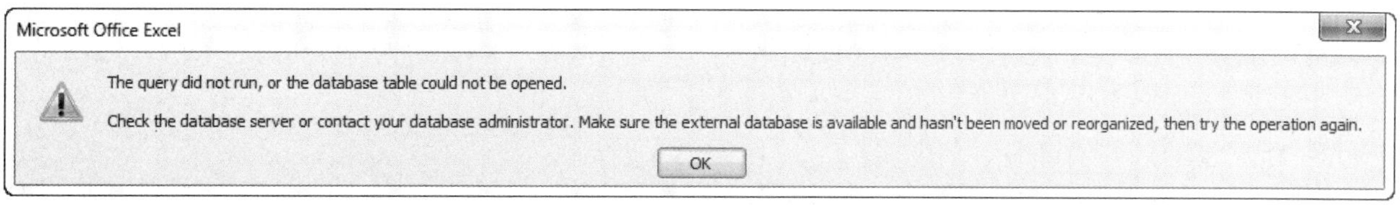

Error when refreshing a Power Query table in Excel 2007.

6 Sorting, Filtering, and Using Slicers

Two very common tasks when working with data are sorting and filtering. This chapter details how they apply to Tables. Generally speaking, it's not a good idea to have multiple Tables stacked horizontally when filtering. This is because a filtered row hides the entire sheet row, not just the rows of the Table being filtered. If Tables are to be stacked, it's generally recommended to stack them vertically; however, if you do this, their dimensions should be identical, or potential errors may arise when inserting Table rows. This chapter describes sorting and filtering pertaining to Tables; for more information on best practices related to these tasks, see Chapter 3.

Sorting

Tables provide sorting tools via the AutoFilter controls. When a Table is sorted, Excel automatically constrains the effects of the sort to the Table's data body range.

Sorting is an integral part of data analysis. Whether you're sorting text or numbers or sorting by color, Excel offers a wide variety of sorting methods to view Table data in many ways. In terms of the sort options available, there is no difference between sorting a standard range of cells and sorting a Table. There are three basic types of sorts:

- **Ascending**—Numeric values sort low to high, and text values sort A to Z.
- **Descending**—Numeric values sort high to low, and text values sort Z to A.
- **By color**—You can sort a specific fill color to the top or sort using a custom order of cell fill colors.

> ***NOTE***
>
> Excel 2007 introduced sorting by color.

Sorting by Color

When you're sorting by color, Excel displays a list of all cell fill colors used in the selected column. Excel lists only the cell fill colors applied—whether manually applied or applied with conditional formatting. When a manually applied cell fill color is overridden with a conditionally applied cell fill color, the underlying manually applied cell fill color is not considered when building the list or sorting the list.

You can see the sorting options by clicking the AutoFilter drop-down control on the right side of each header cell. The next figure shows the sort and filter menu you get when you click the AutoFilter drop-down.

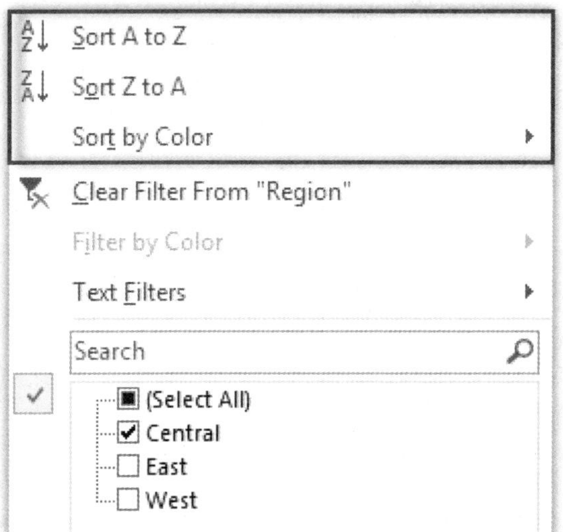

AutoFilter drop-down menu sort commands.

When you expand the *Sort by Color* submenu, you see a list of unique colors in the selected column that are currently visible, including the option *No Fill*, which is any cell with no fill color applied, either manually or with conditional formatting.

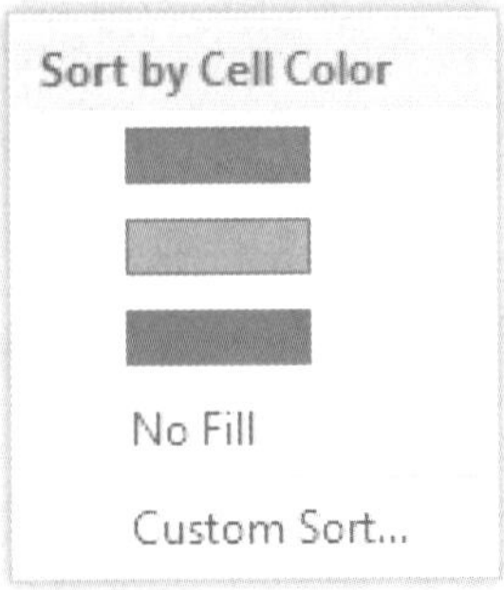

Sort by Cell Color submenu.

> ***TIP***
>
> There are two kinds of drop-down controls associated with cells: validation lists and AutoFilter controls. They look the same but are placed on different sides of the cell's right border. AutoFilter drop-down controls are inside the cell's right border, and validation list drop-down controls are displayed outside the cell's right border. In addition, AutoFilter drop-down controls are always displayed, whether the cell is selected or not; on the other hand, validation list controls are displayed only when the cell is selected and active. The next figure shows these two kinds of drop-down controls on the selected cell.

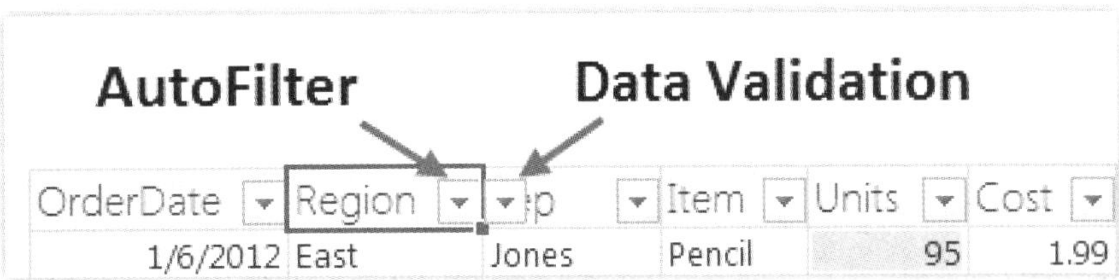

Table headers with AutoFilter drop-downs showing, along with a data validation drop-down control for the selected cell. The AutoFilter control on the left is for filtering, and the validation drop-down on the right is for an in-cell validation list.

You can also access the sorting commands by selecting *HOME | Editing*.

Performing a Custom Sort

At the bottom of the *Sort by Cell Color* submenu is the command *Custom Sort*. If you select this command, Excel opens the *Sort* dialog, which allows you to sort on any number of columns at once (see the next figure).

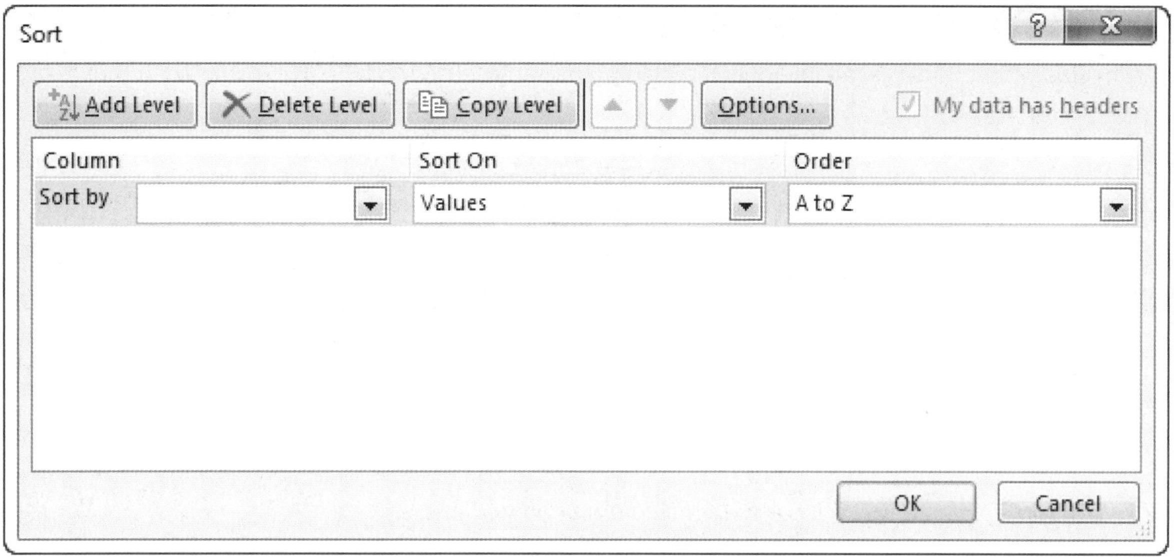

Sort *dialog box for custom sorting.*

> ***TIP***
>
> By default, a protected worksheet does not allow sorting in a Table, even if you choose to allow sorting when protecting the worksheet. A workaround is to turn off the *Locked* property of every cell in the header and data body range. You do this by selecting the header range and data body, right-clicking any cell in the selection, and selecting *Format Cells*. Then you navigate to the *Protection* tab, uncheck *Locked*, and click *OK*. Alternatively, you can select *HOME | Cells | Format* and uncheck *Lock Cell*.

Determining the Sort State

To determine whether a column is sorted, you can inspect the images in the AutoFilter drop-down controls. When a column is sorted, the icon changes to show an upward- or downward-pointing arrow.

Filters

In addition to allowing you to sort, the AutoFilter drop-down controls also provide access to tools for filtering a Table in a variety of ways. Each column supports AutoFilter conditions. You can filter a Table by making column filters active.

Filtering Tables works the same way as filtering standard worksheet cells. When you filter a Table, Excel automatically constrains the effects of the filter to the Table's data body range.

> ***TIP***
>
> Excel allows only a single AutoFilter per worksheet, but Tables have their own AutoFilter in addition to the worksheet's AutoFilter. It is therefore possible to have an AutoFilter for every Table plus one additional AutoFilter for the worksheet on a standard range.

You get the AutoFilter options the same way you get the sort options: by clicking the AutoFilter drop-down control on the right side of each header cell.

Excel allows you to filter in a number of ways, including these:

- By color
- By various text, number, and date filters
- By value

Filtering by Color

The *Filter by Color* command is available only if a column has any cells with fill colors other than those applied with the Table style (see the next figure).

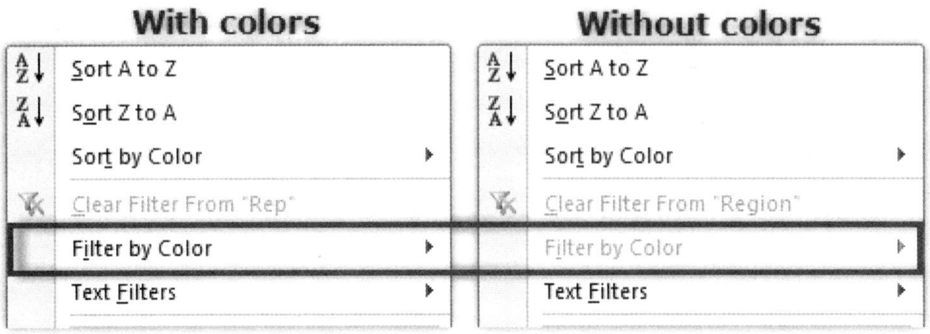

The AutoFilter drop-down menu, with colors in the column and without.

Filtering Text

When a column contains mostly text values, Excel displays the *Text Filters* menu, with these filter options:

- *Equals* (a value)
- *Does Not Equal* (a value)
- *Begins With* (a value)
- *Ends With* (a value)
- *Contains* (a value)
- *Does Not Contain* (a value)

Filtering Numbers

When a column contains mostly number values, Excel displays the *Number Filters* menu, with these filter options:

- *Equals* (a value)
- *Does Not Equal* (a value)
- *Greater Than* (a value)
- *Greater Than Or Equal To* (a value)
- *Less Than* (a value)
- *Less Than Or Equal To* (a value)
- *Between* (two values)
- *Top 10* (shows the top/bottom number items/percent, where number can be set to any value or percentage)
- *Above Average* (shows the values above the average value)
- *Below Average* (shows the values below the average value)

Filtering Dates

When a column contains mostly date values, Excel displays the *Date Filters* menu, with these filter options:

- *Equals* (a specific date)
- *Before* (a specific date)
- *After* (a specific date)

- *Between* (two specific dates)
- *Tomorrow*
- *Today*
- *Yesterday*
- *Next Week*
- *This Week*
- *Last Week*
- *Next Month*
- *This Month*
- *Last Month*
- *Next Quarter*
- *This Quarter*
- *Last Quarter*
- *Next Year*
- *This Year*
- *Last Year*
- *Year to Date*
- *All Dates in the Period* (with options for quarters 1–4 and with the months of the year displayed in a subordinate menu)

> **NOTE**
>
> For most of the text, number, and date cases, Excel displays a dialog for entering one or more values pertinent to the filter. The type of filters provided depends on the number of value types in that column (text, numbers, or dates); the value type that occurs most determines the type of filter.

Filtering Values

At the bottom of the AutoFilter menu is a list of all the unique values in that column. If the column contains mostly date or time values, the list is organized in a hierarchical manner, starting with years at the highest level, months next, then days, and so on. You can select any combination of values. You can use the search box at the top of the list to quickly narrow down the list of values to a specific set that matches the entered search value.

Determining the Filter State

When a Table is in a filtered state, the row headers on the left side of the worksheet window change from black to blue, as shown in the next figure.

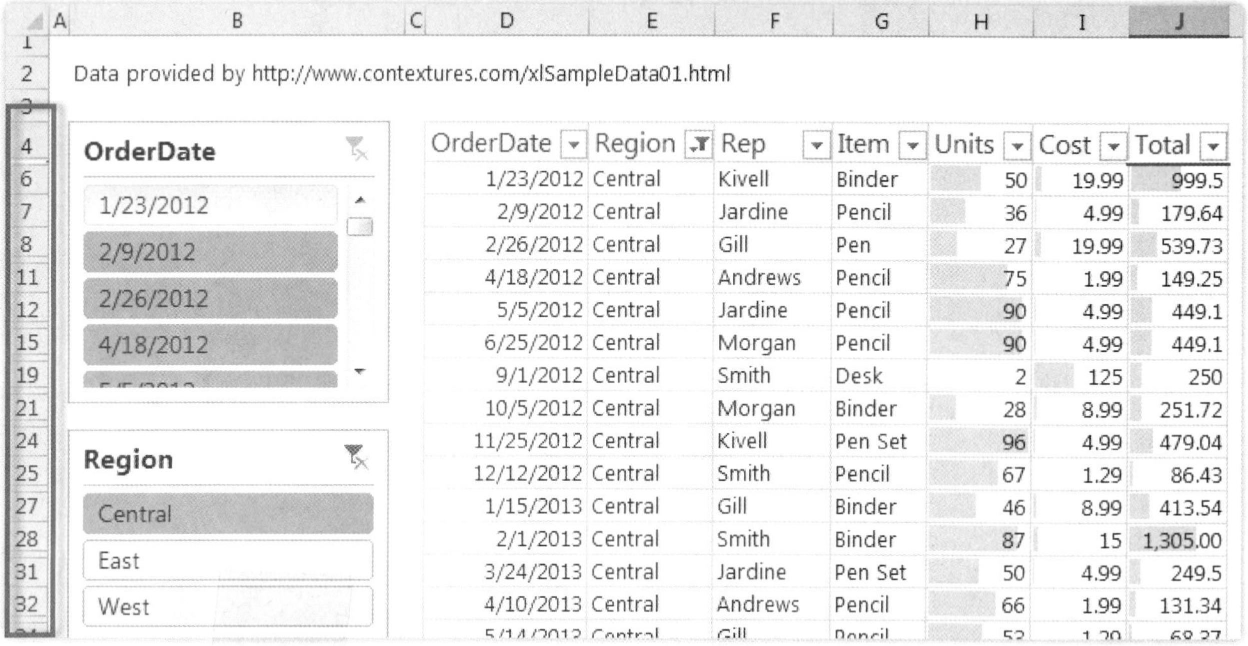

Row headers showing that a filter has been applied.

> ***TIP***
>
> The figure above uses blue to indicate filtered rows, but the Windows color scheme actually controls what color is used here. You can customize these settings to change the look and feel of Excel and any other application that uses these settings.

Another way to tell if a filter is applied (and to tell which columns are filtered) is to inspect the images on the AutoFilter drop-down controls. When a column is filtered, the icon changes to show a funnel, as you can see in the next figure.

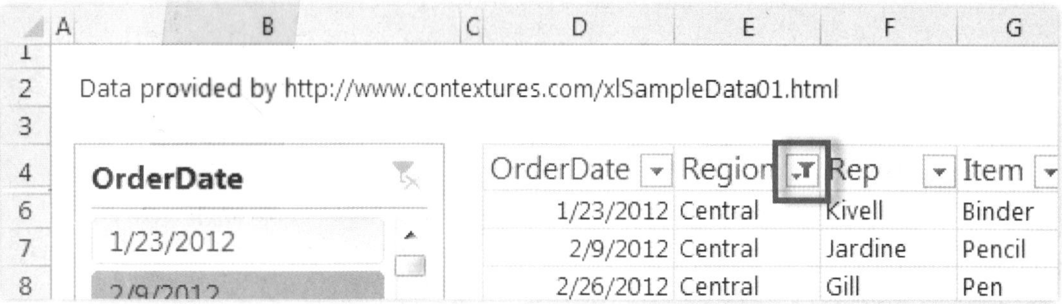

Filter applied to the "Region" column, as indicated by the image on the AutoFilter drop-down control.

> ***NOTE***
>
> When a filter is applied to a Table, if you hide the header row (via *{TABLE TOOLS} DESIGN | Table Style Options | Header Row*), Excel removes the filter and disables the *Filter Button* control. There is no workaround for this.

Removing Filters

You remove a filter from a column by selecting *Clear Filter From "Column Name"* from the AutoFilter drop-down menu. If the column is not filtered, this command is disabled.

Using Slicers

Introduced in Excel 2010 for PivotTables only, Slicers are visual interactive filtering controls. Slicers expose a single column's unique values in a grid of buttons that you can click to include those values in the filter. By default, if you click a button, Excel includes that value and excludes all others. Pressing the CTRL key while clicking maintains the existing set of selected values and toggles the status of the clicked button. Excel 2013 includes Slicers for Tables.

> **NOTE**
>
> Excel Online provides only limited support for Slicers: You can use them, but you can't maintain them.

To add a Slicer, you select *{TABLE TOOLS} DESIGN | Tools | Insert Slicer*. The *Insert Slicers* dialog box appears, as shown in the next figure. In it, you select the column(s) for which you want Slicers and then click *OK*. Excel creates one Slicer for each selected column.

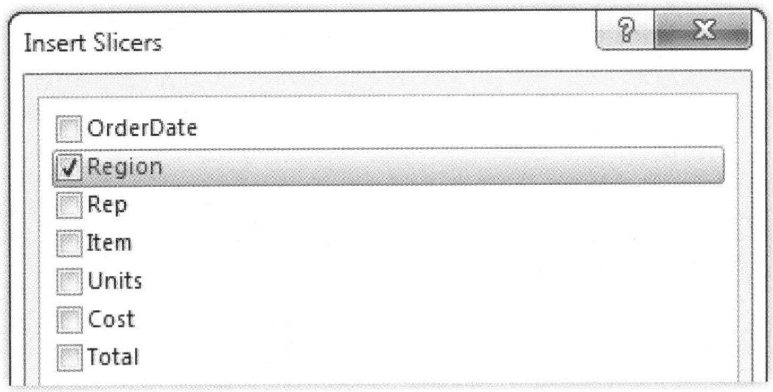

Insert Slicers *dialog box.*

After you create a Slicer, Excel places it on your worksheet. The next figure shows an example of a Slicer for the "Region" field of a Table.

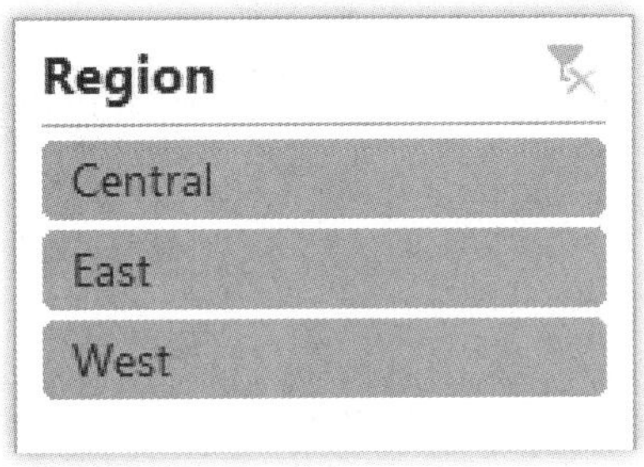

Example of a Slicer on a worksheet.

The next figure shows the *{SLICER TOOLS} OPTIONS* ribbon tab, which is a contextual tab.

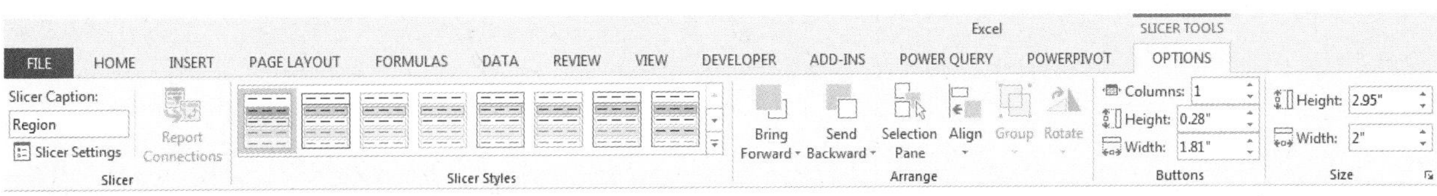

{SLICER TOOLS} OPTIONS *contextual ribbon tab.*

You can add duplicate Slicers for the same column. When you do, by default the Slicers are linked to the same data source, and you cannot change this link.

You cannot filter a column's values that are filtered out by filters in other columns. Slicers have options to indicate what is currently available to be filtered in a column. You can tell Excel what to do with values that are not available by selecting one of the three check boxes in the *Slicer Settings* dialog: *Hide items with no data*, *Visually indicate items with no data*, or *Show items with no data last*. The next figure shows these three controls. In this figure, unchecking *Hide items with no data* enables the next two check boxes. Checking the *Visually indicate items with no data* check box enables the *Show items with no data last* check box.

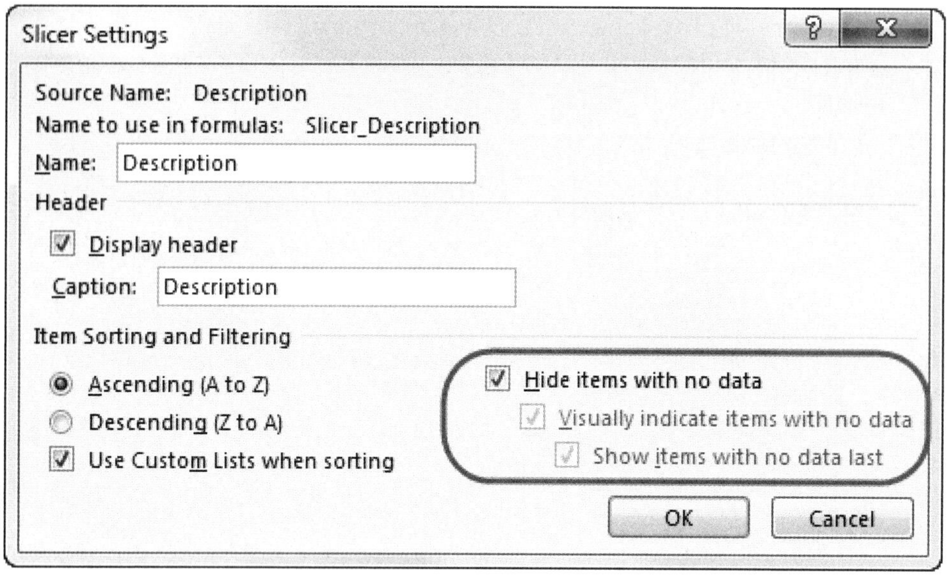

Slicer settings *to hide items with no data.*

The *SLICER TOOLS | OPTIONS* ribbon tab includes options for customizing the visual style of a Slicer, such as the number of columns, dimensions, and other aspects of the Slicer.

Table Slicers are the same as PivotTable Slicers and thus share many things in common in the user interface. For example, the right-click menu of a Table Slicer is the same as the right-click menu of a PivotTable Slicer (see the next figure). The only difference is that the command *Report Connections* is disabled for Tables because this is a feature only of PivotTables.

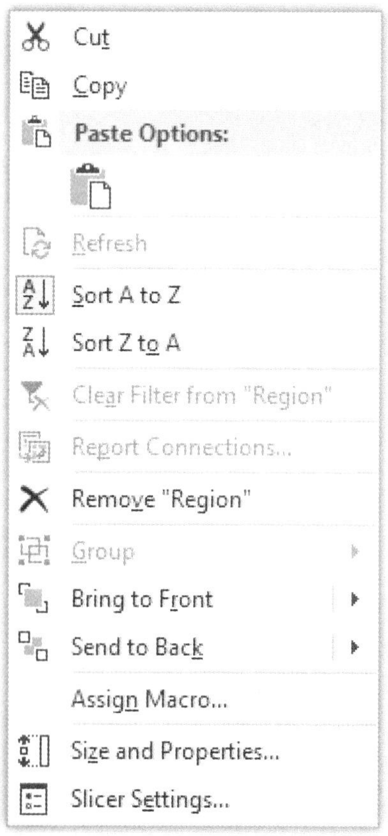

Slicer right-click menu.

Customizing Slicer styles is similar to customizing Table styles. For more information, see Chapter 7.

If a Table's header row is disabled, you cannot use Slicers on that Table. All Slicers that are linked to a Table whose header row is disabled show as *Out-of-date*, with an *UPDATE* button, as shown in the next figure. You can click the *UPDATE* button to enable the Table's header row.

Slicer from a Table with a hidden header row.

> **NOTE**
>
> A Timeline is a variant of a Slicer that is specifically for dates. Timelines are available only for PivotTables, not for Excel Tables.

7 Table Formatting

Excel allows you to use Table styles to apply font, border, and fill style elements to entire Tables. You can use them to format rows and columns in a banded manner that makes it easier to work with the Table data.

The most common Table style is banded rows, where every odd visible row has one cell fill color and every even visible row has a different cell fill color. Applying banding like this makes it easier to follow a single row the length of the Table. As rows are added, removed, sorted, and filtered, Excel continuously applies a Table style so that, regardless of what actions are taken and which rows are visible, every odd visible row is displayed with one cell fill color and every even visible row is displayed with the other cell fill color.

Table Styles

Excel provides 61 different built-in Table styles: 22 light, 28 medium, and 11 dark. You can add any number of custom Table styles to the list of available styles.

Table Styles Gallery

The existing built-in and custom Table styles are presented in the *Table Styles* gallery. You can reach this gallery by selecting *HOME | Format as Table* or *{TABLE TOOLS} DESIGN | Table Styles*, as shown in the next figure.

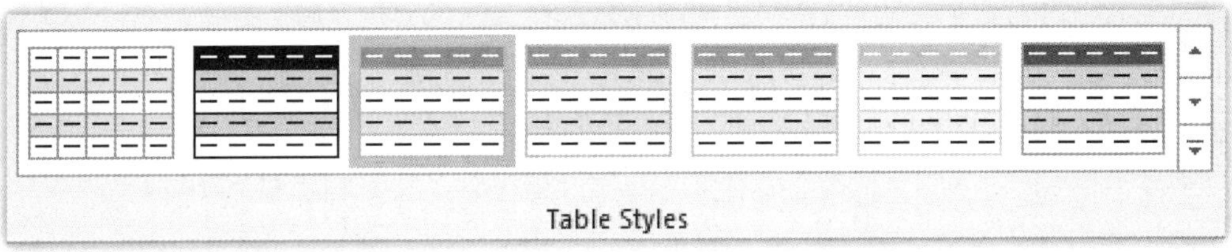

Table Styles *gallery.*

To see the full *Table Styles* gallery, shown in the next figure, you click the *More* button on the right scroll control.

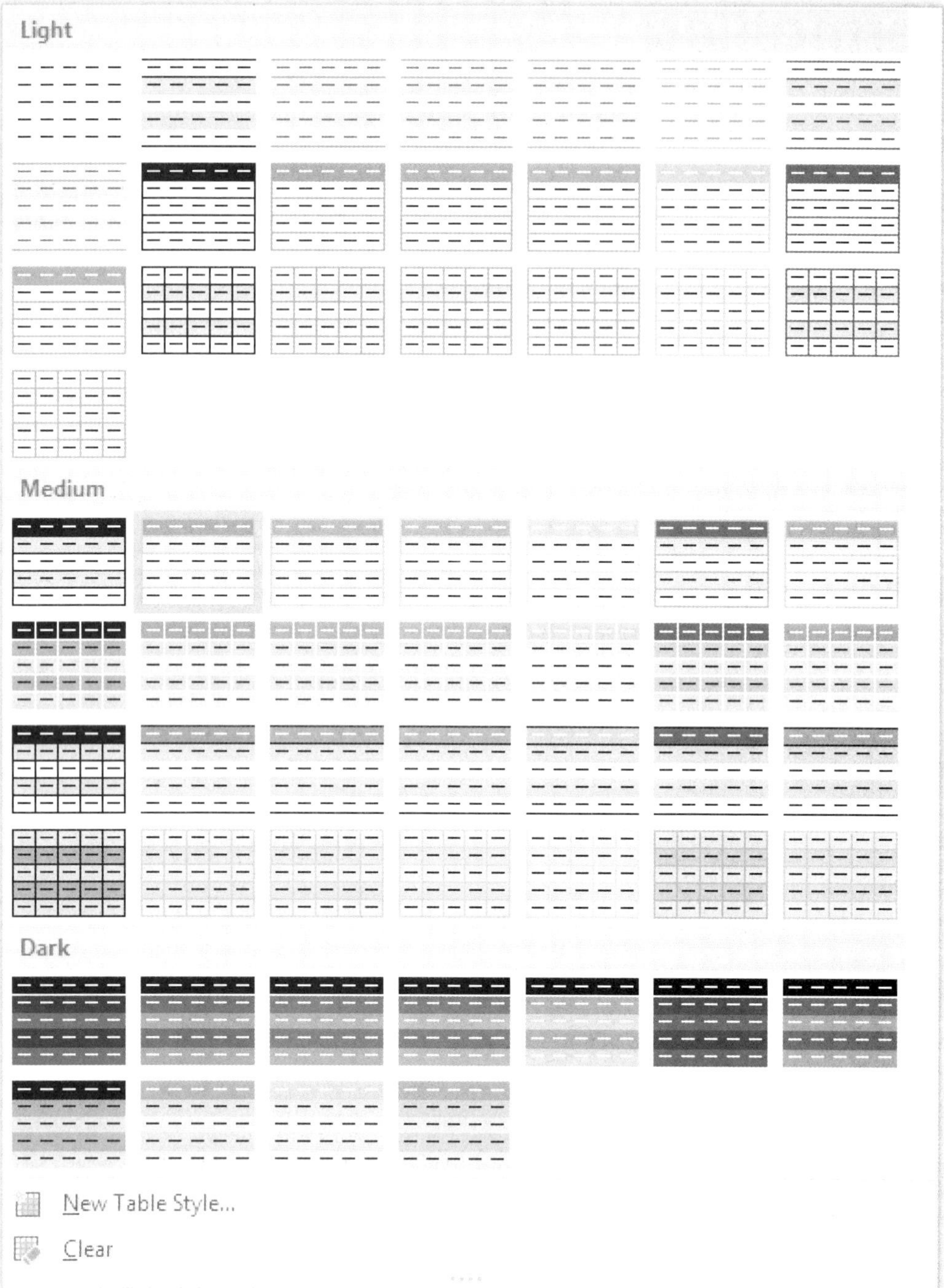

Expanded Table Styles gallery from the {TABLE TOOLS} DESIGN *tab.*

Notice that, as you move the mouse over a styles in any of these views, Excel temporarily applies that style to the selected Table if the *Live Preview* option is enabled (which it is by default). To toggle *Live Preview* mode, you select *FILE | Options | General | Enable Live Preview*.

> **CAUTION**
>
> *Live Preview* may not be available if a computer's hardware doesn't meet minimum specifications. For Office 2013, you need a 1 GHz processor or faster; 1 GB of RAM for 32-bit Office and 2 GB RAM for 64-bit Office; 3.0 GB of free hard disk space; graphics hardware acceleration (DirectX 10 or above supported graphics card); and Windows 7 and above or Windows Server 2008 R2 and above (64-bit only).

Once you apply a Table style to a Table, Excel continuously reapplies the style to the Table as rows and columns are added and removed and as rows are sorted and filtered.

> **TIP**
>
> You can use a Table style to format a regular range of cells by converting that range to a Table, applying the Table style, and converting the Table back to a range. The formatting remains but is not dynamically reapplied as the range of data is modified (adding and removing rows and columns or sorting and filtering rows).

Table Style Options

Four Table options control how a Table style is applied to a Table. You find these options in the group *{TABLE TOOLS} DESIGN | Table Style Options*:

- ***Banded Rows***—Applies the Table style's alternating row format to the data body range.
- ***Banded Columns***—Applies the Table style's alternating column format to the data body range.
- ***First Column***—Applies the Table style's first column format to the data body range.
- ***Last Column***—Applies the Table style's last column format to the data body range.

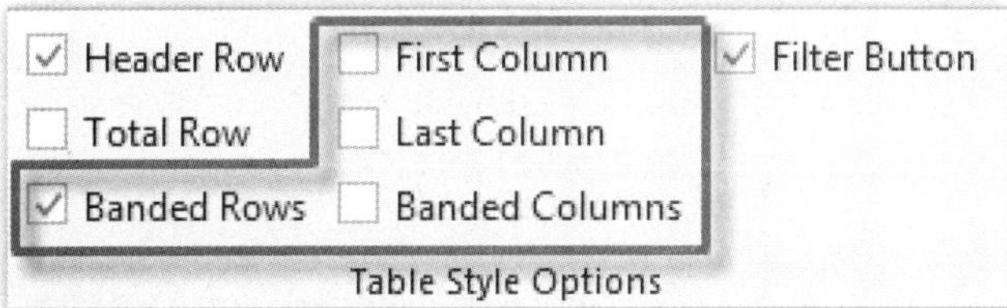

Table Style Options ribbon group used to format Table elements, found by navigating to {TABLE TOOLS} DESIGN | Table Style Options.

By default, *Banded Rows* is selected and the other three are not. Table style options are applied on a Table-by-Table basis; they are independent of the Table style itself. The following figures illustrate the same Table style with different *Table Style Options* settings enabled.

OrderDate	Region	Rep	Item	Units	Cost	Total
1/6/2012	East	Jones	Pencil	95	1.99	189.05
1/23/2012	Central	Kivell	Binder	50	19.99	999.5
2/9/2012	Central	Jardine	Pencil	36	4.99	179.64
2/26/2012	Central	Gill	Pen	27	19.99	539.73
3/15/2012	West	Sorvino	Pencil	56	2.99	167.44
4/1/2012	East	Jones	Binder	60	4.99	299.4
4/18/2012	Central	Andrews	Pencil	75	1.99	149.25

Table with no style options enabled.

OrderDate	Region	Rep	Item	Units	Cost	Total
1/6/2012	East	Jones	Pencil	95	1.99	189.05
1/23/2012	Central	Kivell	Binder	50	19.99	999.5
2/9/2012	Central	Jardine	Pencil	36	4.99	179.64
2/26/2012	Central	Gill	Pen	27	19.99	539.73
3/15/2012	West	Sorvino	Pencil	56	2.99	167.44
4/1/2012	East	Jones	Binder	60	4.99	299.4
4/18/2012	Central	Andrews	Pencil	75	1.99	149.25

Table with Banded Rows enabled.

OrderDate	Region	Rep	Item	Units	Cost	Total
1/6/2012	East	Jones	Pencil	95	1.99	189.05
1/23/2012	Central	Kivell	Binder	50	19.99	999.5
2/9/2012	Central	Jardine	Pencil	36	4.99	179.64
2/26/2012	Central	Gill	Pen	27	19.99	539.73
3/15/2012	West	Sorvino	Pencil	56	2.99	167.44
4/1/2012	East	Jones	Binder	60	4.99	299.4
4/18/2012	Central	Andrews	Pencil	75	1.99	149.25

Table with Banded Columns enabled.

OrderDate	Region	Rep	Item	Units	Cost	Total
1/6/2012	East	Jones	Pencil	95	1.99	189.05
1/23/2012	Central	Kivell	Binder	50	19.99	999.5
2/9/2012	Central	Jardine	Pencil	36	4.99	179.64
2/29/2012	Central	Gill	Pen	27	19.99	539.73
3/15/2012	West	Sorvino	Pencil	56	2.99	167.44
4/1/2012	East	Jones	Binder	60	4.99	299.4
4/18/2012	Central	Andrews	Pencil	75	1.99	149.25

Table with First Column enabled.

OrderDate	Region	Rep	Item	Units	Cost	Total
1/6/2012	East	Jones	Pencil	95	1.99	**189.05**
1/23/2012	Central	Kivell	Binder	50	19.99	**999.5**
2/9/2012	Central	Jardine	Pencil	36	4.99	**179.64**
2/26/2012	Central	Gill	Pen	27	19.99	**539.73**
3/15/2012	West	Sorvino	Pencil	56	2.99	**167.44**
4/1/2012	East	Jones	Binder	60	4.99	**299.4**
4/18/2012	Central	Andrews	Pencil	75	1.99	**149.25**

Table with Last Column enabled.

OrderDate	Region	Rep	Item	Units	Cost	Total
1/6/2012	East	Jones	Pencil	95	1.99	**189.05**
1/23/2012	Central	Kivell	Binder	50	19.99	**999.5**
2/9/2012	Central	Jardine	Pencil	36	4.99	**179.64**
2/26/2012	Central	Gill	Pen	27	19.99	**539.73**
3/15/2012	West	Sorvino	Pencil	56	2.99	**167.44**
4/1/2012	East	Jones	Binder	60	4.99	**299.4**
4/18/2012	Central	Andrews	Pencil	75	1.99	**149.25**

Table with Banded Rows, First Column, and Last Column enabled.

Creating Custom Table Styles

You can add any number of custom Table styles to a workbook. Custom Table styles behave similarly to built-in Table styles, but you can define the style elements as you like. You can't modify built-in Table styles, but you can copy them to custom Table styles, as discussed in the following sections.

Adding a New Custom Table Style

There are three ways to create a custom Table style:

- Select *HOME | Styles | Format as Table | New Table Style*.
- Select *{TABLE TOOLS} DESIGN | Table Styles | New Table Style*.
- Right-click any Table style in the gallery and choose *Duplicate*.

Duplicating an existing style is the easiest way to get started. Otherwise, the Table style is empty. To see how this works, right-click a Table style in the gallery and choose *Duplicate*. Excel gives you the right-click menu shown in the next figure.

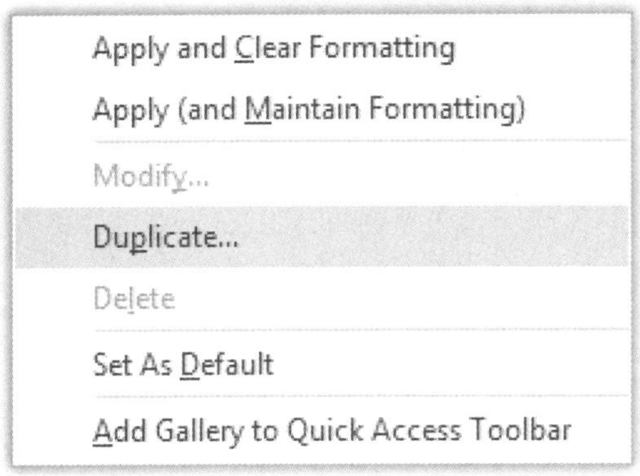

Right-click menu from a style in the Table Styles gallery.

If you choose *Duplicate* from the right-click menu, a *Modify Table Style* dialog appears. The controls for this are identical to those in the *New Table Style* dialog, which is shown in the next figure.

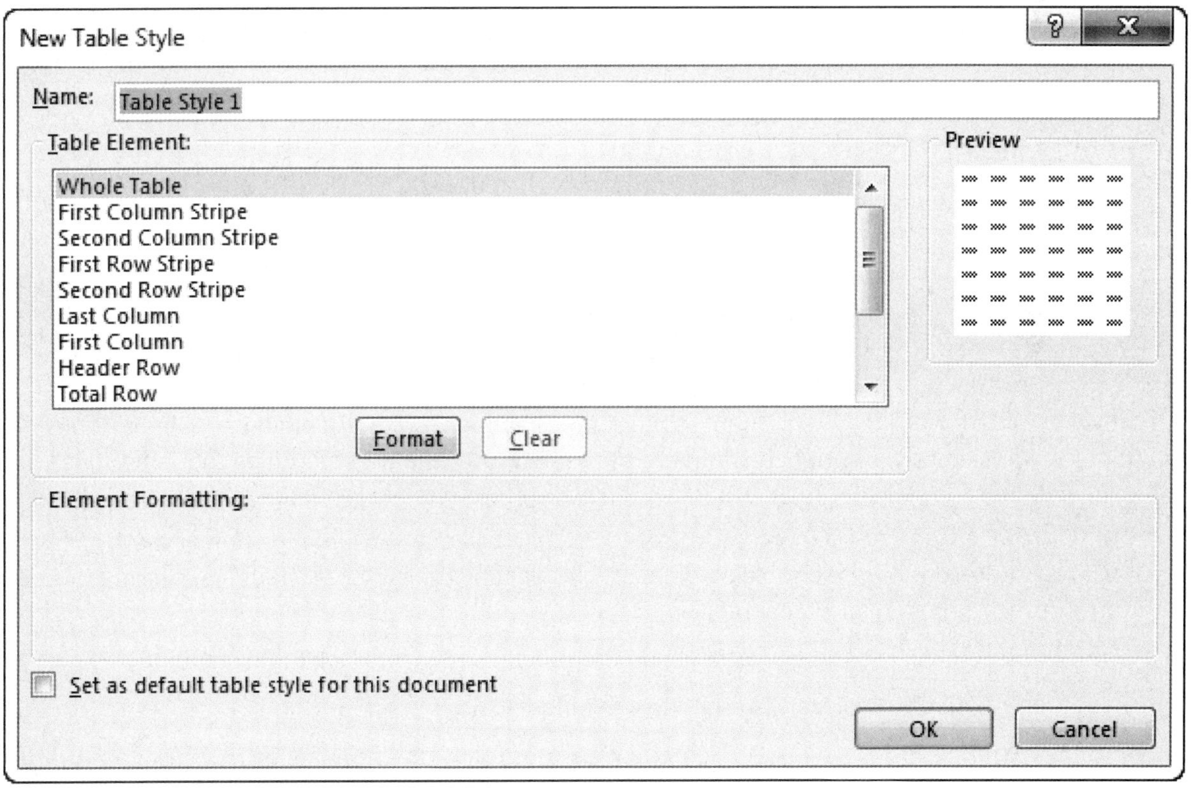

New Table Style *dialog box.*

When you create a new custom Table style, you use the *New Table Style* dialog box, shown in the previous figure, which offers the following items:

- ***Name***—You can fill in any unique Table style name. All custom Table style names must be unique in the workbook; if you try to reuse a name, you get the error message shown in the next figure.
- ***Table Element***—You can choose from this list of 13 style elements (discussed later in this chapter). After you select the element to edit, you can click *Format* to open the *Format Cells* dialog box.

Any style elements that have settings defined appear boldfaced in this list. Clicking *Clear* clears all settings from that style element and removes the boldface from the style element name.

- ***Preview***—This area provides a small representation of what the Table style element looks like when applied.
- ***Element Formatting***—This area shows the formatting applied to the selected element, including font color (specified in RGB format), borders, and fill color/pattern.
- ***Set as default table style for this document***—Select this check box to set the Table style as the default Table style for all new Tables created.

Error message when you try to save a custom Table style with a name that already exists in the workbook.

> **CAUTION**
>
> You can name a custom Table style the same as a built-in Table style name. However, it's not a good idea to do so because it can be confusing.

Table Style Elements

A Table style comprises multiple style elements that format the parts of a Table, such as the header row, odd and even rows, and odd and even columns. You can enable or disable each style element. If you disable one, the *Whole Table* style element applies to that part of the Table.

Each element can apply font, border, and fill formatting but not number, alignment, or protection formatting. Only style elements that are defined (enabled) in the Table style are applied when you apply that Table style to a Table. The four Table style options discussed earlier in this chapter also apply to custom Table styles and override how the Table style settings are applied to a Table on a Table-by-Table basis. If a Table style element has not been defined for the part of the Table covered by the Table style option, toggling that Table style option has no effect on how the Table style is applied to the Table.

Each Table style includes 13 style elements. You can enable each element by defining one or more style properties (font, border, or fill). You disable an element by selecting that style element and clicking the *Clear* button. These are the 13 style elements:

- ***Whole Table***—Applies to the entire Table, unless superseded in another Table element.
- ***First Column Stripe***—Applies to alternating columns.
- ***Second Column Stripe***—Applies to alternating columns following the column(s) affected by the *First Column Stripe* style element.
- ***First Row Stripe***—Applies to alternating rows.
- ***Second Row Stripe***—Applies to alternating rows following the row(s) affected by the *First Row Stripe* style element.
- ***Last Column***—Applies to the rightmost column in the data body range unless the Table contains a single column. If this element is defined, it supersedes the settings in the *First Column Stripe* and *Second Column Stripe* style elements.

- ***First Column***—Applies to the leftmost column. If this element is defined, it supersedes the settings in the *First Column Stripe* and *Second Column Stripe* style elements.
- ***Header Row***—Applies to the header row if the *Header Row* style is enabled.
- ***Total Row***—Applies to the total row if the *Total Row* style is enabled.
- ***First Header Cell***—Applies to the leftmost header cell if the header is enabled. If this element is defined, it supersedes the settings in the *Header Row* style element.
- ***Last Header Cell***—Applies to the rightmost header cell if the header is enabled. If this element is defined, it supersedes the settings in the *Header Row* style element.
- ***First Total Cell***—Applies to the leftmost total row cell if the total row is enabled. If this element is defined, it supersedes the settings in the *Total Row* style element.
- ***Last Total Cell***—Applies to the rightmost total row cell if the total row is enabled. If this element is defined, it supersedes the settings in the *Total Row* style element.

Note that some of these style elements refer to a **stripe** rather than to a **column** or **row**. This is because they can apply to more than one column and more than one row. The default is a single column and a single row, but as many as nine (contiguous and visible) columns and nine (contiguous and visible) rows can be affected by changing the style element's *Stripe Size* setting (see the next figure).

How the first and second stripes are applied depend on each style element's stripe size. When the default of one is used for both the first and second stripes, the first stripe is applied to all odd columns or rows, and the second stripe is applied to all even columns or rows. If either the first or second stripe's stripe size is more than a single column or row, the results are different. For example, if the first stripe size is two and the second stripe size if three, the first two columns or rows are formatted with the first stripe style, the next three columns or rows the second stripe style, the next two columns or rows the first stripe style, and so on, alternating between the first and second stripe styles.

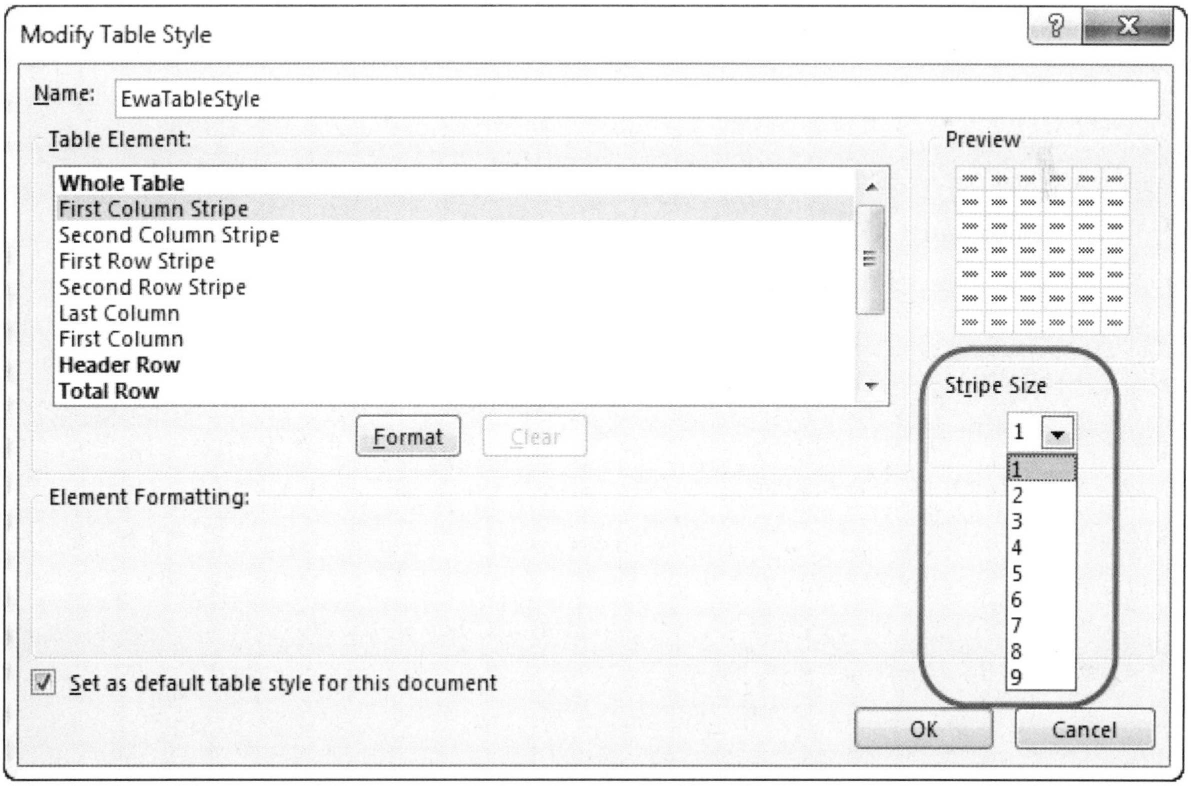

Stripe Size settings: 1 through 9.

> **NOTE**
>
> Stripe formatting is applied only to visible columns and rows. Any hidden columns or rows are not counted in the stripe size.

> **NOTE**
>
> Most built-in Table styles define only the *First Column Stripe* and *First Row Stripe* elements. The striping effect is generally achieved by relying on the *Whole Table* element to format the columns and rows that are not affected by the first stripe element (that is, any columns and rows that would be affected by the second stripe element defined). Regardless of whether one or both of the first and second stripe elements are defined, toggling the Table style options *Banded Rows* and *Banded Columns* affects both style elements at the same time.

> **TIP**
>
> When you create custom Table styles, unless you have a good reason to do otherwise, it is easiest to follow the strategy used in the built-in Table styles and define only the first stripe element and let the *Whole Table* element format the other columns or rows.

Each style element can apply font, border, and fill properties:

- As shown in the next figure, the *Font* tab lets you set these options:
    - *Font style*
    - *Underline*
    - *Color*
    - *Effects* (*Strikethrough* only)
- The *Border* tab lets you set these options:
    - *Line style*
    - *Color*
    - *Border part*
- The *Fill* tab lets you set these options:
    - *Color*
    - *Effects*
    - *Pattern*

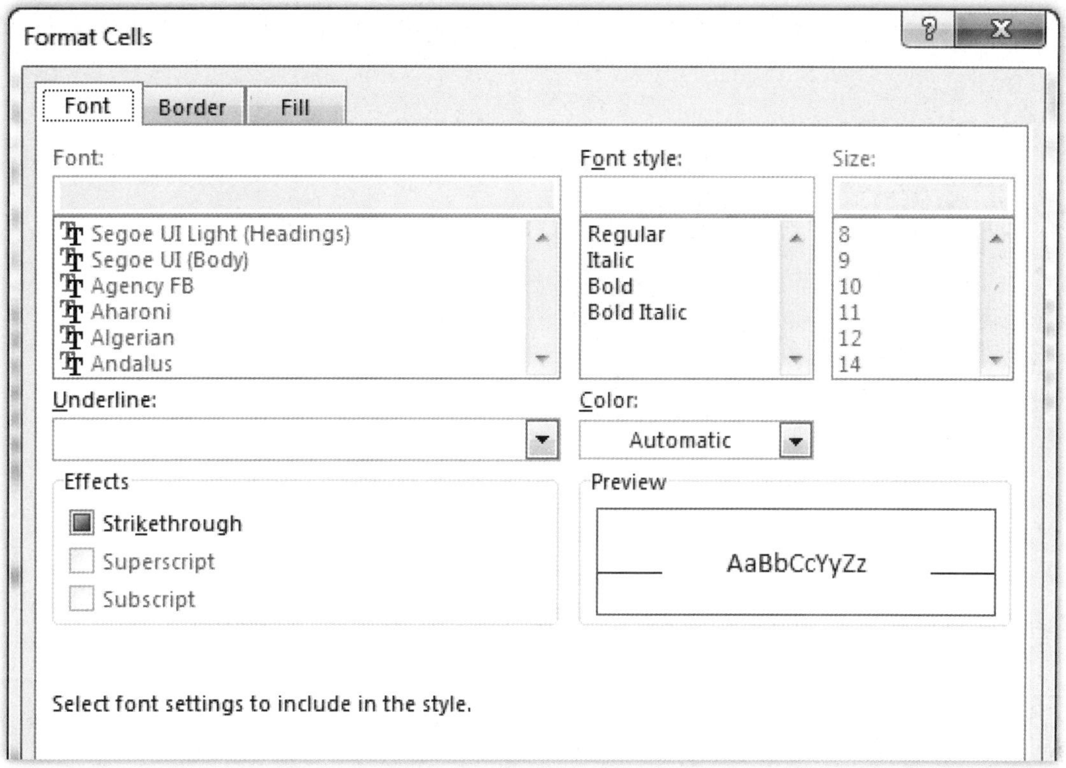

Format Cells *dialog box for customizing a Table style element.*

If you want to apply cell format attributes that are not available in a Table style, you can do so by applying a cell style or manually applying any cell format settings.

> ***TIP***
>
> You can change the accent colors available to a Table style element (font color, border color, and fill color) by selecting *PAGE LAYOUT | Themes | Colors* and choosing the desired color set. You can define a custom theme color palette by selecting *PAGE LAYOUT | Themes | Colors | Customize Colors*, which opens the *Create New Theme Colors* dialog box, shown in the next figure. To edit an existing custom theme color palate, you right-click the theme and select *Edit*.

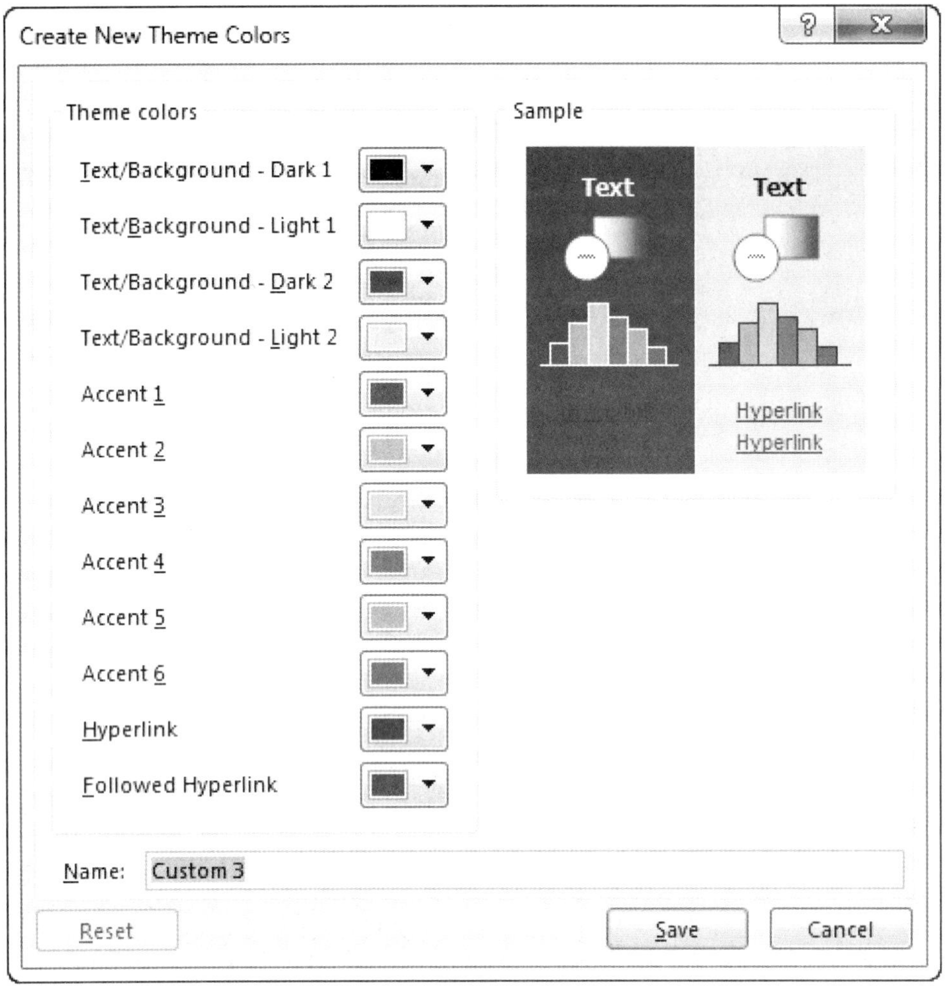

Create New Theme Colors *dialog box.*

> **NOTE**
>
> You can create custom styles for regular cells, PivotTables, Slicers, and Timelines. Creating and maintaining these styles is similar to creating and maintaining Table styles.

Setting the Default Table Style

By default, the Table style *Table Style Medium 2* is applied to all new Tables. However, you can change the default Table style for a workbook at any time; you can select any built-in or custom Table style as the default Table style. To change the default Table style, right-click the Table style you want in the *Table Styles* gallery and select *Set As Default*.

> **TIP**
>
> When you customize a Table style by using the *New Table Style* or *Modify Table Style* dialog box, you can make that Table style the default Table style by selecting the check box *Set as default table style for this document*, as illustrated in the next figure.

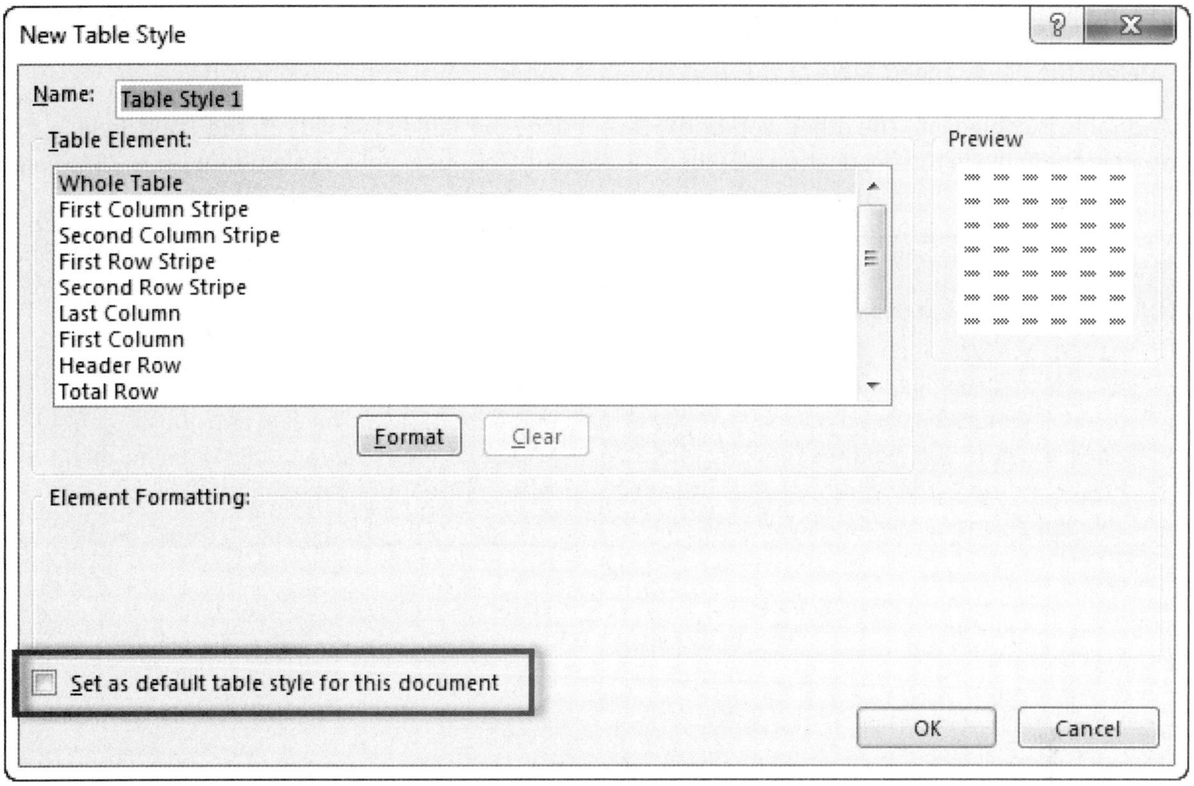

Check box to set a Table style as the default. All new Tables created will then use this style.

Modifying an Existing Custom Table Style

You modify an existing custom Table style by right-clicking that Table style in the *Table Styles* gallery and selecting *Modify*, as shown in the next figure. The *Modify Table Style* dialog box appears.

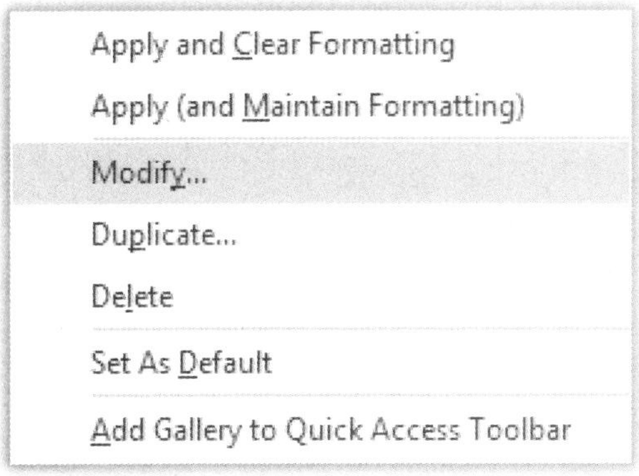

Right-click menu from a style in the Table Styles *gallery.*

Table Style Portability

When you create a custom Table style, it is saved to the workbook in which you created it. Unlike with workbook colors, fonts, effects, and themes, there is no native way to easily copy a Table style to another workbook. However, you can follow these steps to copy a Table style from one workbook to another:

1. Select the entire source Table with the desired Table style applied.
2. Copy the range (using CTRL+C).
3. Activate the destination workbook.
4. Add a new worksheet (optional).

5. Paste the source Table (using CTRL+V).
6. Delete the newly added Table or the worksheet into which it was copied (optional).

When the Table is copied into the other workbook, Excel brings the Table style with it; the Table Style remains after the Table in the destination workbook is deleted. This method is implemented as a VBA macro in Chapter 9.

> **NOTE**
>
> The new file formats allow you to go under the hood of an Excel file. With the file closed, change the extension from XLSX or XLSM to ZIP. (XLSB files are handled differently.) Then you can open the file and navigate to see different parts of the spreadsheet, which is stored in Extensible Markup Language (XML). As a precaution, save a backup copy of your file before you explore. The XML for custom Table styles, Slicer styles, and Timeline styles is stored in the workbook file in the same node ("//styleSheet/tableStyles/tableStyle"), inside the "/xl/styles.xml" file.

8 Working with External Data

External data is any data from outside Excel. You may get external data from a SQL Server database, an Oracle data set, an Access database, or a Sybase database, for example. If Excel can connect to such an external source, you can pull that data into a Table. Excel offers a number of functions to query and manage data from external sources.

Why External Data Is Important

Acquiring and housing massive quantities of data has become an important part of the modern business landscape, and analyzing such big data has become increasingly challenging. To address this trend, Microsoft continues to add more powerful data querying and analysis tools to Excel. The latest addition is a suite of what Microsoft calls BI (business intelligence) tools to pull, aggregate, and transform very large data sets. These tools allow Excel users to present that data with traditional tools such as Tables, PivotTables, and charts to effectively tell a story.

The majority of this book to this point has focused on how to use Tables within the scope of a workbook. This chapter discusses how Excel extends the reach of Tables to data originating outside the workbook. It presents three scenarios covering three different kinds of sources: external databases, text files, and the Azure Marketplace. The data in these sources can be from any entity capable of producing data in a tabular form: from point-of-sale systems, accounting and finance departments, or other business sources anywhere there is Internet connectivity.

How Excel Exposes External Data Connections

Excel devotes an entire tab to data. The *DATA* tab provides functions for pulling data into Excel from external sources as well as transforming and working with local data. You can access the following external data sources via Excel's *DATA* ribbon tab:

- Access databases
- Web services and pages
- Text files
- SQL Server databases
- SSAS (SQL Server Analysis Services)
- Windows Azure Marketplace data sources
- OData data feeds
- XML data import files
- other OLEDB or ODBC connections, including Microsoft Query

> ***NOTE***
>
> The *Get External Data* group on the *DATA* tab is disabled if a Table is selected or if the destination of an existing query is selected, as shown in the figure below. This is because you can't place a new query into a destination that already has a defined structure.

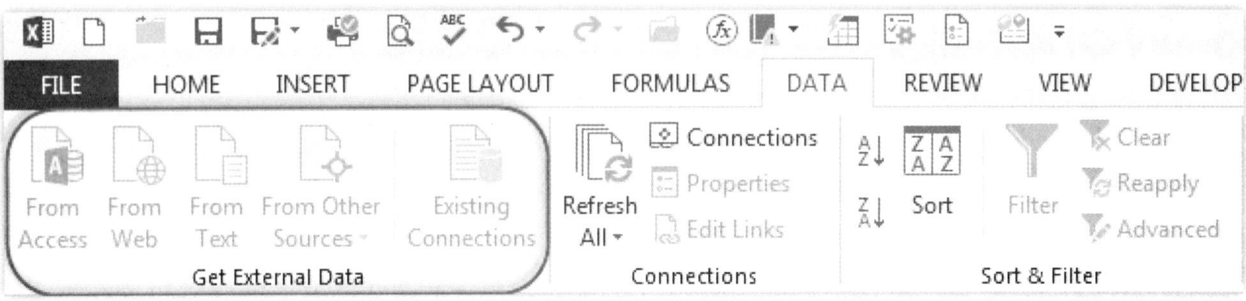

Disabled Get External Data *group on the* DATA *tab.*

Data connections are stored with the workbook, and you can view them by selecting *DATA | Get External Data | Existing Connections* and navigating to the *Connections* tab. The *Tables* tab of this dialog box shows existing Data Model connections that use a Table as a source, such as when a PivotTable is created using a Table as a source. (See Chapter 5 for more on this.)

> **CAUTION**
>
> Data connections may be disabled on your computer. To enable data connections, select *FILE | Options | Trust Center | Trust Center Settings | External Content* and ensure that either *Enable all Data Connections (not recommended)* or *Prompt user about Data Connections* is enabled.

Refreshing External Data Connections

When you use Tables with data connections, you can rearrange and delete columns without affecting a query. Excel continues to map the queried data to the correct columns. Column widths, however, are typically not maintained and AutoFit on refresh.

> **TIP**
>
> To stop Excel from AutoFitting Table columns with every refresh, right-click anywhere on the Table and select *Table | External Data Properties* and then uncheck *Adjust column width*. Two other options are *Preserve column sort/filter/layout* and *Preserve cell formatting*. They are both selected by default. These options are not available to all types of external data connections.

Working with Data from a Database

Every desktop Excel installation provides many different drivers for connecting to external data sources. A **driver** is software that knows about a specific kind of data source, including how to query it and how to interpret the query result and transform the result into a form compatible with Excel. Older drivers use ODBC application API technology, and newer drivers use the Object Linking and Embedding, Database (OLEDB) application API methodology. The differences between these two methodologies are beyond the scope of this book, but basically, you should use the newer OLEDB whenever possible.

The database example in this chapter focuses on SQL Server, but there are drivers for just about any database source, including Oracle, MySQL, Access, Hadoop, SSAS, OData data feeds, and many others.

> **NOTE**
>
> When you're connecting to an Access database, you cannot connect to a crosstab query. Chapter 9 presents a VBA solution to this problem.

Connecting to SQL Server

To connect to a SQL Server database, select *DATA | Get External Data | From Other Sources | From SQL Server*. The *Data Connection Wizard* appears, offering controls for specifying the server name and the type of login to use to open the connection. Contact your SQL Server or IT administrator to determine how to enter the login credentials.

> **NOTE**
>
> The following example uses the AdventureWorks2012 sample SQL Server database, which is freely available from Microsoft.

Creating the Query

Making a connection is only part of the process of pulling data out of a database. Once a connection is established, a query is defined to find and return the desired data in a meaningful form. Many databases support custom routines on the server that do a lot of the querying. A database administrator is responsible for creating tables and custom routines. A query originating from an external location such as Excel can be as simple as a query for the entire contents of a single table in the database, or it can be a query for a complex joining of many tables and filtering on specific values. How much or little support an Excel developer has from the database administrator determines how simple or complex the query on the Excel side of the connection will be.

Fortunately, Excel provides many powerful tools for performing virtually all the data transformation tasks that the database administrator can do in a stored routine. While this book does not delve into the many nuances of relational database queries, this example does present the basic process.

With an active connection to the source database, Excel asks for the database to which to connect. (Each SQL Server instance can house any number of databases, which may or may not be related to each other.) When a database is selected, the tables and views are displayed for selection, and you can select any number of them. When you click the button *Select Related Tables*, you select every table with any known relationship to any currently selected table. By clicking this button again, you add more tables to the selection if there are more relationships defined in the database.

When you import a single table, by default the destination is a new Excel Table, and the data is not loaded into the Data Model. There are two ways to load the queried data into the Data Model:

- Select the check box *Enable selection of multiple tables.*
- In the *Import Data* dialog box, select the check box *Add this data to the Data Model*. Note that Excel selects this check box by default if the check box *Enable selection of multiple tables* is also selected.

> **TIP**
>
> When you import data into an Excel workbook, loading it into the Data Model has the advantage of exposing that data to other analysis tools, such as Power Pivot.

If the database administrator for a database has created a stored routine (call a stored procedure in SQL Server) for your use, then you need a custom query, often specifying parameters. To define a custom query, select any table on the *Select Database and Table* page of the *Data Connection Wizard* (it doesn't matter which one), click *Next*, and click *Finish* to display the *Import Data* dialog box. Then click *Properties* to open the *Connection Properties* dialog box and navigate to its *Definition* tab. The default query command text is displayed in the *Command text* text box. Change the *Command type* to "SQL" and enter the custom query string in the *Command text* text box. Click *OK* to execute the query.

By default, creating a query connection to SQL Server creates an ODC (Office Database Connection) file, which is, by default, stored in the folder "C:\Users\USERNAME\MyDocuments\My Data Sources\".

There are many different types of data sources available, and sometimes the default connection templates that Excel presents do not work. In these cases, Excel provides tools to define custom connections. A helpful website for determining connection strings for these custom connections is www.connectionstrings.com. Many examples of connection strings are available there, along with articles and Q&A forums.

Table Names

Excel imports each database table selected into a new Excel Table on a new sheet in the active workbook. It creates Table names using the format "Table_Name", where "Name" is the name of the database table or view in the SQL Server database. If you import a single table, the Table's name is "Table_ServerName_DatabaseName_TableName", where "ServerName" is the name of the server, "DatabaseName" is the name of the database, and "TableName" is the name of the Table or view imported.

> ***NOTE***
>
> Crosstab queries cannot be returned natively when you connect to Access from Excel. There are two workarounds: Use Microsoft Query by selecting *DATA | Get External Data | From Other Sources | From Microsoft Query* or use VBA.

Working with Data from Text Files

Sometimes data comes in the form of simple text files. While this is not common these days, many applications still export data in text file format. Text files are usually in the form of a CSV (comma-separated value) file, a TXT (tab-delimited) file, or a PRN (fixed-field or space-delimited) file.

Excel still creates a data connection when importing text files, but it does not put data into a Table, as it does with other data connections. This is due to the lack of information about the data contained in a text file. Databases have certain rules, like Excel Tables, such as unique field/column names, whereas text files are not bound by these rules. Excel loads data as it finds it in the text file into a range of cells without any formatting; it does not try to force the data into a Table or other structured format.

> ***CAUTION***
>
> If a Table is inserted on data that is connected to a text file, Excel displays a warning, as shown in the next figure. The warning states that the connection will be severed if the Table is inserted.

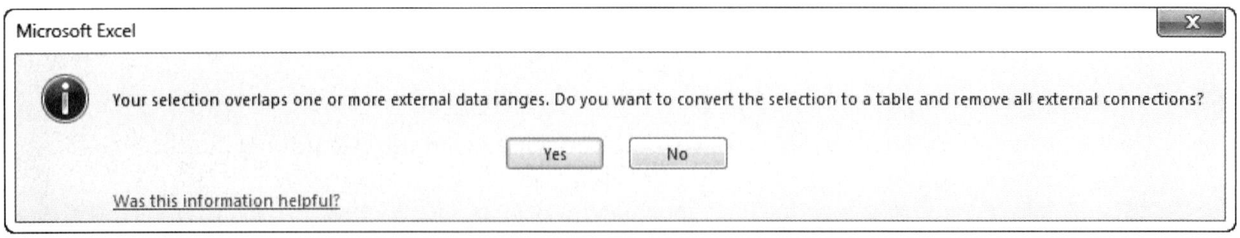

Error that appears when you insert a Table over a text file data connection.

Connecting to a Text File

To choose the text file to import, you select *DATA | Get External Data | From Text*. Default file formats are PRN, TXT, and CSV. After the file is selected, Excel opens the *Text Import Wizard* dialog box. The wizard walks you through three steps:

1. Select *Delimited* for CSV and TXT files or select *Fixed width* for PRN flies. Then click *Next*.
2. For a CSV or TXT file, select *Comma* for a CSV file or *Tab* for a TXT file. Then click *Next*. For a PRN file, define the column breaks and click *Next*.

3. Define the format to be used to interpret each column in the text file. Click *Finish*. The *Import Data* dialog box appears, as shown in the next figure. Enter the destination range and click *OK* to import the data.

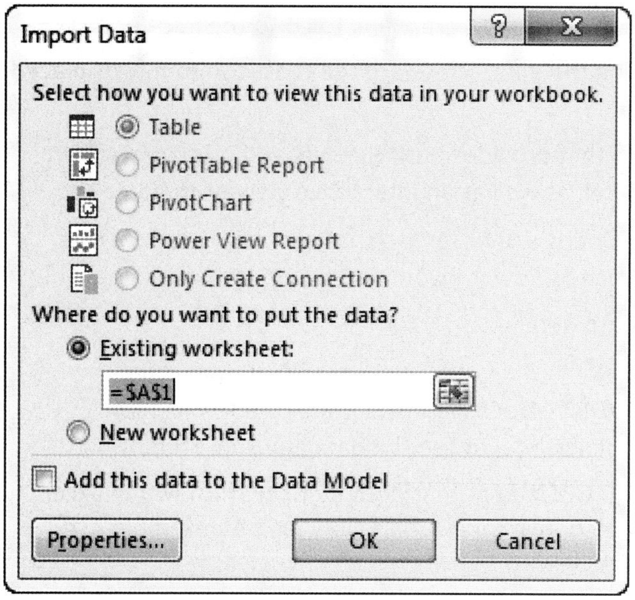

Import Data *dialog box.*

> **NOTE**
>
> To refresh a data connection to a text file, you need to go through the import process again.

Working with Data from Azure Marketplace

The Azure Marketplace (datamarket.azure.com) is a repository of data and data mining applications. It is a cloud infrastructure and platform that is used to build, deploy, and manage cloud-based services. Data available from the Azure Marketplace can be exported to text files, pulled into a Power Pivot Data Model, or imported directly into a Table. If a queried record set is large, it may have to be imported directly into the Data Model, which supports many more rows than a worksheet.

> **NOTE**
>
> Connecting to the Azure Marketplace from Excel requires both the URL for the data and a primary *Account Key*. Both are available from the Azure site. If an *Account Key* is missing or invalid you will be prompted to verify it, as shown in the next figure.

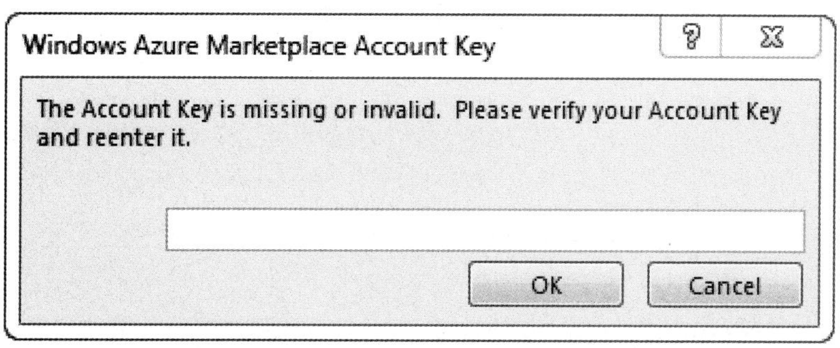

An error message with a missing or invalid Account Key when connecting to an Azure data source.

At the Azure Marketplace home page, click the *Data* link in the top menu bar. The data page appears, listing all the catalogs or data sets available; some of them are free and some have an associated fee. Select one of these data sources to view that product's page, which displays the cost per transaction (query) and information about the data. Click the *Signup* link to open the *Signup* page. Click the check box stating that you agree to the terms of the agreement and click the *Signup* link to go to the *Receipt* page.

On the *Receipt* page, you see one or more links for using the data. These are the most commonly displayed links:

- ***EXPLORE THIS DATASET***—Opens a browser tab that provides both the URL and primary *Account Key* required to access the data from within Excel, as well as an interactive view of the data set.
- ***MICROSOFT POWERPIVOT FOR EXCEL 2010***—Opens a browser tab that enables the export of the data set to other software, such as Power Pivot.
- ***TABLEAU SOFTWARE***—Opens a browser tab with detailed instructions on how to import the data into Tableau.
- ***LEARN HOW TO USE THIS DATA IN VISUAL STUDIO***—Opens a browser tab to the Microsoft Developer Network (MSDN) help topic that explains how to use the data in Visual Studio.

Click any of the displayed download options or use your URL and primary *Account Key* from within Excel to retrieve the data. You then get a standard data connection in Excel. The following is an example of a connection string:

```
Data Source=URL_Goes_Here;Namespaces to Include=*;Max Received Message
Size=4398046511104;Integrated Security=Basic;User ID=AccountKey;Persist Security
Info=false;Base Url=URL_Goes_Here
```

Once you're connected to the Azure Marketplace data set or catalog, the connection is like any other data connection and can be refreshed so you can keep updated with the most current data. Keep in mind that every connection counts as a transaction.

9 Automating Tables with VBA

This chapter discusses how to automate Tables using Visual Basic for Applications (VBA). VBA is a programming language you can use to extend Excel's functionality far beyond what Microsoft provides with the installed application. VBA allows you to automate complex or repetitive tasks. For example, you can use VBA to format a worksheet received daily from an outside source, pull data from a web page once a week, or build a complex function that can be incorporated into a worksheet formula.

The following are some examples of automating Excel Tables:

- You are building an application to be used by less experienced users, and you want to lock down the Table while providing a few simple functions for adding, editing, and deleting records.
- You want to provide functionality to edit groups of records in a user form, such as all the transactions for a single order (initial deposit, payment to factory, freight, duty, final payment, etc.).
- Your Table supports other workbook functionality, such as recording event information in a log, and you want to insert rows into the Table, update existing Table data, and find and retrieve existing rows in the Table.
- You want to audit a Table and display any data and consistency errors that need to be fixed.

To work through this chapter, it's best if you have at least a moderate level of experience programming, are aware of the Excel Object Model, and want to extend Excel's Table functionality beyond what is provided in the Excel application user interface.

> ***TIP***
>
> One of the easiest ways to learn how to automate Excel is to use the macro recorder. You turn on the macro recorder by selecting *DEVELOPER | Code | Record Macro*. When you use the recorder, most actions are recorded in the VBA environment as VBA statements. Remember to turn off the macro recorder when the steps being automated are complete. You can view and edit recorded VBA statements by selecting *DEVELOPER | Code | Macros*, selecting the macro name, and clicking *Edit*. Excel names the recorded macros "Macro1", "Macro2", etc. Note that the code generated by the macro recorder is not the most efficient, and you can very often improve it with some minor editing.
>
> If the *DEVELOPER* tab is not visible, enable it by selecting *FILE | Options | Customize Ribbon* and enabling (checking on) *Developer tab*. In Excel 2007, select *Office Button | Excel Options | Popular | Show Developer tab* in the ribbon.
>
> To record a macro in Excel 2003, select *Tools | Macro | Record New Macro*.

VBA, Excel, and Objects

Before you go any further in this chapter, it is important that you have a basic understanding of what objects are and how to use them when automating Excel using VBA. This section presents a brief review of objects and how to use them in the Excel environment. You can skip this section if you already have experience working with objects in the Excel VBA environment.

In the VBA environment, the Excel application presents the things you can access as the Excel Object Model. Consider these basic Excel objects:

- **Application**—The Excel application.
- **Workbooks**—A collection of all the workbooks currently open in the Excel application. A collection, in a generic sense, is a set of objects. In this case, the `Workbooks` collection is a set of individual `Workbook` objects.
- **Workbook**—A single workbook.

- **Worksheets**—A collection of all the worksheets in a workbook.
- **Worksheet**—A single worksheet or tab in a workbook.
- **Cells**—A collection of all the cells in a sheet.
- **Range**—A set of one or more cells on a single worksheet. The cells can be discontinuous. Any cell reference is a `Range` object.

Notice that the objects in this list correspond to specific things in the Excel application environment that you see when working with workbooks. This is true with any Object Model: Each object refers to a thing that exists (a workbook, a person, a place) and that has properties (a person's age, a place's address.)

Every object belongs to a parent object; for example, a `Workbook` object's parent is the `Application` object, and a `Cell` object's parent is a `Worksheet` object. One exception is the `Application` object, which has no parent; it is the highest-level object available when you're looking at the Excel Object Model. When describing the context of an object or method, these terms are often used:

- **Parent**—The object that exposes the object in question. For example, the `Cell` object's parent is the `Worksheet` object.
- **Member**—A property or method exposed by its parent. For example, the `Cell` object is a member of the `Worksheet` object.

Every object has members. A member can be a simple attribute, such as a cell's value, or it can be another object or collection of objects, such as the `Workbook` object's member `Worksheets`; the `Worksheets` object is a member of the `Workbook` object, and both have a number of properties and methods. A member can also be a method that does an action.

When referencing an object, you have to start with the highest-level parent. You find each subordinate object by typing the parent object followed by a period and then the child member. For example, to reference the value of cell A1 on "Sheet1" in the workbook "My Workbook.xlsx", you use the following VBA syntax:

```
Application.Workbooks("My Workbook.xlsm").Worksheets("Sheet1").Cells(1, 1).Value
```

> **NOTE**
>
> Instead of using the cell reference A1, the example above uses `1, 1`, with the `Cells` object translating to row 1, column 1. There are ways to use the A1 syntax, but we don't cover them here.

Be aware that the Excel Object Model exposes default objects depending on what application element is currently active. Many programmers take advantage of this and use shortcuts in their code. For example, the following syntax references cell A1 in whatever worksheet happens to be active when the code is executing:

```
Cells(1, 1).Value
```

While this syntax works, it is not considered good practice to use it unless you actually want to reference the active worksheet. However, in that case, we recommend using the `ActiveSheet` object to provide documentation to other developers that you did, in fact, intend to reference the active sheet:

```
Application.ActiveSheet.Cells(1, 1).Value
```

The one object that is implied throughout the Excel VBA environment is the `Application` object, and you can omit it with no problem. Therefore, the following references are non-ambiguous anywhere in the Excel VBA environment:

```
Workbooks("My Workbook.xlsm").Worksheets("Sheet1").Cells(1, 1).Value

ActiveSheet.Cells(1, 1).Value
```

And these references are just as non-ambiguous within Excel:

```
Application.Workbooks("My Workbook.xlsm").Worksheets("Sheet1").Cells(1, 1).Value
Application.ActiveSheet.Cells(1, 1).Value
```

You can assign a reference to any object to a variable as long as that variable is the same type as the object or is defined as a generic `Object` type. The primary reason for doing this is convenience. If you're referencing an object repeatedly, then setting a variable to reference that object can result in less code that is both easier to read and maintain. For example, you can assign the reference to "Sheet1" from above to a variable:

```
Dim TargetWorksheet As Worksheet
Set TargetWorksheet = Workbooks("My Workbook.xlsm").Worksheets("Sheet1")
```

Now the reference to A1 becomes:

```
TargetWorksheet.Cells(1, 1).Value
```

There are two things to note from this example. First, the `Set` keyword assigns the reference. VBA requires the use of the `Set` keyword when assigning references to objects. Also, the variable is a reference to the object, not a copy of the object. You can have any number of variables containing a reference to the same object instance.

> **NOTE**
>
> You may have noticed that we're now using the term **object reference** rather than just **object**. As you learn more about object-oriented programming, you will learn about objects, object instances, and object references. An object includes the Object Model (properties and methods that belong to it) and the code that governs how it behaves. An example of an object is the `Worksheet` object. An object instance is a specific instance of that object and includes the data and property values associated with that object instance. Worksheets "Sheet1" and "Sheet2" are examples of object instances; both are instances of the `Worksheet` object. A variable that references that object contains an object reference.

When you define variables that reference objects, you must define a variable as the same type as the object being referenced or as a generic `Object` type. In general, you should use the generic `Object` type only if that same variable will be assigned references to other objects of different types; when you use a generic `Object` type, the VBA editor can't assist you with IntelliSense. (IntelliSense presents a list of an object's properties and methods as you enter the object reference followed by a period.)

For the rest of the discussion on automating Tables, we use the following references (objects):

- **ThisWorkbook**—The workbook in which the code is running. This is convenient when the only workbook being referenced is the one in which the code resides. `ThisWorkbook` is easier to work with than `Workbooks("My Workbook.xlsm")`, especially when the workbook name may change.
- **Me**—When the code resides in a worksheet's code module, Me is a convenient way to reference the `Worksheet` object in which the code resides.

> **CAUTION**
>
> Excel Online does allow Excel automation with VBA to exist in a file (when viewed in a browser), but it does not execute the code. Any code written behind a workbook is ignored when you open that workbook in the Excel Online application, but the code is retained.

ListObject Object

Excel uses the ListObject object to expose a Table in the Excel Object Model. It is contained in the collection ListObjects, which belongs to the Worksheet object. Use this syntax to reference a specific Table on a worksheet:

```
ThisWorkbook.Worksheets("Sheet1").ListObjects("Table1")
```

> ***TIP***
>
> Name your Table something other than the default name. Doing so will help you both when writing your code and later, when you are looking at your code trying to figure out what you did. It will also be helpful to someone else looking at your code.

Because ListObjects is a collection of Tables, you can also access it with an index number:

```
ThisWorkbook.Worksheets("Sheet1").ListObjects(1)
```

The index (or position) of a ListObject in the ListObjects collection is determined by the order in which the ListObject objects were created on the worksheet. The ListObject object can be assigned to a variable that has been defined as a ListObject type. The ListObject object has a number of properties and methods used to access and manipulate Tables. The following sections present the most commonly used of these properties and methods.

Table Part Properties

Five properties represent the main parts of a Table. Each of these properties is a Range object. Two additional properties or collections provide access to the rows and columns in a Table. Each collection provides access to all the ListRow and ListColumn objects in the Table. Each ListRow and each ListColumn object has properties and methods.

Range Property

The Range **property returns the entire Table, including the header and total rows.** It is a Range object type. **The property cannot be set.**

HeaderRowRange Property

The HeaderRowRange property returns the Table's header row. It is a Range object type. The property cannot be **set**. The range is always a single row—the header row—and extends over all Table columns. When the header row is disabled, this property is set to Nothing.

DataBodyRange Property

The DataBodyRange property returns the Table's body. It is a Range object type. The property cannot be **set**. The range is every row between the header and the total row and extends over all Table columns.

When a Table does not contain any rows, the DataBodyRange property returns Nothing (and ListRows.Count returns 0). This is the only case when the property InsertRowRange returns a Range object that can be used to insert a new row. When in this state, the Table appears to have one row, without any values in it. As soon as one cell in the Table is set to a value, InsertRowRange is set to Nothing, and DataBodyRange is set to the data rows in the Table.

TotalRowRange Property

The TotalRowRange property returns the Table's total row. It is a Range object type. The property cannot be set. The range is always a single row—the total row—and extends over all Table columns. When the total row is disabled, this property is set to Nothing.

InsertRowRange Property

The InsertRowRange property returns the Table's current insertion row. It is a Range object type. The property cannot be set. While this range was always the first free row below the Table in Excel 2003 (the row with the asterisk), it was partially deprecated in Excel 2007 and remains so in 2013. In Excel 2007 and later versions, InsertRowRange only returns the first data row and only when the Table does not contain any data. Otherwise, it returns Nothing and is effectively useless.

ListRows Property

The ListRows property returns a collection of all rows in the Table's DataBodyRange. It is a ListRows object type that behaves very much like a Collection object and contains a collection of ListRow objects. The property cannot be set. Rows are referenced only by a one-based index number relative to the first row. An empty Table has no rows. The ListRows object's Add method is used to insert one new row at a time.

ListColumns Property

The ListColumns property returns a collection of all columns in the Table. It is a ListColumns object type that behaves very much like a Collection object and contains a collection of ListColumn objects. The property cannot be set. Columns are referenced by a one-based index number relative to the first column. A Table always contains at least one column.

Table Structure Properties

The following sections describe properties that you use to manipulate a Table's structure. All these properties are members of the ListObject object.

ShowAutoFilter Property

The ShowAutoFilter property returns or sets whether the Table's AutoFilter is enabled. It is a Boolean type. When it is set to True, the Table's AutoFilter is enabled. When it is set to False, the AutoFilter is disabled. This property is presented in the Excel user interface as the button *DATA | Sort & Filter | Filter.*

ShowAutoFilterDropDown Property

The ShowAutoFilterDropDown property returns or sets whether the Table's AutoFilter drop-down controls are displayed. It is a Boolean type. When it is set to True, the Table's AutoFilter drop-down controls are displayed. When it is set to False, they are hidden. If ShowAutoFilter is set to False, the ShowAutoFilterDropDown property cannot be changed. This property is presented in the Excel user interface as the button *{TABLE TOOLS} DESIGN | Table Style Options | Filter Button.*

ShowHeaders Property

The ShowHeaders property returns or sets whether the Table's header row is enabled. It is a Boolean type. When it is set to True, the Table's header row is enabled. When it is set to False, it is disabled. This property is presented in the Excel user interface as the check box *{TABLE TOOLS} DESIGN | Table Style Options | Header Row.*

ShowTotals Property

The ShowTotals property returns or sets whether the Table's total row is enabled. It is a Boolean type. When it is set to True, the Table's total row is enabled. When it is set to False, it is disabled. This property is presented in the Excel user interface as the check box *{TABLE TOOLS} DESIGN | Table Style Options | Total Row.*

Table Style Properties

The following sections describe properties that you use to manipulate a Table's style. All these properties are members of the `ListObject` object.

`TableStyle` Property

The `TableStyle` property returns or sets the Table's style name. It is a `Variant` type. To change the Table's style, you set the value to the desired style's name as a string. When you assign a Table style to a Table, only the style elements defined in that style are applied; see Chapter 7 for more information. To determine a style's name, move the mouse curser over the desired style in the *Table Styles* gallery until Excel displays that style's name, as shown in the next figure.

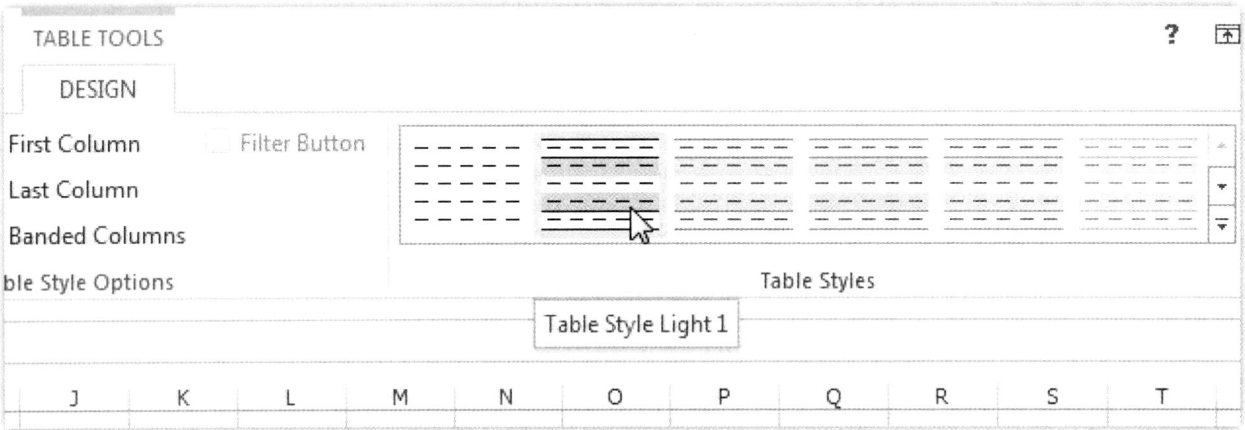

Determining a Table style's name.

This figure shows the Table's style displayed as "Table Style Light 1". To assign that style name to the `StyleName` property, you just remove the spaces:

```
ListObject.TableStyle = "TableStyleLight1"
```

> **NOTE**
>
> The internal names of all built-in styles do not contain spaces even though the names displayed on the ribbon do contain spaces.

The `TableStyle` property is presented in the Excel user interface as the array of buttons in the group *{TABLE TOOLS} DESIGN | Table Styles*.

`ShowTableStyleColumnStripes` Property

The `ShowTableStyleColumnStripes` property returns or sets whether the Table's odd columns are formatted differently than the even columns. It is a `Boolean` type. When it is set to `True`, the Table's odd columns are formatted differently than the even columns, as defined in the assigned Table style; the odd columns are formatted using the Table style's *First Column Stripe* settings, and the even rows are formatted using the Table style's *Second Column Stripe* settings. When `ShowTableStyleColumnStripes` is set to `False`, the Table's columns are not formatted using the assigned Table style. The `ShowTableStyleColumnStripes` property is presented in the Excel user interface as the check box *{TABLE TOOLS} DESIGN | Table Style Options | Banded Columns*.

Note that the default number of columns in each stripe is one, but you can change this to larger numbers for the *First Column Stripe* and *Second Column Stripe* elements independently. See Chapter 7 for more information.

ShowTableStyleRowStripes Property

The ShowTableStyleRowStripes property returns or sets whether the Table's odd rows are formatted differently than the even rows. It is a Boolean type. When it is set to True, the Table's odd rows are formatted differently than the even rows, as defined in the assigned Table style; the odd rows are formatted using the Table style's *First Row Stripe* settings, and the even rows are formatted using the Table style's *Second Row Stripe* settings. When the ShowTableStyleRowStripes property is set to False, the Table's rows are not formatted using the assigned Table style. This property is equivalent to the check box *{TABLE TOOLS} DESIGN | Table Style Options | Banded Rows.*

Note that the default number of columns in each stripe is one, but you can change this to larger numbers for the *First Column Stripe* and *Second Column Stripe* elements independently. See Chapter 7 for more information.

ShowTableStyleFirstColumn Property

The ShowTableStyleFirstColumn property returns or sets whether the Table's first column is formatted differently. It is a Boolean type. When it is set to True, the Table's first column is formatted as defined in the assigned Table style's *First Column* settings. When it is set to False, the Table's first column is not formatted using the assigned Table style. This property is presented in the Excel user interface as the check box *{TABLE TOOLS} DESIGN | Table Style Options | First Column.*

ShowTableStyleLastColumn Property

The ShowTableStyleLastColumn property returns or sets whether the Table's last column is formatted differently. It is a Boolean type. When it is set to True, the Table's last column is formatted as defined in the assigned Table style's *Last Column* settings. When it is set to False, the Table's last column is not formatted using the assigned Table style. This property is presented in the Excel user interface as the check box *{TABLE TOOLS} DESIGN | Table Style Options | Last Column.*

Other Table Object Properties

The following sections cover Table object properties to use in VBA. These are different than methods.

Active Property

The Active property returns True if the active cell is within the Table's range, including the header and total rows; it returns False otherwise. It is a Boolean type. The property cannot be set.

AlternativeText Property

The AlternativeText property returns or sets the Table's alternative text. It is a String type. Setting this property overwrites any previous value. This property is presented in the Excel user interface in the *Alternative Text* dialog box, which you access by right-clicking anywhere in the Table and selecting *Table | Alternative Text.* This property is displayed and edited in the *Title* text box.

AutoFilter Property

The AutoFilter property is an AutoFilter object with its own properties and methods. It can be used to inspect the AutoFilter settings and reapply or clear the AutoFilter settings to the Table. It is not used to set filters; you use the Range object's AutoFilter method for that. Both the Table object's AutoFilter object and the Range object's AutoFilter method are covered in more detail later in this chapter.

Comment Property

The Comment property returns or sets the Table's comment. It is a String type. This property, which was added in Excel 2007, is presented in the Excel user interface in the *Name Manager* dialog box, which you access by selecting *FORMULAS | Defined Names | Name Manager*. The comment is displayed in the rightmost column, and you change it by editing the name.

DisplayName Property

The DisplayName property returns or sets the Table's name. It is a String type. When you assign a value to this property, the same restrictions apply as when you change a Table's name from the Excel user interface; for example, it can't already be in use, and it can't contain any spaces. This property, which was added in Excel 2007, behaves almost the same as the Name property, but with the DisplayName property, the name being assigned must conform to Table name restrictions, or an error occurs. This property is presented in the Excel user interface as the text entry box *{TABLE TOOLS} DESIGN | Properties | Table Name*.

Name Property

The Name property returns or sets the Table's name. It is a String type. Unlike with the DisplayName property, when you assign a value to the Name property, Excel changes the name so that it follows the Table name rules. For example, it changes spaces to underscores and, if the name already exists, it appends an underscore followed by a number to the name. This property is presented in the Excel user interface as the text entry box *{TABLE TOOLS} DESIGN | Properties | Table Name*.

> ***TIP***
>
> To avoid problems, use the DisplayName property instead of the Name property to name a Table. The DisplayName property generates an error if the name is illegal or already defined elsewhere. On the other hand, Excel will mangle the value assigned to the Name property to make it legal, and thus the name may not end up being exactly what you intended.

Parent Property

The Parent property returns the Table's parent. It is an Object type but is always a Worksheet object. The property cannot be set.

QueryTable Property

The QueryTable property returns the QueryTable object that links to a list server. It is a QueryTable object type. The property cannot be set. The QueryTable object exposes properties and methods that enable you to manipulate the Table.

The following code publishes an existing Table to a SharePoint server and names the published list "Register". It then recovers the QueryTable object for the Table and sets the Table's MaintainConnection property to True:

```
Dim Table As ListObject
Dim QueryTable As QueryTable
Dim PublishTarget(4) As String
Dim ConnectionString As String
Set Table = ThisWorkbook.Worksheets("Register").ListObjects("tblRegister")
PublishTarget(0) = "0"
PublishTarget(1) = "http://myserver/myproject"
PublishTarget(2) = "1"
PublishTarget(3) = "Register"
ConnectionString = Table.Publish(PublishTarget, True)
Set QueryTable = Table.QueryTable
QueryTable.MaintainConnection = True
```

SharePointURL Property

The SharePointURL property returns the URL of the SharePoint list. It is a String type. The property is set when you create or maintain a SharePoint connection, and you can't change it. This property is presented in the Excel user interface as the button *{TABLE TOOLS} DESIGN | External Table Data | Export | Export Table to SharePoint List*. The following code publishes an existing Table to a SharePoint server by using SharePointURL and names the published list "Register":

```
Dim Table As ListObject
Dim QueryTable As QueryTable
Dim PublishTarget(4) As String
Dim ConnectionString As String
Set Table = ThisWorkbook.Worksheets("Register").ListObjects("tblRegister")
PublishTarget(0) = "0"
PublishTarget(1) = Table.SharePointURL
PublishTarget(2) = "1"
PublishTarget(3) = "Register"
ConnectionString = Table.Publish(PublishTarget, True)
```

Slicers Property

The Slicers property returns the collection of Slicers associated with the Table. It is a Slicers object type that behaves very much like a Collection object and contains a collection of Slicer objects. The property cannot be set. You use the Slicers object to add, manipulate, and delete Slicers associated with the Table. Each Slicer object exposes properties and methods that enable you to manipulate of the Slicer. The Slicers property was added to the ListObject object in Excel 2013. This section provides examples that illustrate how to add, manipulate, and delete a Slicer for a Table.

In the following example, a Slicer is added and placed on the same worksheet as the Table. Note that adding a Slicer is not quite as straightforward as adding other objects to collections; you need to create a SlicerCache object at the same time for each Slicer:

```
Dim Table As ListObject
Dim SlicerCache As SlicerCache
Dim Slicer As Slicer
Set Table = ThisWorkbook.Worksheets("Register").ListObjects("tblRegister")
Set SlicerCache = ThisWorkbook.SlicerCaches.Add(Table, "Category")
SlicerCache.RequireManualUpdate = False
Set Slicer = SlicerCache.Slicers.Add(Table.Parent, ,
    "tblRegisterCategory", "Category", 100, 400)
```

Note that the SlicerCache object is tied to the Table and the column being filtered. The Slicer itself is the visual representation of the Slicer cache and has a parent, a name, a caption, and a position; it also has a size, but the default size is used in the above example. The SlicerCache object's RequireManualUpdate property is set to False to avoid the "Out-Of-Date" message in the Slicer.

In the following example, the Slicer is configured to show the category "Expense" and hide the category "Income":

```
Dim Table As ListObject
Dim Slicer As Slicer
Set Table = ThisWorkbook.Worksheets("Register").ListObjects("tblRegister")
Set Slicer = Table.Slicers("tblRegisterCategory")
With Slicer.SlicerCache
    .SlicerItems("Expense").Selected = True
    .SlicerItems("Income").Selected = False
End With
```

In the following example, the Slicer is configured to show only one category. This technique is useful when there are many different values and you want only one of them:

```
Dim Table As ListObject
Dim Slicer As Slicer
Dim SlicerItem As SlicerItem
Set Table = ThisWorkbook.Worksheets("Register").ListObjects("tblRegister")
Set Slicer = Table.Slicers("tblRegisterCategory")
With Slicer.SlicerCache
    .ClearManualFilter
    For Each SlicerItem In .SlicerItems
        If SlicerItem.Name <> "Expense" Then
            SlicerItem.Selected = False
        End If
    Next SlicerItem
End With
```

In the following example, the Slicer's filter is cleared:

```
Dim Table As ListObject
Dim Slicer As Slicer
Set Table = ThisWorkbook.Worksheets("Register").ListObjects("tblRegister")
Set Slicer = Table.Slicers("tblRegisterCategory")
Slicer.SlicerCache.ClearManualFilter
```

In the following example, the Slicer is deleted. Note that the Slicer cache is also deleted when the Slicer is deleted:

```
Dim Table As ListObject
Dim Slicer As Slicer
Set Table = ThisWorkbook.Worksheets("Register").ListObjects("tblRegister")
Set Slicer = Table.Slicers("tblRegisterCategory")
Slicer.Delete
Table.ShowAutoFilter = False
```

Note that the Table's `ShowAutoFilter` property is set to `False` to hide the drop-down that remains after the Slicer is deleted. If the Table's AutoFilter was enabled when the Slicer was created, then this step isn't necessary. If the Table's AutoFilter was not enabled before the Slicer was added, then only the column being sliced has the AutoFilter drop-down control remain after the Slicer is deleted.

Sort Property

The `Sort` property returns the Table's `Sort` object. It is a `Sort` object type. The property cannot be set. The `Sort` object exposes properties and methods that enable the sorting of a Table. The `Sort` property was added in Excel 2007.

The following example sorts a Table by date and description:

```
Dim Table As ListObject
Set Table = ThisWorkbook.Worksheets("Register").ListObjects("tblRegister")
With Table
    .Sort.SortFields.Add .ListColumns("Date").DataBodyRange,_
        xlSortOnValues, xlAscending
    .Sort.SortFields.Add .ListColumns("Description")._
        DataBodyRange, xlSortOnValues, xlAscending
    .Sort.Apply
    .Sort.SortFields.Clear
```

```
End With
```

> **CAUTION**
>
> On a protected worksheet, you cannot sort a Table unless all cells in the Table's header and data body are unlocked or unless the worksheet is unprotected and then protected again.

`SourceType` Property

The `SourceType` property returns the Table's current source. It is an `XlListObjectSourceType` type. The property cannot be set. The following are `XlListObjectSourceType` constants:

- **xlSrcExternal or 0**—The source is an external data source, such as a Microsoft SharePoint Foundation site.
- **xlSrcModel or 4**—The source is a Power Pivot model.
- **xlSrcQuery or 3**—The source is a query.
- **xlSrcRange or 1**—The source is a Range object.
- **xlSrcXml or 2**—The source is XML.

`Summary` Property

The `Summary` property returns or sets the descriptive text used for the alternate text when the Table is published. It is a `String` type and was introduced in Excel 2010. Setting this property overwrites any previous value. This property is presented in the Excel user interface in the *Alternative Text* dialog box, which you access by right-clicking anywhere in the Table and selecting *Table | Alternative Text*. It is displayed and edited in the *Description* text box.

`TableObject` Property

The `TableObject` property returns the Table's `TableObject` object. It is a `TableObject` object type. The property cannot be set. The `TableObject` object exposes properties and methods that enable you to manipulate the Table's objects. `TableObject` is an object built from data retrieved from a Power Pivot model. It was introduced in Excel 2013.

`XmlMap` Property

The `XmlMap` property returns the Table's `XmlMap` object, which provides access to the Table's XML schema map. It is an `XmlMap` object type. The `XmlMap` object exposes properties and methods that enable you to manipulate the XML map. The property cannot be set.

Other Properties

The following sections describe other common Table properties.

`ListColumn` Property

The `ListColumn` property is an item in the `ListColumns` property or collection. `ListColumn` is an object with a number of useful properties, including these:

- **Range**—References the cells in a column, including the header and total rows, if enabled.
- **DataBodyRange**—A Range object type that references the column's range, excluding the header row and the totals row. It is the intersection of the ranges represented by the `ListObject`'s Range property and the `ListObject`'s DataBodyRange range.
- **Index**—The relative index number of a column represented by the `ListColumn` object.

- **Parent**—The `ListObject` that owns a column.

`ListColumn` also has a useful method:

- **Delete**—Deletes the column from the Table.

`ListRow` Property

Each `ListRow` object in a collection of rows has three commonly used properties: a `Range` property that references the cells in that row, an `Index` property that is the relative index number of that row, and a `Parent` property that refers to the `ListObject` that contains the row. The Row object also has one method, `Delete`, which deletes the row from the Table.

Table Object Methods

The following sections describe properties for performing actions with `ListObject`.

`Delete` Method

The `Delete` method deletes a Table, including all the Table's values, formulas, and formatting. Do not confuse this method with the `Unlist` method, which converts a Table to a regular range of cells and maintains the values and formulas in the Table.

`ExportToVisio` Method

The `ExportToVisio` method exports to and opens in Visio a dynamic PivotDiagram in a new drawing document. This method was added in Excel 2007. An error is generated if Visio is not installed on the same system on which the method is invoked. To export the Excel Table to Visio, the workbook must be saved with no pending changes.

`Publish` Method

The `Publish` method publishes the Table to a SharePoint service. It returns the URL of the published list on SharePoint as a string. Here is its syntax:

```
expression.Publish(Target, LinkSource)
```

Where:

- **expression**—A variable that represents a `ListObject` object.
- **Target**—A single-dimension `Variant` array that contains two to three elements: the URL of SharePoint server, the display name of the list, and, optionally, the description of the list.
- **LinkSource**—A `Boolean` that, when set to `True`, creates a new link to a new SharePoint list and that, when set to `False`, keeps the link to the current SharePoint list and replaces that list, or, if there is no current link, creates a new list on SharePoint without linking to it.

`Refresh` Method

The `Refresh` method refreshes the Table from its external source, if linked. If the Table is not linked to an external data source, an error is generated. Any changes made to the Table since the last refresh are lost.

`Resize` Method

The `Resize` method changes the Table range to the range provided. The method takes one parameter, `Range`, which specifies the new Table range. If the header row is enabled, the new range must include at least one header row cell. If the header row is disabled, the new range must include at least one cell in the first data body range row. Columns can be added and removed from either end, and rows can be added and removed from the bottom. When you remove rows and columns, any existing data in the removed rows and columns remains but is now outside the Table. When you add rows and columns, any data in the additional cells is added to the Table. After resizing, structured references in formulas in cells no longer in the Table are converted to absolute standard cell referencing.

If a Table is linked to a SharePoint list, you can add and remove only rows. Trying to add or remove columns in a linked Table generates an error.

`Unlink` Method

The `Unlink` method removes any external data link if it exists.

`Unlist` Method

The `Unlist` method converts a Table to a regular range of cells. It is the equivalent of selecting *{TABLE TOOLS} DESIGN | Tools | Convert to Range*. Structured references in formulas are converted to absolute standard cell referencing.

Other Methods

The following sections describe more common methods used when writing code for Tables. These methods are often primary tools used when working with Tables in VBA. Having a basic understanding of how they work will help you write more robust and efficient code.

`ListObject` Object's Add Method

The `ListObject` object's Add method adds a new Table, using an existing list of data or another source. When you use an existing header, numeric values are converted to text, and any duplicate headers are made unique by appending integer values. Here is the syntax for this method:

```
expression.Add(SourceType, Source, LinkSource, XlListObjectHasHeaders,
Destination, TableStyleName)
```

Where:

- **expression**—A variable that represents a `ListObjects` object.
- **SourceType**—Passes an `XlListObjectSourceType` constant that specifies the kind of source used to create the Table. It is optional. If omitted, `xlSrcRange` is assumed.
- **Source**—When `SourceType` is `xlSrcRange`, then pass a Range object that represents the range of data values to convert into a Table. It is optional. If omitted, the current selection is used. When `SourceType` is `xlSrcExternal`, pass an array of string values specifying a connection to the source, where the elements in the array are:
  - **0**—The URL of the SharePoint site
  - **1**—The SharePoint list name
  - **2**—The ViewGUID
- **LinkSource**—A `Boolean` value that indicates whether an external data source is to be linked to the `ListObject` object. If `SourceType` is `xlSrcExternal`, then the default is `True`, and this parameter does not need to be passed. If a value is passed and `SourceType` is `xlSrcRange`, then an error is generated.
- **XlListObjectHasHeaders**—Passes an `XlYesNoGuess` constant type (`xlYes`, `xlNo`, or `xlGuess`), which indicates whether the data being imported has column labels. If `Source` does not contain headers, Excel automatically generates headers. It is optional. If omitted, `xlGuess` is assumed. Note that this parameter's name should be `HasHeaders` but, when the method was implemented, the developers mistakenly used `XlListObjectHasHeaders` instead.
- **Destination**—Passes a Range object that specifies a single-cell reference as the destination for the top-left corner of the Table. An error is generated if the range refers to more than one cell. This

parameter must be specified if `SourceType` is `xlSrcExternal`. It is ignored if `SourceType` is set to `xlSrcRange`. The destination range must be on the worksheet that contains the `ListObjects` collection specified by the expression. Columns are inserted before the destination range to fit the new list, preventing existing data from being overwritten. It is optional.

- **TableStyleName**—Passes the name of the style name to be applied to the Table when created. It is optional. If `TableStyleName` is omitted, the default style is applied.

This method returns a `ListObject` object that represents the new list object.

The following are the `XlListObjectSourceType` constants:

- **xlSrcExternal or 0**—The source is an external data source (for example, Microsoft SharePoint Foundation site).
- **xlSrcModel or 4**—The source is a Power Pivot Data Model.
- **xlSrcQuery or 3**—The source is a query.
- **xlSrcRange or 1**—The source is a range of existing data.
- **xlSrcXml or 2**—The source is XML.

ListRows Object's Add Method

The `ListRows` object's Add method inserts one new row into the Table at the position specified. Here is the syntax for the method:

```
expression.Add(Position, AlwaysInsert)
```

Where:

- **expression**—A variable that represents a `ListRows` object.
- **Position**—An `Integer` that specifies the relative position of the new row. The new row is inserted above the current row at that position. It is optional. If omitted, the new row is appended to the bottom of the Table.
- **AlwaysInsert**—A `Boolean` that specifies whether to always shift data in cells below the last row of the Table when the new row is inserted, regardless of whether the row below the Table is empty. If `True`, the cells below the Table are shifted down one row. If `False`, if the row below the Table is empty, the Table expands to occupy (append) that row without shifting cells below it; if the row below the Table contains data, those cells are shifted down when the new row is inserted.

The Add method returns a `ListRow` object that represents the new row.

ListRow Object's Delete Method

The `ListRow` object's `Delete` method deletes the Table row represented by the `ListRow` object.

ListColumns Object's Add Method

The `ListColumns` object's Add method inserts one new column into the Table at the position specified. Here's the syntax for this method:

```
expression.Add(Position)
```

Where:

- **expression**—A variable that represents a `ListColumns` object.
- **Position**—An `Integer` that specifies the relative position of the new column. The new column is inserted before the current column at that position. It is optional. If omitted the new column is appended to the right side of the Table.

This method returns a `ListColumn` object that represents the new column.

ListColumn Object's Delete Method

The ListColumn object's Delete method deletes the Table column represented by the ListColumn object.

Range Object's AutoFilter Method

You can use the AutoFilter method to create AutoFilter criteria for a column, clear the filter criteria for a column, or toggle the AutoFilter status for the range. To inspect the AutoFilter status and settings, use the ListObject object's AutoFilter property, which has the following syntax:

```
expression.AutoFilter(Field, Criteria1, Operator, Criteria2, VisibleDropDown)
```

Where:

- **expression**—An expression that returns a Range object.
- **Field**—The Integer offset of the field on which to base the filter from the left of the list, where the leftmost field is field 1. It is optional. If omitted, the AutoFilter status (enabled/disabled) is toggled for the entire range. Disabling the AutoFilter removes the AutoFilter drop-down controls.
- **Criteria1**—The criteria as a number, a string, or an array—for example, 20 or Expense. Use = to find blank fields. Use <> to find nonblank fields. To find multiple strings, use the Array function with an Operator value of xlFilterValues—for example, Array("Value 1", "Value 2"). The wildcard characters * (one or more characters) and ? (any single character) can be used. If the Operator is xlTop10Items, Criteria1 specifies the number of items, such as 10. When Operator is xlFilterDynamic, Criteria1 is an XlDynamicFilterCriteria constant. (See the description below.) It is optional. If this argument is omitted, the criteria for the column is cleared.
- **Operator**—Passes an XlAutoFilterOperator constant specifying the type of filter. It is optional. If omitted, then 0 is assumed, which has no value, and Crtiteria1 is treated as a simple value to find; in this case, if an array of values is passed in Criteria1, then only the last value is used. When omitted and Criteria1 is not specified, the effect is to clear the filter for the specified column.
- **Criteria2**—The second criteria as a number, a string, or an array. It is used with Criteria1 and Operator to construct compound criteria or when Operator is xlFilterValues and date and times are filtered. (See the description for xlFilterValues below for details on filtering date and time values.) It is optional.
- **VisibleDropDown**—Passes True to display the AutoFilter drop-down arrow for the filtered field and False to hide the AutoFilter drop-down for the filtered field. It is optional. If omitted, True is assumed.

If setting filter criteria, then the value returned is the Field value. If toggling the AutoFilter status, then True is returned.

These are the XlAutoFilterOperator constants:

- **xlAnd or 1**—Filters with a logical AND of Criteria1 and Criteria2. Both Criteria1 and Criteria2 are strings specifying a condition—for example, ">0" and "<100" for greater than zero and less than 100.
- **xlBottom10Items or 4**—Finds the lowest-valued items displayed, where the number of items is specified as a number or string in Criteria1—for example, 5 or "5", meaning the five smallest items. The column specified by Field must contain at least one number, or an error occurs.
- **xlBottom10Percent or 6**—Find the lowest-valued items displayed, where the percentage is specified as a number or string in Criteria1—for example, 20 or "20" for the items in the bottom 20%. The column specified by Field must contain at least one number, or an error occurs.

- **xlFilterCellColor or 8**—Finds the color of the cell where the color is specified as an RGB value in `Criteria1`.
- **xlFilterDynamic or 11**—A dynamic filter where the filter criteria is specified as an `XlDynamicFilterCriteria` value in `Criteria1`. A dynamic filter is one that changes depending on some other value, such as today's date or the average of the values in the column.
- **xlFilterFontColor or 9**—Finds the color of the font, where the color is specified as an RGB value in `Criteria1`.
- **xlFilterIcon or 10**—Finds the icon, where the icon is specified in `Criteria1`. Icons are retrieved from `ActiveWorkbook`'s `IconSets` property. The `IconSets` property is a collection of `IconSets` objects where each `IconSet` is a collection of a series of icons, such as the "3 Arrows (Colored)" set. The example below retrieves the first icon in the "3 Arrows (Colored)" set:

```
ActiveWorkbook.IconSets(XlIconSet.xl3Arrows).Item(1)
```

> ***TIP***
>
> Note the use of the enumerated list identifier `XlIconSet`, which provides an easy way to remember the name of each icon set: Entering "XlIconSet." (including the period) invokes an IntelliSense pop-up list of all available icon set references.

- **xlFilterValues or 7**—Finds multiple values specified as an array in `Criteria1` or `Criteria2`. `Criteria1` is used when finding a simple list of values, such as "Value 1" and "Value 2". The values in the array must each be a string and must match exactly the displayed value if numeric; for example, if matching values displayed as "$25.00", the value passed must be "$25.00". `Criteria2` is used when finding dates and times. When finding dates and times, the array is passed as an array of pairs of values, where the first value of each pair is a type of search and the second value is a date. The types of date/time searches are:
    - **0**—Finds items in the same year as the following paired date/time value.
    - **1**—Finds items in the same month as the following paired date/time value.
    - **2**—Finds items on the same date as the following paired date/time value.
    - **3**—Finds items in the same hour as the following paired date/time value.
    - **4**—Finds items in the same minute as the following paired date/time value.
    - **5**—Finds items in the same second as the following paired date/time value.
- Any number of search type and date/time value pairs can be passed. All search type values must be in odd positions in the array (1, 3, 5, etc.), and all date/time values must be in even positions (2, 4, 6, etc.). Any value passed for a search type that is not in the above list generates an error. Any value passed for a date/time value that is not a date/time value passed as a string generates an error. Any date/time value that can be entered in a cell and recognized as a date is valid. Below are some examples of `Criteria2` values.
- Show all items in the year 2014:

```
Array(0, "1/1/2014")
```

- Show all items in the year 2014 when the current year is 2014:

```
Array(0, "1/1")
```

- Show all items in the month January 2014:

```
Array(1, "1/1/2014")
```

- Show all items on the day January 15, 2014:

```
Array(2, "1/15/2014")
```

- Show all items on the days January 15, 20, and 25, 2014:

  ```
  Array(2, "1/15/2014", 2, "1/20/2014", 2, "1/25/2014")
  ```

- Show all items in the year 2013 and in the month January 2014:

  ```
  Array(0, "1/1/2013", 1, "1/1/2014")
  ```

- Show all items in the same hour as 3 PM on January 15, 2014:

  ```
  Array(3, "1/15/2014 15:0")
  Array(3, "1/15/2014 3 PM")
  ```

- Show all items in the same minute as 3:01 PM on January 15, 2014:

  ```
  Array(3, "1/15/2014 15:1")
  Array(3, "1/15/2014 3:01 PM")
  ```

- **xlOr or 2**—Logical OR of `Criteria1` or `Criteria2`. Both `Criteria1` and `Criteria2` are strings that specify a condition, such as `"<0"` and `">100"` for less than zero or greater than 100.
- **xlTop10Items or 3**—Finds the highest-valued items displayed, where the number of items is specified as a number or string in `Criteria1`, such as 5 or `"5"`, meaning the five largest items. The column specified by `Field` must contain at least one number, or an error occurs.
- **xlTop10Percent or 5**—Finds the highest-valued items displayed, where the percentage is specified as a number or string in `Criteria1`, such as `20` or `"20"` for items in the top 20%. The column specified by "`Field`" must contain at least one number, or an error occurs.

The following are `XlDynamicFilterCriteria` constants:

- **xlFilterToday**—Filters all date values equal to today.
- **xlFilterYesterday**—Filters all date values equal to yesterday.
- **xlFilterTomorrow**—Filters all date values equal to tomorrow.
- **xlFilterThisWeek**—Filters all date values in the current week.
- **xlFilterLastWeek**—Filters all date values in the last week.
- **xlFilterNextWeek**—Filters all date values in the next week.
- **xlFilterThisMonth**—Filters all date values in the current month.
- **xlFilterLastMonth**—Filters all date values in the last month.
- **xlFilterNextMonth**—Filters all date values in the next month.
- **xlFilterThisQuarter**—Filters all date values in the current quarter.
- **xlFilterLastQuarter**—Filters all date values in the last quarter.
- **xlFilterNextQuarter**—Filters all date values in the next quarter.
- **xlFilterThisYear—**Filters all date values in the current year.
- **xlFilterLastYear—**Filters all date values in the last year.
- **xlFilterNextYear—**Filters all values related to next year.
- **xlFilterYearToDate—**Filters all date values from today until a year ago.
- **xlFilterAllDatesInPeriodQuarter1—**Filters all date values in Quarter1.
- **xlFilterAllDatesInPeriodQuarter2—**Filters all date values in Quarter2.
- **xlFilterAllDatesInPeriodQuarter3—**Filters all date values in Quarter3.
- **xlFilterAllDatesInPeriodQuarter4—**Filters all date values in Quarter4.
- **xlFilterAllDatesInPeriodJanuary**—Filters all date values in January.

- **xlFilterAllDatesInPeriodFebruary**—Filters all date values in February.
- **xlFilterAllDatesInPeriodMarch**—Filters all date values in March.
- **xlFilterAllDatesInPeriodApril**—Filters all date values in April.
- **xlFilterAllDatesInPeriodMay**—Filters all date values in May.
- **xlFilterAllDatesInPeriodJune**—Filters all date values in June.
- **xlFilterAllDatesInPeriodJuly**—Filters all date values in July.
- **xlFilterAllDatesInPeriodAugust**—Filters all date values in August.
- **xlFilterAllDatesInPeriodSeptember**—Filters all date values in September.
- **xlFilterAllDatesInPeriodOctober**—Filters all date values in October.
- **xlFilterAllDatesInPeriodNovember**—Filters all date values in November.
- **xlFilterAllDatesInPeriodDecember**—Filters all date values in December.
- **xlFilterAboveAverage**—Filters all above-average values.
- **xlFilterBelowAverage**—Filters all below-average values.

Accessing Table Parts

While the `ListObject`, `ListColumns`, and `ListRows` properties provide access to the main parts of a Table, there are other ways to access parts of a Table, using the same structured referencing syntax described in Chapter 4. These forms of referencing can be more convenient, depending on programming style and preferences. The examples below assume the following: a Table named "tblRegister" on a worksheet named "Register" with column names "Date", "Description", "Category", and "Amount".

Date	Description	Category	Amount
1/3/1900	Transaction 1	Expense	-100.00
1/15/2014	Transaction 4	Income	350.00
2/1/2014	Transaction 2	Income	150.00
3/1/2014	Transaction 3	Expense	-75.00
Total			**325.00**

A sample Table.

To use a structured reference, use the Range object to retrieve the range described by the reference. The `Range` object is a child object of many Excel objects, including the `Application` and `Worksheet` objects. When you use `Range` with the `Application` object, the reference must have global scope. When you use `Range` with the `Worksheet` (or `Sheet`) object, the reference can have global or local (`Worksheet`) scope.

> ***NOTE***
>
> The scope of a name determines from where it can be accessed. A reference with global scope can be accessed from any object. A reference with local scope can be referenced only from the worksheet to which the specific reference refers.

Table names have global scope, which means you can access them from any code module without qualifying the reference with the `Worksheet` object in which the Table resides. For example, this reference:

```
ThisWorkbook.Worksheets("Register").Range("tblRegister[Date]")
```

Is equivalent to:

```
Application.Range("tblRegister[Date]")
Range("tblRegister[Date]")
```

```
[tblRegister[Date]]
```

To support this convention, Excel enforces the rule that every Table in a workbook must have a unique name. This rule governs all globally scoped names, not just names of Tables.

> ***TIP***
>
> To reduce the probability of a name collision, an option is to preface all Table names with a common prefix—often referred to as "Hungarian notation" and described in Chapter 2—such as "tbl".

> ***CAUTION***
>
> Excel 2003 does not support structured references. There are also some differences between Excel 2007, 2010, and 2013 in terms of support for structured references. For more information, see the section "Forward and Backward Compatibility" in Chapter 2.

Creating and Naming a Table

You create Tables by using the `ListObjects` object's `Add` method. After you create a new Table, the `ListObject` object's `DisplayName` property is set to the new Table's name. The `DisplayName` property is used instead of the `Name` property because Excel is stricter about what can be assigned to the `DisplayName` property; instead of altering the name when it is not valid, Excel generates an error, which produces more predictable results than when using the `Name` property.

The following sections provide examples of creating Tables with four different sources: `xlSrcRange` (a range of existing data), `xlSrcExternal` (external data source), `xlSrcModel` (Power Pivot Data Model), and `xlSrcQuery` (query). The source type `xlSrcXml` (XML source) is not covered, but workarounds are shown.

Using a Range of Existing Data (SourceType Set to xlSrcRange)

This example creates a new Table, using an existing range of data with headers. The `SourceType` parameter is set to `xlSrcRange`:

```
Dim TableRange As Range
Dim Table As ListObject
Set TableRange = ThisWorkbook.Worksheets("Register").Range("A1").CurrentRegion
Set Table = ThisWorkbook.Worksheets("Register").ListObjects.Add(xlSrcRange,
TableRange, , xlYes)
Table.DisplayName = "tblRegister"
```

Note that the fourth parameter, `xlYes`, tells Excel that the list of data has existing headers. In this example, the Table is named as soon as it is created; this helps you locate the `ListObject` later.

Using a Power Pivot Data Model (SourceType Set to xlSrcModel)

This example uses a `TableObject` to create a connection to a SQL Server database. The SQL table "Product" is added to the Power Pivot Data Model. The Table is placed into the worksheet "Sheet1" at cell "A1". Because the interaction is with the Data Model, the `TableObject` must be used instead of a `ListObject` with `xlSrcModel` passed for `SourceType`. Change the text "YourServerName" to the name of the desired SQL server. The database used is AdventureWorks2012:

```
Dim SQLConnection As WorkbookConnection
Dim TargetWorksheet As Worksheet
Dim Table As TableObject
```

```
Dim ConnectionString As String
Set TargetWorksheet = ThisWorkbook.Worksheets("Sheet1")
ConnectionString = "OLEDB;Provider=SQLOLEDB.1;Integrated Security=SSPI;" _
    & "Initial Catalog=AdventureWorks2012;Data Source=YourServerName"
Set SQLConnection = ActiveWorkbook.Connections.Add2("FriendlyName",
"Description", _
    ConnectionString, "Product", 3, True)
With TargetWorksheet
    Set Table = .ListObjects.Add(SourceType:=xlSrcModel, Source:=SQLConnection,
_
        Destination:=.Range("A1")).NewTable
End With
Table.ListObject.DisplayName = "tblNewTable"
```

The `xlSrcModel` constant was added in Excel 2013.

This next example assumes that the workbook already has a SQL Server connection with a table in the Power Pivot Data Model, and the objective is to pull the data out of the Data Model table into a new Excel Table. The source type is `xlSrcModel` and assumes that the Data Model table name is "Product". This example works only in Excel 2013:

```
Dim ModelSource As Model
Dim SourceTable As ModelTable
Dim TargetWorksheet As Worksheet
Dim Table As TableObject
Set TargetWorksheet = ThisWorkbook.Worksheets("Sheet1")
Set ModelSource = ThisWorkbook.Model
Set SourceTable = ModelSource.ModelTables("Product")
Set Table = TargetWorksheet.ListObjects.Add(SourceType:=xlSrcModel, _
    Source:=SourceTable.SourceWorkbookConnection, _
    LinkSource:=True, Destination:=DestinationSheet.Range("A1")).TableObject
Table.Refresh
```

Using an External Data Source or Query (`SourceType` Set to `xlSrcExternal` or `xlSrcQuery`)

This example uses a `QueryTable` object to create a connection to a SQL Server database. The Table "Product" is added to the worksheet "Sheet1" at cell "A1". Change the text "YourServerName" to the name of the desired SQL server. The database used is AdventureWorks2012:

```
Dim TargetWorksheet As Worksheet
Dim Table As QueryTable
Dim ConnectionString As String
Set TargetWorksheet = ThisWorkbook.Worksheets("Sheet1")
ConnectionString = "OLEDB;Provider=SQLOLEDB.1;Integrated Security=SSPI;" _
    & "Initial Catalog=AdventureWorks2012;Data Source=YourServerName"
Set Table = TargetWorksheet.ListObjects.Add(SourceType:=xlSrcExternal,
Source:=ConnectionString, _
    LinkSource:=True, Destination:=DestinationSheet.Range("A1")).QueryTable
Table.CommandText = Array("""AdventureWorks2012"".""Production"".""Product""")
Table.CommandType = xlCmdTable
Table.Refresh BackgroundQuery:=False
Table.ListObject.DisplayName = "tblNewTable"
```

The `xlSrcQuery` constant was added in Excel 2007.

This example uses the SourceType of xlSrcExternal, which is used for any external data connection. Passing xlSrcQuery for the SourceType parameter produces the same result. Typically, xlSrcQuery is used for database connections, and xlSrcExternal is used for SharePoint connections. There is a lot of latitude in data connections.

> **CAUTION**
>
> When using xlSrcExternal, you must specify the Destination parameter. When using a QueryTable object, you must set the CommandText and CommandType properties before refreshing the connection.

Using an XML Source (SourceType Set to xlSrcXml)

By design, the ListObjects object's Add method with the xlSrcXml source type is supposed to create a ListObject object by using an XML file as the source. However, this method is unreliable, and there are no known working examples of using it. Two methods are recommended for importing an XML source file into a Table. The first is to import an XML file into a new, blank workbook:

```
Workbooks.OpenXML Filename:="C:\XML File Name.xml",
LoadOption:=xlXmlLoadImportToList
```

The second is to import an XML file into the existing worksheet at the specified range:

```
ActiveWorkbook.XmlImport URL:="C:\XML File Name.xml", ImportMap:=Nothing,
Overwrite:=True, _
    Destination:=Range("A1")
```

> **NOTE**
>
> In both of these examples, if the specified XML source doesn't refer to a schema, Excel creates one based on what it finds in the referenced XML file.

Table Information

The following examples assume that DataBodyRange is a valid Range object. If there are no existing rows in the Table (that is, if ListRows.Count equals 0), any reference to DataBodyRange generates an error.

Determining Whether a Table Exists

Determining whether a Table exists is not a straightforward operation. It requires some error handling because an error occurs when a Table name that doesn't exist is used with the ListObjects collection. The following code illustrates how to use error handling to determine whether a Table exists:

```
Dim Table As ListObject
Set Table = Nothing
On Error Resume Next
Set Table = ThisWorkbook.Worksheets("Register").ListObjects("tblRegister")
On Error GoTo 0
If Table Is Nothing Then
    Debug.Print "Table does not exist"
Else
    Debug.Print "Table exists"
End If
```

> ***TIP***
>
> Why set the object variable to `Nothing` before attempting to assign it a value? In the case above, it's not necessary because VBA initializes every variable when it is defined with the `Dim` statement. But it's included above as an example of writing robust code because, if an error occurs, the variable is not touched and, if it already contains a reference to another object, the following test will not produce the desired result.

Determining a Table's Address

This example displays a Table's address and the Table's `DataBodyRange` address in the *Immediate* window:

```
Dim Table As ListObject
Set Table = ThisWorkbook.Worksheets("Register").ListObjects("tblRegister")
Debug.Print "Table's address: " & Table.Range.Address
Debug.Print "Table's data body range address: " & Table.DataBodyRange.Address
```

Determining the Number of Rows

You determine the number of rows in a Table by using the `ListRows` object's `Count` property:

```
Dim Table As ListObject
Set Table = ThisWorkbook.Worksheets("Register").ListObjects("tblRegister")
Debug.Print "Number of rows: " & Table.ListRows.Count
```

The `Count` property returns `0` if the Table is empty (that is, has one row ready for data entry and no data in any cells).

Determining the Number of Columns

You determine the number of columns in a Table by using the `ListColumns` object's `Count` property:

```
Dim Table As ListObject
Set Table = ThisWorkbook.Worksheets("Register").ListObjects("tblRegister")
Debug.Print "Number of columns: " & Table.ListColumns.Count
```

Determining Whether a Column Exists

Determining whether a column exists is not a straightforward operation. It requires some error handling because an error occurs when a column name that doesn't exist is used with the `ListColumns` collection. The following code illustrates how to use error handling to determine whether a column exists:

```
Dim Table As ListObject
Dim ListColumn As ListColumn
Set Table = ThisWorkbook.Worksheets("Register").ListObjects("tblRegister")
Set ListColumn = Nothing
On Error Resume Next
Set ListColumn = Table.ListColumns("Description")
On Error GoTo 0
If ListColumn Is Nothing Then
    Debug.Print "Column does not exist"
Else
    Debug.Print "Column exists"
End If
```

Adding Rows

There are a few ways to add new rows to a Table. If you're adding one row, use the ListRows object's Add method, which returns a ListRow object that can then be used to add values to that new row:

```
Dim Table As ListObject
Dim NewRow As ListRow
Set Table = ThisWorkbook.Worksheets("Register").ListObjects("tblRegister")
Set NewRow = Table.ListRows.Add
With NewRow.Range
    .Columns(1).Value = #1/1/2015#
    .Columns(2).Value = "Transaction 20"
    .Columns(3).Value = "Expense"
    .Columns(4).Value = -75
End With
```

Note that in this example, the Position parameter was not passed to the Add method, which resulted in the new row being appended to the end of the Table. To insert the new row at a specific position in the Table, use the Position parameter.

To append more than one row to the bottom of a Table, it's more efficient to add the rows in one step than to invoke the ListRows object's Add method multiple times. In the next example, the total row is disabled, the new data is copied into the empty cells immediately below the Table, and the Total row is enabled; if the TotalRow is not disabled, the Table does not recognize the new rows and therefore does not expand to include them. The new data is copied from the range "A2:D11" on the "Data" worksheet:

```
Dim Table As ListObject
Dim NewValues As Variant
Set Table = ThisWorkbook.Worksheets("Register").ListObjects("tblRegister")
NewValues = ThisWorkbook.Worksheets("Data").Range("A2:D11").Value
Table.ShowTotals = False
With Table.DataBodyRange
    .Resize(10).Offset(.Rows.Count).Value = NewValues
End With
Table.ShowTotals = True
```

To insert multiple rows into the middle of a Table, you use the Range object's Insert method to insert empty cells, and then those cells are filled with the new row data. In the next example, 10 rows of data are inserted after the existing row 2 (and before row 3):

```
Dim Table As ListObject
Dim NewValues As Variant
Set Table = ThisWorkbook.Worksheets("Register").ListObjects("tblRegister")
NewValues = ThisWorkbook.Worksheets("Data").Range("A2:D11").Value
With Table.DataBodyRange
    .Resize(10).Offset(2).Insert Shift:=xlShiftDown
    .Resize(10).Offset(2).Value = NewValues
End With
```

Deleting Rows

The following sections show different methods for deleting rows from a Table by using VBA. The method you use depends on how many rows you want to delete.

Deleting One Row

You use the ListRow object's Delete method to delete a single row:

```
Dim Table As ListObject
Dim ListRow as ListRow
Set Table = ThisWorkbook.Worksheets("Register").ListObjects("tblRegister")
Set ListRow = Table.ListRows(3)
ListRow.Delete
```

In this example, the variable `ListRow` is assigned the third `ListRow` object in the `ListRows` collection, and then the `ListRow` object's `Delete` method is invoked. Here is an alternative, shorter version of the example that does not require the `ListRow` variable:

```
Dim Table As ListObject
Set Table = ThisWorkbook.Worksheets("Register").ListObjects("tblRegister")
Table.ListRows(3).Delete
```

Deleting Multiple Rows

Deleting multiple rows at once requires use of the `Range` object's `Delete` method. In the next example, 10 rows are deleted, starting at row 3:

```
Dim Table As ListObject
Set Table = ThisWorkbook.Worksheets("Register").ListObjects("tblRegister")
Table.DataBodyRange.Resize(10).Offset(2).Delete
```

Deleting All Rows

The next example deletes all the rows in a Table:

```
Dim Table As ListObject
Set Table = ThisWorkbook.Worksheets("Register").ListObjects("tblRegister")
Table.DataBodyRange.Delete
```

> ***CAUTION***
>
> In this example, the `DataBodyRange` object is set to `Nothing` after the code completes. Any subsequent references to this object returns an error unless at least one row is added to the Table.

Looping

The following sections show methods for looping through rows and columns utilizing Table objects. You could also accomplish this by using row or column numbers, which is beyond the scope of this book.

Looping Through Rows

This example loops through all rows of the Table, adding each amount to the `TotalExpenses` variable for any row with "Expense" in the third column and printing the output to the *Immediate* window:

```
Dim Table As ListObject
Dim ListRow As ListRow
Dim TotalExpenses As Double
Set Table = ThisWorkbook.Worksheets("Register").ListObjects("tblRegister")
For Each ListRow In Table.ListRows
    If ListRow.Range.Columns(3).Value = "Expense" Then
        TotalExpenses = TotalExpenses + ListRow.Range.Columns(4).Value
    End If
Next ListRow
Debug.Print "Total expenses: " & TotalExpenses
```

The following is an alternative method that uses the column names:

```
Dim Table As ListObject
Dim ListRow As ListRow
Dim TotalExpenses As Double
Set Table = ThisWorkbook.Worksheets("Register").ListObjects("tblRegister")
For Each ListRow In Table.ListRows
    If Intersect(ListRow.Range, Table.ListColumns("Category").Range)_
        .Value = "Expense" Then
        TotalExpenses = TotalExpenses + Intersect(ListRow.Range, Table.
ListColumns("Amount").Range).Value
    End If
Next ListRow
Debug.Print "Total expenses: " & TotalExpenses
```

Looping Through Columns

This example loops through the columns of a Table, printing each column's name to the *Immediate* window by using the `ListColumns` collection and a `For/Each` statement:

```
Dim Table As ListObject
Dim ListColumn As ListColumn
Set Table = ThisWorkbook.Worksheets("Register").ListObjects("tblRegister")
For Each ListColumn In Table.ListColumns
    Debug.Print ListColumn.Name
Next ListColumn
```

Filtering

One of the most powerful features of Tables is their ability to filter rows so that only the rows of interest are displayed. The Excel Object Model exposes the `AutoFilter` object (a child member of the `ListObject` object) and the `AutoFilter` method (a child member of the Range object), enabling complete control of the filtering process from VBA. You use the `ListObject.AutoFilter` object to inspect the current AutoFilter settings, refresh the AutoFilter, and clear the AutoFilter. You use the `Range.AutoFilter` method to set AutoFilter criteria.

Turning AutoFilter On and Off

You turn AutoFilter on and off by setting the `ShowAutoFilter` property to `True` (on) and `False` (off). The following example shows how to turn on the AutoFilter:

```
Dim Table As ListObject
Set Table = ThisWorkbook.Worksheets("Register").ListObjects("tblRegister")
Table.ShowAutoFilter = True
```

> ***TIP***
>
> Since `AutoFilter` is an object that is set to `Nothing` when the AutoFilter is disabled, any code that references any of the `AutoFilter` object's properties and methods will generate an error if the AutoFilter is disabled. To prevent errors, check that the AutoFilter is enabled and access the `AutoFilter` object's properties and methods only if it is. The code examples in this section demonstrate this check.

> **NOTE**
>
> You can also enable and disable the AutoFilter by repeatedly invoking the Range object's `AutoFilter` method without any parameters. But using this technique alone only toggles the AutoFilter state and, without checking another property, does not provide any control if a specific state is desired.

Determining the Filtering State

You use the `AutoFilter` object to determine whether the AutoFilter is enabled:

```
Dim Table As ListObject
Set Table = ThisWorkbook.Worksheets("Register").ListObjects("tblRegister")
If Table.ShowAutoFilter Then
    Debug.Print "AutoFilter is on"
Else
    Debug.Print "AutoFilter is off"
End If
```

If the AutoFilter is enabled, you use the `AutoFilter` object's `FilterMode` property to determine whether filtering criteria is in place:

```
Dim Table As ListObject
Set Table = ThisWorkbook.Worksheets("Register").ListObjects("tblRegister")
If Table.ShowAutoFilter Then
    If Table.AutoFilter.FilterMode Then
        Debug.Print "Filtering is active"
    Else
        Debug.Print "Filtering is inactive"
    End If
Else
    Debug.Print "AutoFilter is off"
End If
```

Determining Whether a Column Is Filtered

As shown in the following example, if the AutoFilter is enabled, you can use the `Filter` object's On property to determine whether a column has an active filter criteria. The `Filter` object is an item in the `AutoFilter` object's `Filters` property:

```
Dim Table As ListObject
Set Table = ThisWorkbook.Worksheets("Register").ListObjects("tblRegister")
If Table.ShowAutoFilter Then
    If Table.AutoFilter.Filters(3).On Then
        Debug.Print "Column 3 is being filtered"
    End If
Else
    Debug.Print "AutoFilter is off"
End If
```

Creating Filters

You create (apply) filters one column at a time. You use the Range object's `AutoFilter` method to add and remove filter criteria. (The Range object's `AutoFilter` method is described earlier in this chapter.) When an AutoFilter criterion is applied, the header row is automatically enabled. The following are some examples, each of which begins with these lines of code and assumes that the Table has no active filter criteria:

```
Dim Table As ListObject
Set Table = ThisWorkbook.Worksheets("Register").ListObjects("tblRegister")
```

This example shows only rows with "Expense" in the third column:

```
Table.Range.AutoFilter Field:=3, Criteria1:="Expense"
```

This example shows only rows with "Expense" or "Income" in the third column:

```
Table.Range.AutoFilter Field:=3, Criteria1:=Array("Expense", "Income"),
Operator:=xlFilterValues
```

This example shows only rows with values in the third column that start with "Transaction":

```
Table.Range.AutoFilter Field:=2, Criteria1:="Transaction*"
```

This example shows only rows with values in the fourth column that are greater than zero:

```
Table.Range.AutoFilter Field:=4, Criteria1:=">0"
```

This example shows only rows with "Income" in the third column and values in the fourth column that are greater than 100:

```
Table.Range.AutoFilter Field:=3, Criteria1:="Income"
Table.Range.AutoFilter Field:=4, Criteria1:=">100"
```

Reapplying the Active Filter Criteria

The visibility of rows in a filtered Table can become out of sync with the filter criteria as data is changed and new rows added. You can correct this situation by reapplying the active filter criteria, as shown in the following example:

```
Dim Table As ListObject
Set Table = ThisWorkbook.Worksheets("Register").ListObjects("tblRegister")
If Table.ShowAutoFilter Then
    Table.AutoFilter.ApplyFilter
End If
```

Clearing One Column's Filter

You can clear one column's filter by using the `AutoFilter` method and specifying only the `Field` parameter. The following example clears the third column's filter criteria:

```
Dim Table As ListObject
Set Table = ThisWorkbook.Worksheets("Register").ListObjects("tblRegister")
Table.Range.AutoFilter Field:=3
```

Clearing All Column Filters

You can clear the filter criteria for all columns in one step without disabling AutoFilter by invoking the `ShowAllData` method, as shown here:

```
Dim Table As ListObject
Set Table = ThisWorkbook.Worksheets("Register").ListObjects("tblRegister")
If Table.ShowAutoFilter Then
    Table.AutoFilter.ShowAllData
End If
```

Hiding Drop-Down Controls by Column

You can hide AutoFilter drop-down controls in specific columns. The following example illustrates how to hide the AutoFilter drop-down control in the Table's second column:

```
Dim Table As ListObject
Set Table = ThisWorkbook.Worksheets("Register").ListObjects("tblRegister")
If Table.ShowAutoFilter Then
    Table.Range.AutoFilter Field:=2, VisibleDropDown:=False
End If
```

Custom Routines

The following sections provide some custom routines to make your projects a little easier. More robust versions of these routines and a number of other routines plus useful utilities and code libraries are available at www.exceltables.com.

Doing a Bulk Insert

The following function inserts an array of values into a Table and returns the new rows as a range. If a row is specified, then the values are inserted above that row; otherwise, the values are appended to the bottom of the Table. The function also maps columns of values to columns in the Table by using the `ColumnAssignments` parameter. See the comments in the routine for more details on the parameters.

```
Public Function BulkInsertIntoTable( _
        ByVal Table As ListObject, _
        ByVal Values As Variant, _
        Optional ByVal Position As Long = -1, _
        Optional ByVal ColumnAssignments As Variant _
    ) As Range

' Insert an array of values into a Table. Optionally specify the row before
' which the new rows are inserted. Optionally specify how the columns are
' assigned. The new rows in the Table are returned as a Range.
'
' Syntax
'
' BulkInsertIntoTable(Table, Values, Position, ColumnAssignments)
'
' Table - A Table object.
'
' Values - A single value, a single dimension array of values, or a two
'   dimension array of values.
'
' Position - The row number before which the new rows are inserted. Optional.
'   If omitted then the new rows are appended to the end of the Table.
'
' ColumnAssignments - A single dimension array of integer values specifying
'   which Table column receives what column of values in the Values parameter.
'   Each element in the array is a column number in the Table. The position of
'   the element in the array corresponds to the column in the Values array.
'   Optional. If omitted then the values are placed in column order starting in
'   the first Table column. For example, passing Array(2,3,1) results in this
'   column mapping:
'
'   Values column 1 is placed in Table column 2.
'   Values column 2 is placed in Table column 3.
```

```
'   Values column 3 is placed in Table column 1.

    Dim Calculation As XlCalculation
    Dim ScreenUpdating As Boolean
    Dim Result As Long
    Dim TwoDimensionArray As Boolean
    Dim WorkArray As Variant
    Dim Column As Long
    Dim SourceColumn As Long
    Dim TargetColumn As Long
    Dim ShowTotals As Boolean
    Dim InsertRange As Range

    ' Exit if no values to insert
    If IsEmpty(Values) Then Exit Function

    Calculation = Application.Calculation
    Application.Calculation = xlCalculationManual
    ScreenUpdating = Application.ScreenUpdating
    Application.ScreenUpdating = False

    ' Normalize Values parameter - must be a two-dimension array
    On Error Resume Next
    Result = LBound(Values, 2)
    TwoDimensionArray = Err.Number = 0
    On Error GoTo 0
    If Not TwoDimensionArray Then
        If Not IsArray(Values) Then
            Values = Array(Values)
        End If
        ReDim WorkArray(1 To 1, 1 To UBound(Values) - LBound(Values) + 1)
        For Column = 1 To UBound(WorkArray, 2)
            WorkArray(1, Column) = Values(Column - 1 + LBound(Values))
        Next Column
        Values = WorkArray
    End If

    ' Normalize Position parameter
    If Position < 0 Then
        Position = Table.ListRows.Count
    End If
    Position = Application.Max(1, Application.Min(Position, Table.ListRows.Count
+ 1))

    ' Save total row setting and disable total
    ShowTotals = Table.ShowTotals
    Table.ShowTotals = False

    ' Insert the new rows
    If Table.ListRows.Count > 0 And Position <= Table.ListRows.Count Then
```

```
        Table.DataBodyRange.Resize(UBound(Values)).Offset(Position - 1).Insert
Shift:=xlShiftDown
    End If
    If Table.ListRows.Count > 0 Then
        Set InsertRange = Table.DataBodyRange.Resize(UBound(Values)).
Offset(Position - 1)
    Else
        Set InsertRange = Table.InsertRowRange.Resize(UBound(Values))
    End If
    If IsEmpty(ColumnAssignments) Or IsMissing(ColumnAssignments) Then
        InsertRange.Value = Values
    Else
        For TargetColumn = LBound(ColumnAssignments) To _
            UBound(ColumnAssignments)
            SourceColumn = TargetColumn - LBound(ColumnAssignments) + 1
            If ColumnAssignments(TargetColumn) >= 1 And _
                ColumnAssignments(TargetColumn) <= _
                Table.ListColumns.Count Then
                InsertRange.Columns(ColumnAssignments(TargetColumn)) _
                     .Value = Application.Index(Values, , SourceColumn)
            End If
        Next TargetColumn
    End If
    Set BulkInsertIntoTable = InsertRange

    ' Restore the total row setting
    Table.ShowTotals = ShowTotals

    Application.Calculation = Calculation
    Application.ScreenUpdating = ScreenUpdating

End Function
```

Repairing Formatting and Formulas

Normally, a Table maintains the same formatting and formulas across all rows, excluding the header and total rows. When the formatting or formula is changed in a cell in a Table's column, Excel applies that new formatting or formula to the entire column. The formatting and formulas are automatically applied to new rows as they are added.

A Table's formatting or formulas can become inconsistent when you're manually editing formatting or applying different formulas in the same Table column. You can fix the Table column by reapplying the formatting to the entire column plus one additional row at the bottom. (The total row must be disabled to make this adjustment.) You can fix a formula (convert the column back to a calculated column) by applying the formula to the entire column.

The routine below accomplishes this by using the Table's `Resize` method. First, the Table is resized to be just one row. Next, the formatting and formulas are cleared from all Table rows from row 2 down to the last row plus one row. Finally, the Table's range is set back to what it was. This final step instructs Excel to apply the formatting and formulas in the first row to all rows below the first row. The result is a consistently formatted Table, using the first data row as the template for all other rows. The code assumes that there is at least one row of data in the Table:

```
Public Sub RepairTable( _
        ByVal Table As ListObject _
    )

' Repair the Table's formatting and formulas by making them consistent down the
' entire length of each column.
'
' Syntax
'
' RepairTable(Table)
'
' Table - A Table object (ListObject object).

    Dim RowCount As Long
    Dim ListColumn As ListColumn
    Dim ShowTotals As Boolean

    RowCount = Table.ListRows.Count
    If RowCount < 2 Then Exit Sub

    With Table
        ShowTotals = .ShowTotals
        .ShowTotals = False
        .Resize .HeaderRowRange.Resize(2)
        For Each ListColumn In .ListColumns
            With ListColumn.DataBodyRange.Resize( _
                Application.Max(RowCount, 1)).Offset(1)
                If Left(.Rows(1).Formula, 1) = "=" Then
                    .Cells.Clear
                Else
                    .Cells.ClearFormats
                End If
            End With
        Next ListColumn
        .Resize .HeaderRowRange.Resize(1 + RowCount)
        .ShowTotals = ShowTotals
    End With

End Sub
```

Copying a Table Style to a New Workbook

There is no easy way to copy a Table style from one workbook to another. The following sample code copies the Table style assigned to the Table named "tblRegister" to the workbook "Destination Workbook.xlsx":

```
Sub ExportTableStyle()

    Dim Source As Workbook
    Dim Target As Workbook
    Dim Table As ListObject

    Set Source = ThisWorkbook
    Set Target = Workbooks("Destination Workbook.xlsx")
    Set Table = Source.Worksheets("Register").ListObjects("tblRegister")
    Target.Worksheets.Add Before:=Target.Worksheets(1)
    Table.Range.Copy Target.Worksheets(1).Range("A1")
    Target.Worksheets(1).Delete

End Sub
```

Retrieving an Access Crosstab Query

In Excel there is no native way to return a crosstab query from Access. In essence, a crosstab query is a type of SELECT query that pivots specified fields across columns and aggregates in the intersection of row and column fields. You can think of it as a PivotTable in an Access query.

In the following example, GetCrosstabQueryFromAccess uses an ADO (ActiveX Data Objects) method to create a crosstab query from a table that resides in a known database table. These three routines utilize this same example code to return the query into a Table:

- "**TestCrosstabQuery1**"—Returns a crosstab query into a new worksheet
- "**TestCrosstabQuery2**"—Returns a crosstab query into an existing Table and overwrites header values
- "**TestCrosstabQuery3**"—Returns a crosstab query into an existing Table but does not overwrite header values

All the routines in this example utilize a constant that expresses the SQL statement needed for the crosstab query.

> **NOTE**
>
> This example uses a reference to "Microsoft ActiveX Data Objects 6.1 library". To set this, you select *Tools | References* in the Visual Basic Editor, enable this reference, and click *OK*.

```
Const TestSQL As String = "TRANSFORM Sum(tblSampleData.Total) AS SumTotal " & _
      "SELECT tblSampleData.Region " & _
      "FROM tblSampleData " & _
      "GROUP BY tblSampleData.Region " & _
      "PIVOT Format([Date],""mmm"") In " & _
(""Jan"",""Feb"",""Mar"", ""Apr"",""May"",""Jun"", ""Jul"",""Aug"",""Sep"",
""Oct"",""Nov"",""Dec"");"

Sub TestCrosstabQuery1()
    'Bring crosstab query into a new table created on a new worksheet
    Call GetCrosstabQueryFromAccess(TestSQL)
```

```
End Sub

Sub TestCrosstabQuery2()
    'Bring crosstab query into an existing table
    'Overwrite headers with field names
    Call GetCrosstabQueryFromAccess(TestSQL, True, ThisWorkbook.
Worksheets("Query").ListObjects("qryCrosstab"))
End Sub

Sub TestCrosstabQuery3()
    'Bring crosstab query into an existing table
    'Do not overwrite headers
    Call GetCrosstabQueryFromAccess(TestSQL, False, ThisWorkbook.
Worksheets("Query").ListObjects("qryCrosstab"))
End Sub

Sub GetCrosstabQueryFromAccess( _
        ByVal SQL As String, _
        Optional ByVal OverwriteHeaders As Boolean, _
        Optional ByVal Table As ListObject _
    )

    Dim DataConnection As ADODB.Connection
    Dim DataRecordset As ADODB.Recordset
    Dim DestinationSheet As Worksheet
    Dim DestinationTable As ListObject
    Dim DestinationRange As Range
    Dim ShowTotalRow As Boolean
    Dim ShowHeaderRow As Boolean
    Dim ColumnHeader As Long

    'Make sure database is found
    If Dir(ThisWorkbook.Path & "\SampleDatabase.accdb", vbNormal) = vbNullString
Then
        MsgBox "Database not found", vbExclamation, "Whoops!"
        Exit Sub
    End If

    'Create and open connection
    Set DataConnection = New Connection
    Set DataRecordset = New Recordset
    DataConnection.CursorLocation = adUseClient
    DataConnection.ConnectionString = "Provider=Microsoft.ACE.OLEDB.12.0;Data
Source=" & _
        ThisWorkbook.Path & "\SampleDatabase.accdb"
    DataConnection.Open

    'Get the recordset via query
    Set DataRecordset = DataConnection.Execute(SQL)
```

```
    'Set destination table
    If Table Is Nothing Then
        'Use a new table created on a new worksheet in the active workbook
        Set DestinationSheet = ActiveWorkbook.Worksheets.Add(After:=ActiveSheet)
        Set DestinationRange = DestinationSheet.Range("A1").
Resize(DataRecordset.RecordCount + 1, _
            DataRecordset.Fields.Count)
        DestinationSheet.Activate
        DestinationRange.Select
        Set DestinationTable = DestinationSheet.ListObjects.Add( _
                               SourceType:=xlSrcRange, _
                               XlListObjectHasHeaders:=xlYes, _
                               Destination:=DestinationRange _
                               )
    Else
        'Use existing table passed to routine, which assumes the Table columns
        'already match the query field results
        Set DestinationTable = Table
        If Not DestinationTable.DataBodyRange Is Nothing Then DestinationTable.
DataBodyRange.Delete
        DestinationTable.InsertRowRange.Insert
    End If

    'Save header/total row status
    ShowHeaderRow = DestinationTable.ShowHeaders
    ShowTotalRow = DestinationTable.ShowTotals
    DestinationTable.ShowTotals = False
    DestinationTable.ShowHeaders = True

    'Copy recordset to table
    DestinationTable.DataBodyRange(1, 1).CopyFromRecordset DataRecordset

    'Get column headers
    If OverwriteHeaders Or Table Is Nothing Then
        For ColumnHeader = 0 To DataRecordset.Fields.Count - 1
            DestinationTable.HeaderRowRange(1, ColumnHeader + 1) =
DataRecordset.Fields(ColumnHeader).Name
        Next ColumnHeader
    End If

    'Close recordset from database
    DataRecordset.Close

    'Set table header/total rows how they were originally
    DestinationTable.ShowTotals = ShowTotalRow
    DestinationTable.ShowHeaders = ShowHeaderRow

End Sub
```

Automating Tables with .NET

This section is for experienced .NET developers. It assumes that you are able to create and compile a .NET Visual Basic or C# project.

Accessing the `ListObject` with a .NET solution is very similar to doing so in VBA. This section provides examples in both Visual Basic and C# using the .NET framework to check whether a Table exists. Each solution is built as an Excel COM add-in, although the logic could be applied to many other situations and projects. These projects are available for download at www.exceltables.com.

Each example below has two code parts: the `TableExists` function and a custom ribbon button click event handler. Both routines reside in a *Ribbon (Visual Designer)* class called `MyRibbon`. The button name on the ribbon is "button1". The code presents the user with an input box to enter a Table name and then presents a message box with the result `True` if the Table exists in the active workbook or `False` if it does not exist. The code does very little error handling.

> **NOTE**
>
> The code examples below were created in Visual Studio 2012 with Visual Studio Tools for Office (VSTO).

The following reference must be included to reference the Excel Object Model in the project:

```
Microsoft.Office.Interop.Excel
```

This reference is created when the project is specified as an Excel add-in. The following steps detail how to set up a new project for the code examples below:

1. **Create a new project in Visual Studio.** Select *Templates | Language | Office/SharePoint | Office Add-ins | Excel 2013 Add-in*.
2. **Add a new ribbon item to the project.** Select *PROJECT | Add New Item*, select *Ribbon (Visual Designer)* and change the name to "MyRibbon", and then click *Add*.
3. **Set the ribbon to "Custom".** In the *Properties* pane, expand the *ControlId* group and change the *ControlIdType* from "Office" to "Custom".
4. **Add a ribbon button.** From the *Toolbox*, drag a ribbon button onto the ribbon group.
5. **Open the "MyRibbon" class.** Right-click *MyRibbon* in the *Solution Explorer* and select *View Code*.
6. **Copy the appropriate sample code from below.** Copy the code below for the desired language into the solution's `MyRibbon` class. (In C# projects, the default name is "MyRibbon.cs", and in Visual Basic projects, the default name is "MyRibbon.vb".)

> **TIP**
>
> You expose the Excel application with the property `Globals.ThisAddin.Application`.

Finding Whether the Table Exists by Using C#

The following code is contained in the ribbon class MyRibbon, in a project named "TableExample_C":

```
using System;
using System.Collections.Generic;
using System.Linq;
using System.Text;
using System.Windows.Forms;
using Microsoft.Office.Tools.Ribbon;
using Excel = Microsoft.Office.Interop.Excel;

namespace TableExample_C
{
    public partial class MyRibbon
    {
        private void button1_Click_1(object sender, RibbonControlEventArgs e)
        {
            // Set variables
            var xlApp = Globals.ThisAddIn.Application;
            var xlBook = xlApp.ActiveWorkbook;
            const string Prompt = "Enter a Table name to check if it exists in
the active workbook:";

            // Get table name
            var CheckName = xlApp.InputBox(Prompt, "Table Exists");

            // Run TableExists function, notify user
            bool bExists;
            bExists = TableExists(CheckName, xlBook);
            MessageBox.Show(bExists.ToString(),  "Result", MessageBoxButtons.
OK);
        }

        public static bool TableExists(string TableName, Microsoft.Office.
Interop.Excel.Workbook WKB)
        {
            try
            {
                // Loop through all worksheets in the specified workbook
                foreach (Excel.Worksheet WKS in WKB.Worksheets)
                {
                    // Loop through all Tables in the iterated worksheet
                    foreach (Excel.ListObject LO in WKS.ListObjects)
                    {
                        if (LO.DisplayName == TableName) return true;
                    }
                }
                // In case no Table names match
                return false;
            }
```

```
            catch
            {
                // If an error occurred, default to false
                return false;
            }
        }

    }
}
```

Finding Whether the Table Exists by Using VB

The following code is contained in the ribbon class MyRibbon, in a project named "TableExample_VB":

```
Imports System.Windows.Forms
Imports Microsoft.Office.Tools.Ribbon
Imports Excel = Microsoft.Office.Interop.Excel

Public Class MyRibbon

    Private Sub Button1_Click(sender As Object, e As RibbonControlEventArgs)
Handles Button1.Click

        Try

            'Set variables
            Dim xlApp As Excel._Application = Globals.ThisAddIn.Application
            Dim xlBook As Excel.Workbook = xlApp.ActiveWorkbook
            Const Prompt As String = "Enter a Table name to check if it exists
in the active workbook:"

            'Get table name
            Dim CheckName As String = xlApp.InputBox(Prompt, "Table Exists")

            'Run TableExists function, notify user
            Dim bExists As Boolean = TableExists(CheckName, xlBook)
            MessageBox.Show(bExists.ToString(), "Result", MessageBoxButtons.OK,
MessageBoxIcon.Information)

        Catch ex As Exception
            MessageBox.Show("An error occurred.", "Whoops!", MessageBoxButtons.
OK, MessageBoxIcon.Exclamation)
        End Try

    End Sub

    Public Function TableExists(ByVal TableName As String, WKB As Excel.
Workbook) As Boolean
        Try
            'Loop through all worksheets in the specified workbook
            For Each xlSheet As Excel.Worksheet In WKB.Worksheets
                'Loop through all Tables in the iterated worksheet
```

```
                For Each xlTable As Excel.ListObject In xlSheet.ListObjects
                    If xlTable.DisplayName = TableName Then Return True
                Next
            Next
            'In case no Table names match
            Return False
        Catch ex As Exception
            'If an error occurred, default to false
            Return False
        End Try
    End Function

End Class
```

10 Tables in Excel Online

The first version of Office Online, released in summer 2007, was called Office Web Apps. Office Online is a browser-based limited version of the Office suite of applications. Office Online provides the basic functionality of Office, and you can access it on any device, with any operating system, as long as you have an Internet connection and use a compliant browser.

The Office Online application is hosted on Microsoft servers. The advantage of using it is that you need nothing but a browser; you don't have to install an application, and users do not have to worry about updating the application or applying hotfixes. Similar to Google Spreadsheets and Google Docs, Office Online is ideal for students and those not wanting to pay a fee for the desktop version of Office.

Office Online is compatible with most major browsers:

- Internet Explorer (7 or later)
- Firefox
- Chrome
- Safari

> ***TIP***
>
> We recommend using the latest available version of your preferred browser. Office Online makes use of many of the latest features implemented in browsers, so it's important that you use the latest browser version available and keep it up-to-date to make the most of your Office Online experience.

This chapter refers to two modes of Office:

- **Office Online/Excel Online**—In this case, the Office application runs on a server as a hosted service and is used with a browser.
- **Office Desktop/Excel Desktop**—In this case, the Office application is installed and runs on a workstation.

With a subscription to Office 365, you can access a version of Office Online that you can install on a private network. It functions the same as Office Online run from Microsoft servers (that is, it runs within a web browser), but the service is hosted on servers within a company's firewall, thus avoiding security issues that can arise when using public services.

> ***NOTE***
>
> In February 2014, Microsoft changed SkyDrive to OneDrive. This is Microsoft's cloud-based storage service, which ties together the features of Office Online and Outlook.com and gives consumers free availability to these services.

To create an Excel workbook on OneDrive (https://onedrive.live.com), you select *Create | Excel workbook*, as shown in the next figure. A free Microsoft account is required to log in. If you have a hotmail.com, outlook.com, or Xbox Live account, you can use those credentials to log in to OneDrive. When you create a new OneDrive account, you can use any valid email address.

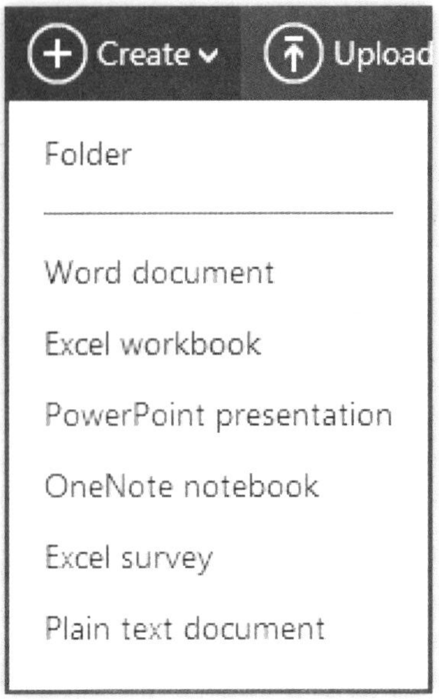

Create a new Excel workbook in Excel Online.

The workbook appears in Office Online (in your browser), and it looks much the same as it does in Office Desktop, with the ribbon displaying the familiar tabs *FILE*, *HOME*, *INSERT*, *DATA*, and *VIEW*. However, you also see *Excel Online* displayed at the top of the window, as shown in the next figure.

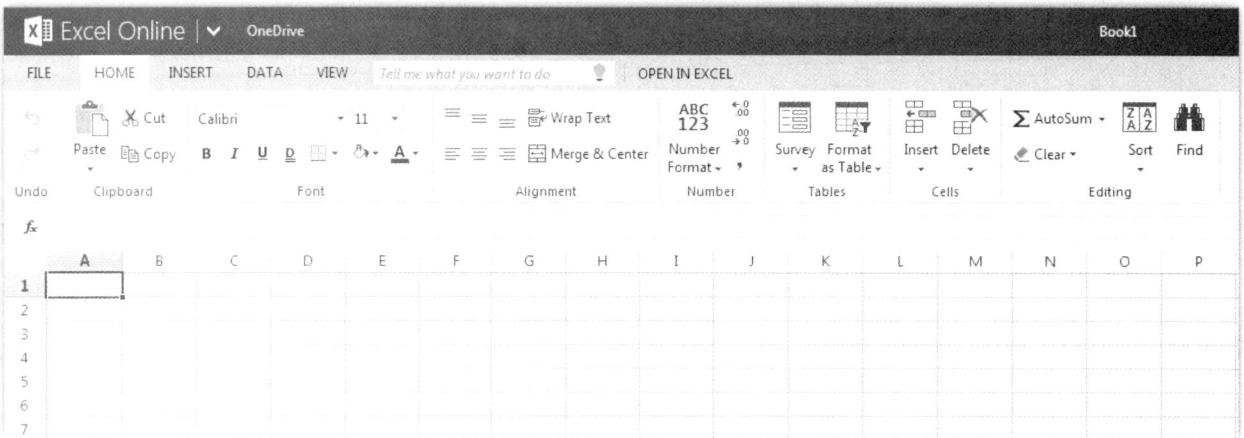

A blank workbook in Excel Online.

A drop-down control to the right of the *Excel Online* title provides quick access to the Office Online applications. When you click it, a gallery of Office Online applications appears, as shown in the next figure. Options include Outlook.com (previously known as Hotmail), People (that is, contacts), Calendar, OneDrive, Word Online, Excel Online, PowerPoint Online, and OneNote Online.

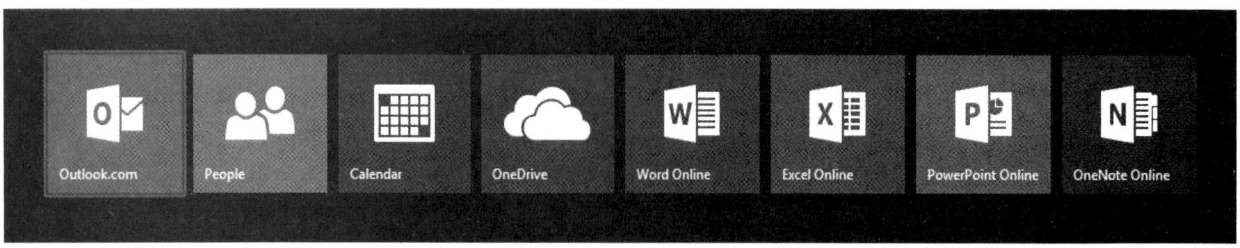

Office Online quick switch menu.

Excel Online Functionality

Excel Online displays Tables the same way as Desktop Excel. However, not all the functionality available in Excel Desktop is available in Excel Online. In particular, the contextual *TABLES* ribbon tab is not available. Another difference is that although you can use the *INSERT* tab to create a Table in Excel Online, you cannot change a Table's name in Excel Online.

Keyboard shortcuts are different, too. This is primarily due to the fact that the browser in which Excel Online is running already exposes a number of keyboard shortcuts. For example, CTRL+T, which creates a Table in the (US English) desktop version of Excel, typically opens a new tab in a browser.

> **TIP**
>
> For a list of keyboard shortcuts that work in Excel Online, visit
>
> http://office.microsoft.com/en-us/office-online-help/keyboard-shortcuts-in-excel-online-HA010378329.aspx.

What Is Available in Excel Online

If a workbook has any unsupported objects—such as shapes, comments, or ink—you cannot edit it in Excel Online. The next figure shows the dialog box you get when you attempt to open such a workbook. If you click *Edit in the browser*, Excel Online creates a copy of the workbook, with all the unsupported objects removed. If you later open this newly copied version in desktop Excel, those features are still removed permanently.

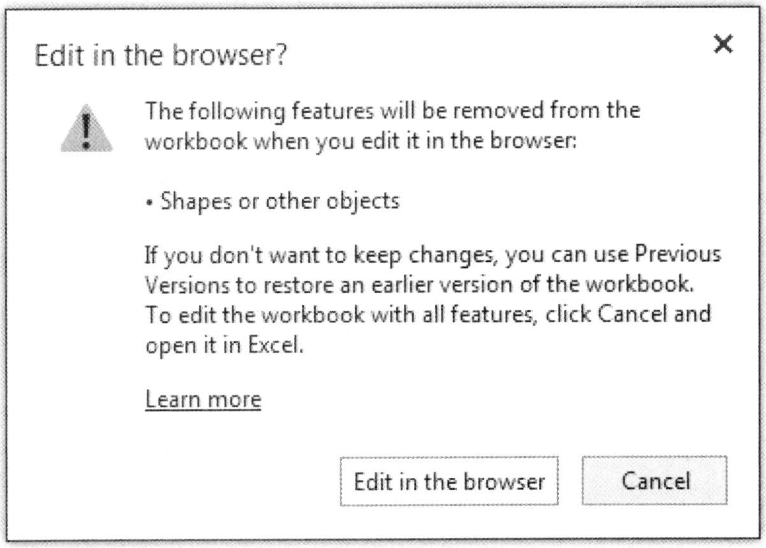

Excel Online error message when you attempt to edit a workbook that contains unsupported features.

If you click *Cancel*, Excel Online displays the workbook, but you cannot edit it. It displays a yellow bar directly under the ribbon to remind you that you can't make changes to the workbook, as shown in the next figure.

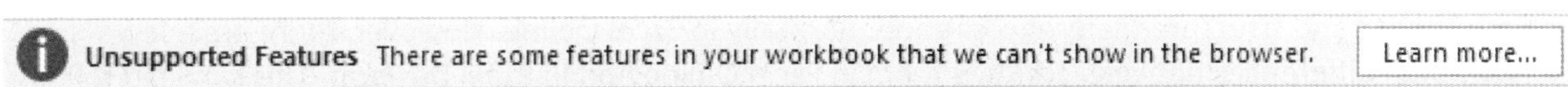

Unsupported features banner in Excel Online.

Another issue with Excel Online is that Tables that are connected to external data (for example, SQL Server) cannot be refreshed. Instead, Excel Online shows the last data pulled with a refresh and then saved using Excel Desktop.

Slicers and Timelines are available in Excel Online and work just as they do in Excel Desktop. However, you cannot create or modify Slicers and Timelines in Excel Online.

Excel Online also offers the distinct advantage of allowing you to view and interact with a workbook that contains a Data Model (for example, Power Pivot). If the file resides on OneDrive, Excel Online does allow you to interact with the Data Model components (Slicers and Timelines). To allow interaction with the Data Model, the file has to reside on a SharePoint server with BI capabilities or a SharePoint Server 2013 with Excel Services. If you want to refresh any external data connections, the file has to reside on SharePoint Server 2013. These are some examples of data sources you can use when a workbook resides on either of these servers:

- Windows Azure SQL Database Tables
- SharePoint lists that are available as OData feeds
- Windows Azure Marketplace data
- External data through Business Connectivity Services
- SQL Server data in Power BI Admin Center (subscription required)

CAUTION

Excel Online imposes file size limitations for viewing files. If you're using an Office 365 subscription that includes SharePoint Online, the file size limit is 10 MB. If your Office 365 subscription includes Power BI, the limit is extended to 250 MB. If you're opening files from Outlook.com, the limit is 5 MB.

There continues to be some confusion about what is and what is not available in Excel Online. Below is a list of some functionalities that are currently available in Excel Online:

- Real-time co-authoring
- Worksheet protection
- Data validation
- Cell drag-and-drop
- Workbook renaming
- Ability to embed a spreadsheet on a web page
- Column AutoFitting
- Printing to HTML
- PivotTable field lists
- Query Tables
- Sharing by email/link
- Sheet hiding/unhiding
- Sorting

Formulas

Table formulas and structured references render normally in Excel Online. However, there are a few fundamental differences between creating them in Excel Online and in Excel Desktop. This can lead to some confusion, but no matter where they're created, these calculations work as expected in all versions of Excel. The following are differences between Excel Online structured formulas and those created in Excel Desktop:

- Excel Online does not provide IntelliSense for Table references. IntelliSense works with Excel Online formulas in general, but it does not display any Table structured references.
- In Excel Online, you cannot insert structured references by clicking on parts of the Table. In Desktop Excel, when you select Table parts while editing a formula, Excel

enters the respective Table structured reference—for example, =[@Column1]—but Excel Online does not do this. Instead, it inserts A1-style addressing. You can enter structured references manually, however, and it will work all the same.

- Although you can't enter array formulas into a cell in Excel Online, Excel Online does calculate preexisting array formulas correctly.

Filtering

Filtering is available in Excel Online but is a more manual process than in Excel Desktop. In Excel Desktop, the AutoFilter displays a list of unique values. In Excel Online, the AutoFilter drop-down list does not display a list of unique values. Sorting and filtering options include *Sort Ascending*, *Sort Descending*, *Clear Filter from 'Worksheet'* (if a filter is applied), a *Filter* command that opens a dialog box of unique values, and *Number Filters*, which provides the following options:

- *Equals*
- *Does Not Equal*
- *Greater Than*
- *Less Than*
- *Between*
- *Top 10*
- *Above Average*
- *Below Average*
- *Custom Filter*

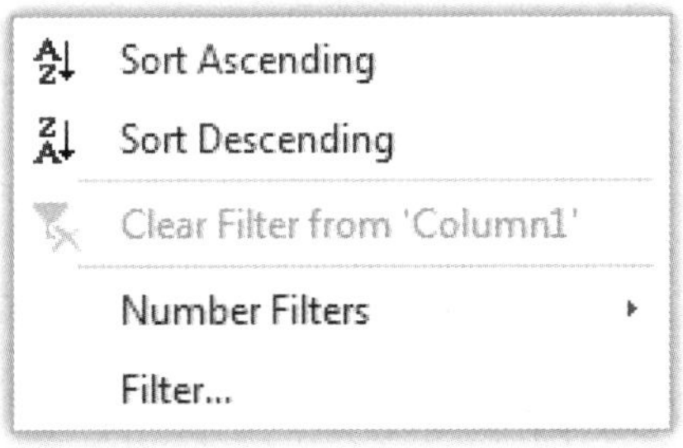

Filter drop-down in Excel Online.

Number Filter submenu in Excel Online.

To set a custom filter on a column, you click the AutoFilter drop-down button. Depending on what type of data that column contains, you either see a *Text Filters* button, a *Date Filters* button, or a *Number Filters* button. At the bottom of this menu, choose *Custom Filter* to open the *Custom Filter* dialog box. As shown in the next figure, this dialog box in Excel Online provides only one condition (instead of than the two in Excel Desktop).

Custom Filter dialog box in Excel Online.

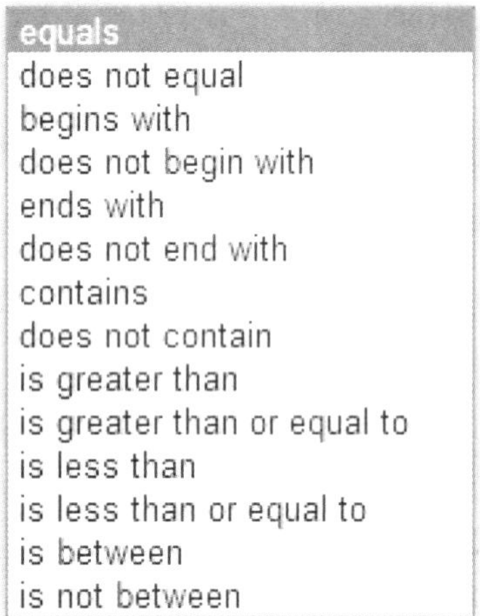

Custom Filter options in Excel Online.

Surveys Using Excel

Excel Online allows you to easily create customized surveys that can be distributed to anyone who has a browser and Internet connectivity. Survey data captured with a survey is saved to OneDrive, where the results are published using a Table in an Excel file. Multiple users can take the same survey at one time.

To create a survey within an existing workbook, select *INSERT | Survey | New Survey* or, in OneDrive, select *Create | Excel survey*. When the survey is created, additional options are displayed in the *Survey* menu, as shown in the next figure.

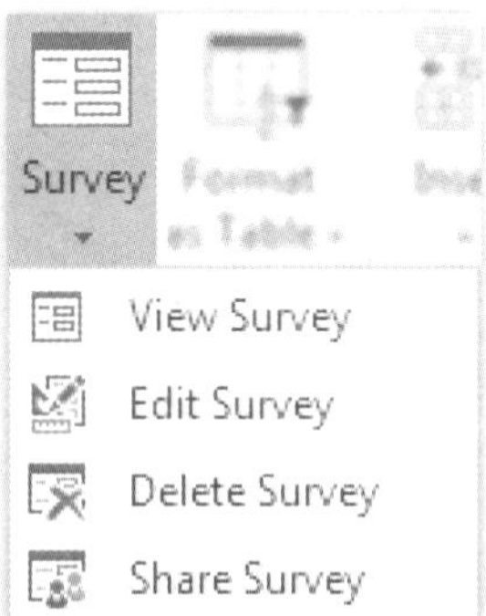

Excel Online Survey *menu.*

The *Edit Survey* dialog box, like the one shown in the next figure, appears. In it you can enter a title and description for the survey.

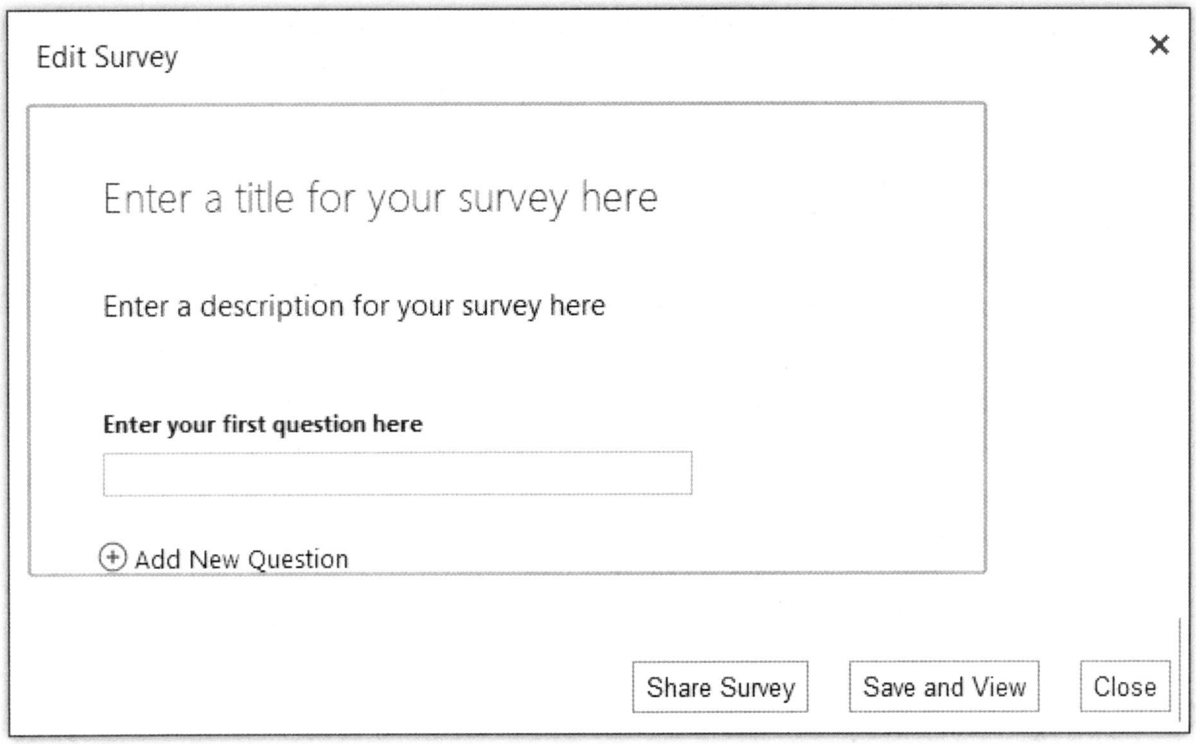

Edit Survey *dialog box.*

After you enter a title and description, you can click *Add New Question* to open the *EDIT QUESTION* dialog box, shown in the next figure, for defining a new question. Enter the question text, a subtitle (shown in smaller font below the question), the response type, whether it is a required question and must be answered before submission, and the specific answer requirements. There is effectively no limit to the number of questions in a survey.

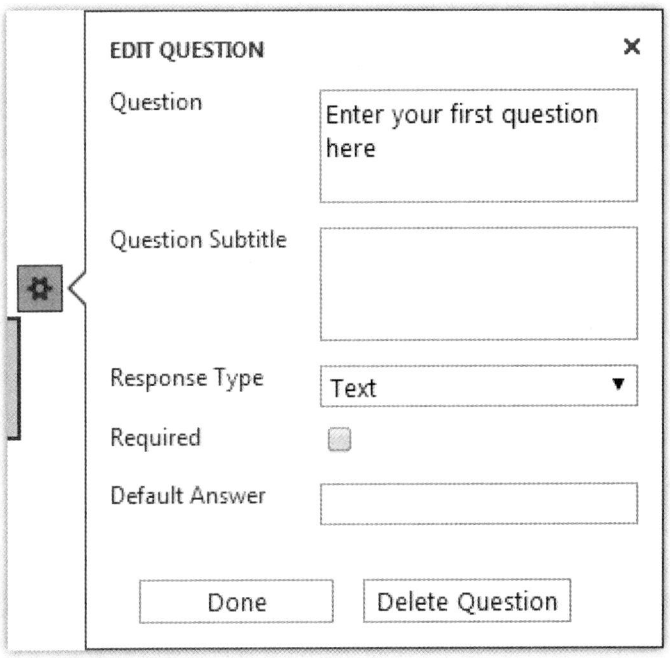

Survey EDIT QUESTION *dialog box.*

These are the possible *Response Type* options:

- ***Text***—A single-line text box.
- ***Paragraph text***—A larger text box that allows multiple lines of text.

- ***Number***—A text box that allows entry of numbers only. Choose a desired number format. For fixed decimal, percentage, and currency types, choose the number of decimal places.
- ***Date***—A text box that allows entry of valid dates only. Excel Online accepts dates in the format determined by the survey taker's locale settings. Dates entered are stored using Excel's internal universal format so that, when the Table containing the survey results is viewed, all the dates are displayed using the viewer's locale settings.
- ***Time***—A text box that allows entry of valid times, without or with seconds.
- ***Yes/No***—A combo box with *Yes* and *No* choices.
- ***Choice***—A combo box with a custom list of choices. When you enter choices, press ENTER to separate the items.

When you're done entering the questions and defining the responses, Excel Online creates a Table on a new worksheet titled "Survey1". The number appended to the Table name increases with each survey added to the workbook. The survey results are appended to the Table, one row per survey completed.

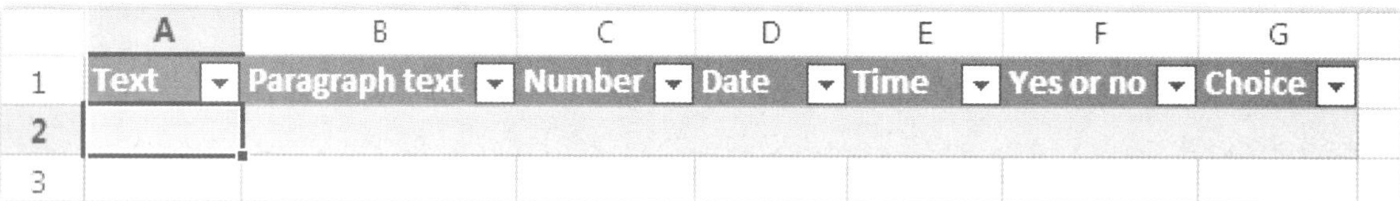

A Table based on a survey.

To help users filling out a survey, Excel shows examples of specific formats in text boxes where formats have been specified. For example, a text box that accepts only dates shows the text "Example: 10/21/2015". The text disappears as soon as the user types a value in the box. The next figure shows two text boxes, one for a date and one for a time, with Excel's examples.

Default view of date and time entry types.

If a survey taker doesn't enter a valid value and moves on to another question, the skipped question and response field are set in a light red background, as shown in the next figure. Regardless of whether the question is marked as required, the survey taker will not be able to submit the survey if the answer is not in a valid format. For an answer that is not required, clearing the answer field allows the survey to be submitted.

Entered survey data that doesn't match the required format.

When the survey taker attempts to submit a survey with incorrect or missing values, Excel displays any errors preventing the submission on the survey form, as shown in the next figure.

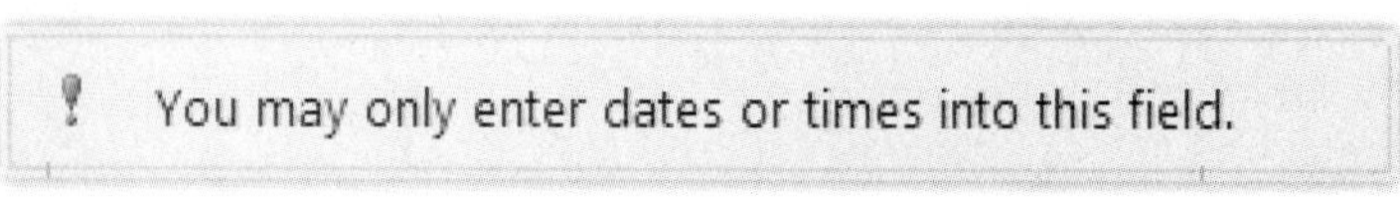

Error message informing the user that the data entered must be a date or time.

Once you complete a survey definition, you share it by clicking the *Share Survey* button and then clicking the *Create link* button shown in the next figure.

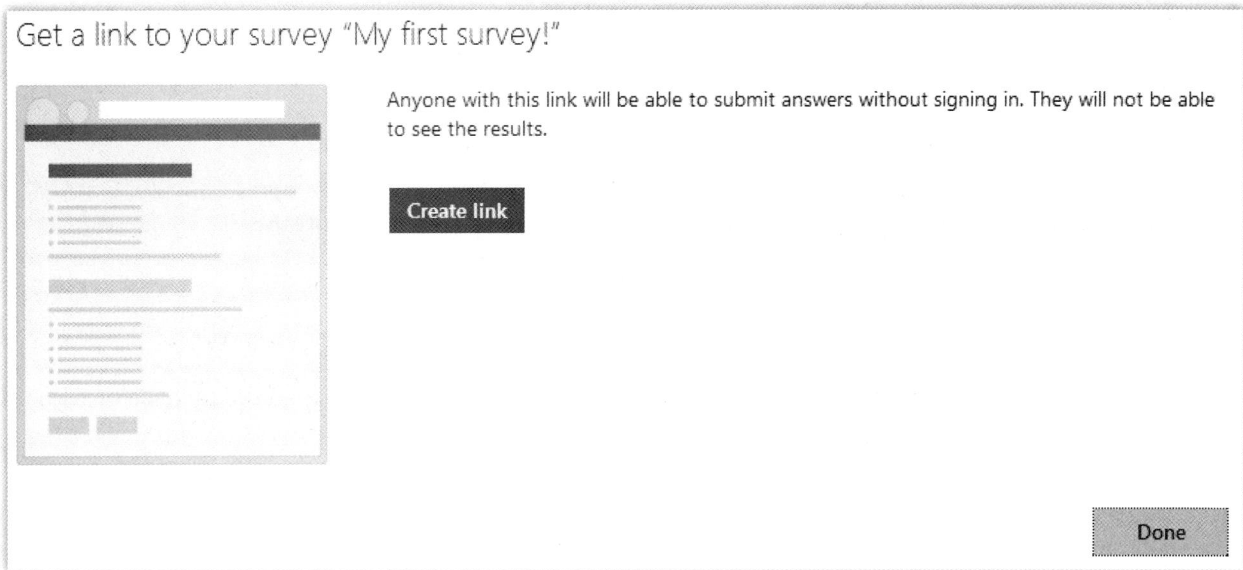

Click Create link *to generate a sharable link to the survey.*

Excel generates a unique link for the survey and displays it for you, as shown in the next figure. If you click the *Shorten link* button, Excel gives you a shorter link as opposed to a hyperlink to the actual file. Both links work identically. Anyone who uses a supported browser and follows the link can take the survey. Survey takers do not need to have a OneDrive account.

Click Shorten *link to get a shorter link provided by OneDrive.*

When users take your survey, at the bottom is a *Submit* button, as shown in the next figure. After the user clicks this button, Excel provides a message saying that the response was received. Excel then puts the answers to the questions into the Table in the Excel file created or used to create the survey.

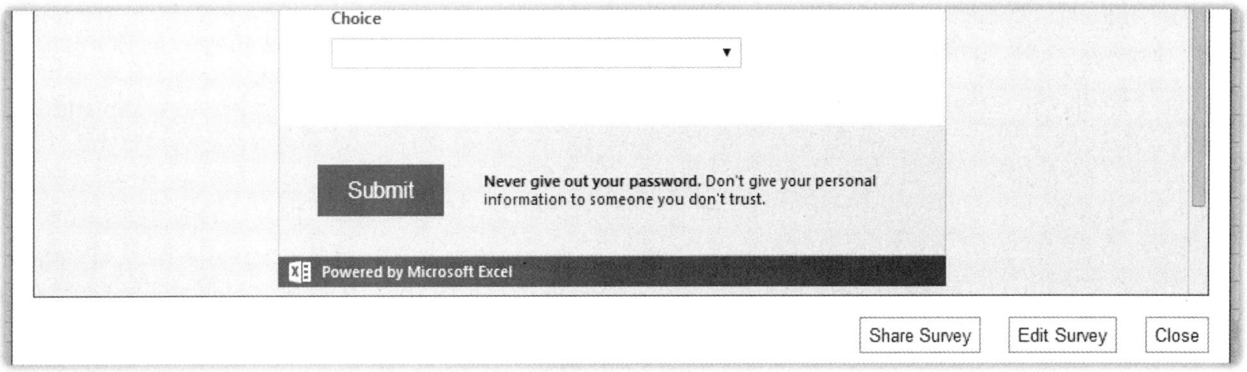

Survey takers click the Submit *button at the bottom of the survey.*

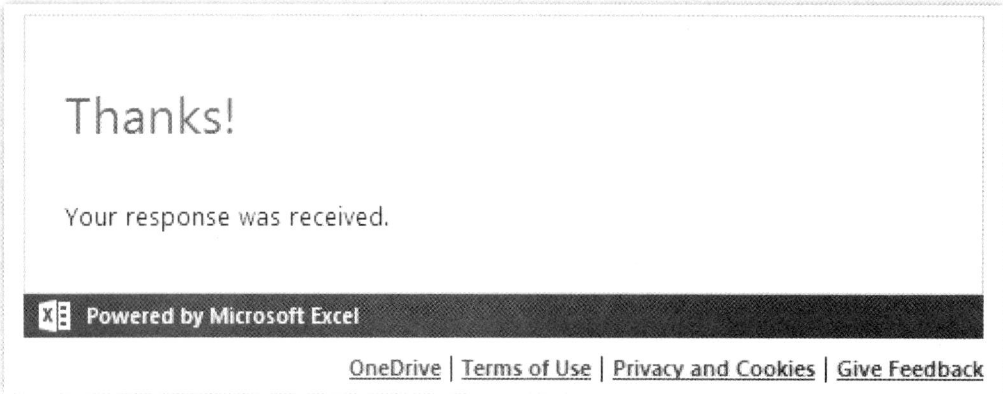

After a user submits survey responses, Excel tells the user the responses have been received.

Because the survey results are stored in an Excel Table, the results can easily be analyzed in place or with a PivotTable or PivotChart.

Updates

A significant advantage with Excel Online is that users never have to worry about having the latest update installed. Microsoft keeps the Office Online servers constantly updated with the latest versions, security patches, etc.

> ***TIP***
>
> The best way to stay informed about what has been updated in Excel Online, or to generally follow its progress, is to follow the Office blog at http://blogs.office.com.

11 Tables on Mac, iPad, and Office Mobile

At this writing, Microsoft supports versions of Office for Mac, iPad, and smart phones (iPhone, Windows Phone, and Android).

Excel 2011 was the first Mac version to offer Tables. Excel 2008 for Mac (like Excel 2003 for Windows) used the term **Lists** for what it now calls **Tables**. Though there are some fundamental differences between the Mac and Windows versions, most of the functionality is the same. In 2013 Microsoft released a version of Office, Office Mobile, for iOS (Apple's operating system for mobile platforms) and for Windows Phone and Android. In March 2014 Microsoft released Excel for iPad, along with Word and PowerPoint.

The various Office versions have many unique functional differences compared to each other and the Windows desktop version. This chapter discusses the differences in Table functionality provided by each of these versions. In the rest of this chapter, we refer to Excel 2011 for Mac as the **Mac version**, Excel for iPad as the **iPad version**, and Excel 2013 for Windows as the **Windows version**.

Tables in Excel for Mac

This section discusses the major differences between Tables in the Mac version and Tables in the Windows version, as well as user interface differences.

Tables Tab

As shown in the next figure, in the Mac version, the *Tables* ribbon tab is always present and is not contextual, as it is in the Windows version. There are some slight differences in the controls on the *Tables* tab in the Mac version. Because it is not contextual and is always present, there is a *New* button on the far left; this button is on the *INSERT* tab in the Windows version. Also, there is no *Filter Button* control, as there now is in the Windows version. Most Table operations—such as inserting rows and columns, deleting rows and columns, removing duplicates, using a Table as source data for a PivotTable, converting to a range, and renaming a Table—are available in both the Mac and Windows versions. One minor difference is that the Mac version gives you a command button rather than a text box for renaming a Table.

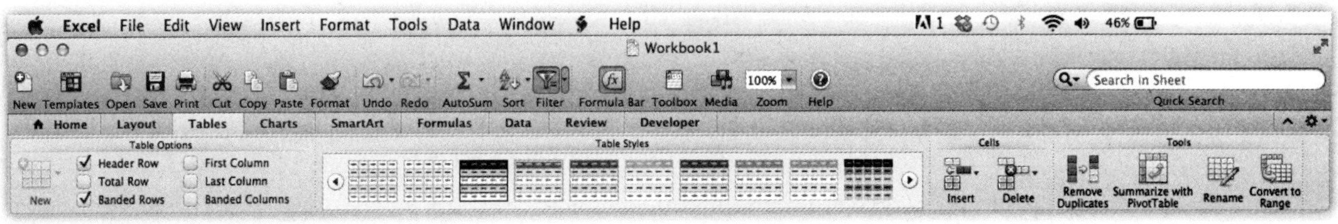

Tables ribbon tab in the Mac version.

The Mac version does not have anything equivalent to the Windows version's *TABLE TOOLS* tab group or *DATA* tab but, because the Mac version still has a menu bar, some of the commands on these two tabs are available in the *Data* menu, as shown in the next two figures.

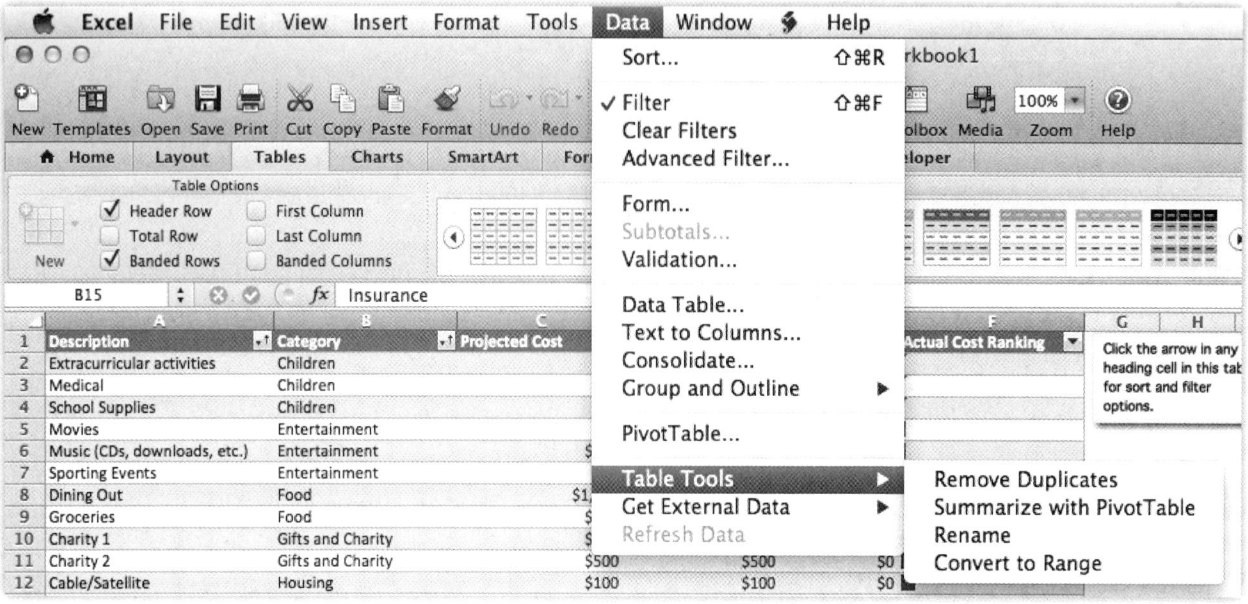

Table Tools *submenu of the* Data *menu.*

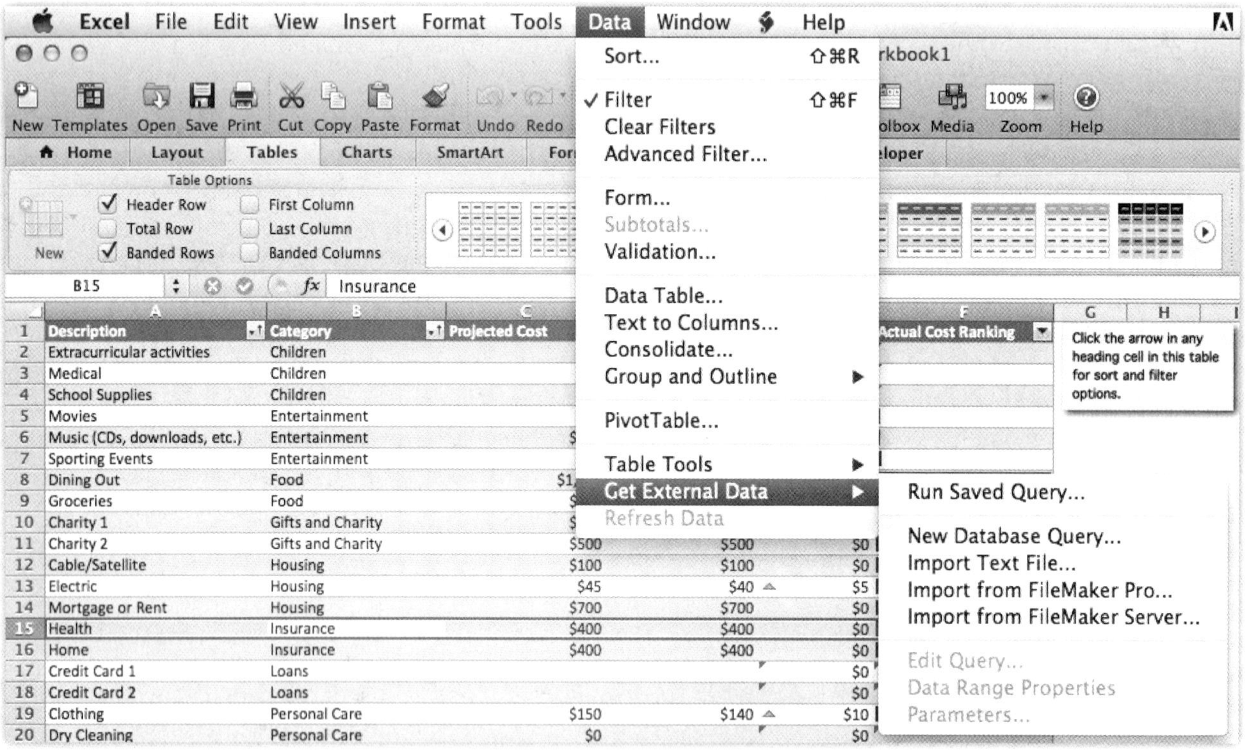

Get External Data *submenu of the* Data *menu.*

Filtering

There are minor differences between filtering a Table in the Mac version and in the Windows version. When you click the AutoFilter button for a column, the *Result* floating dialog box appears, as shown in the next figure. The *Result* dialog box stays open while you enter and change the filtering criteria, and the Mac version instantly applies the criteria to the Table. (On the other hand, in the Windows version, you must click *OK* to close the AutoFilter pop-up and perform the action.) The *Result* dialog box stays open until you close it by clicking the close control in the upper-left corner or by clicking any cell on the worksheet.

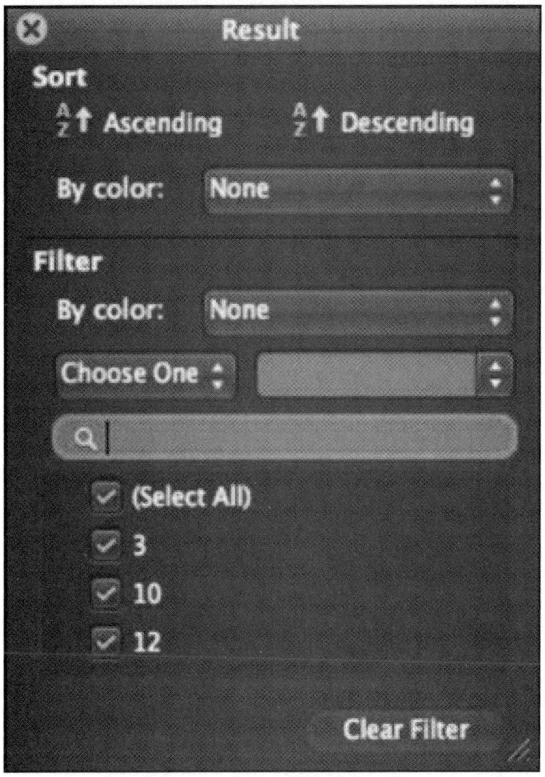

Result *dialog box for a Table in the Mac version.*

> ***NOTE***
>
> Slicers are not available in the Mac version.

Tables in Excel for Office Mobile

Office Mobile is often confused with Excel Online or Excel for iPad. But Office Mobile is an app that is available only for smart phones. The app is free to download and install, and you can use it to view files without paying a service fee. However, to edit files in Office Mobile, you must have one of these Office 365 subscriptions:

- Office 365 Home Premium
- Office 365 Small Business Premium
- Office 365 Midsize Business
- Office 365 Enterprise E3 and E4 (Enterprise and Government)
- Office 365 Education A3 and A4
- Office 365 ProPlus
- Office 365 University
- Office 365 Trial Subscription

The Office 365 ProPlus subscription includes a single desktop installation. All other subscriptions include five desktop installations, which can be either Windows or Mac versions.

> ***NOTE***
>
> An Office Mobile installation does not count against the allotted number of desktop installations.

When you run the Office 365 application, it presents a login screen, as shown in the next figure.

Office 365 login screen.

You get a message like the one shown in the next figure when your Office 365 login is successful.

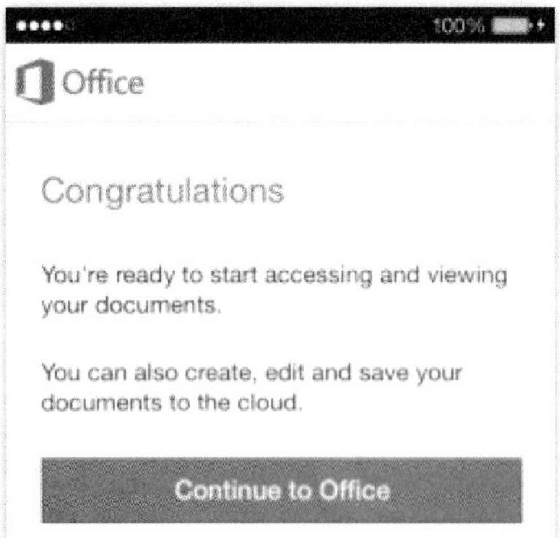

Confirmation of successful Office 365 login.

Once you're logged in to Office 365, you can connect to various cloud-based storage locations, including:

- OneDrive (still listed as SkyDrive in version 1.1)
- Office 365 SharePoint
- SharePoint

For each location, you must enter additional login credentials. Once you're connected to a service, that service is listed in the *PLACES* view that appears when you click the *Open* button at the bottom of the application. The next figure shows Office connected to three of Zack's locations.

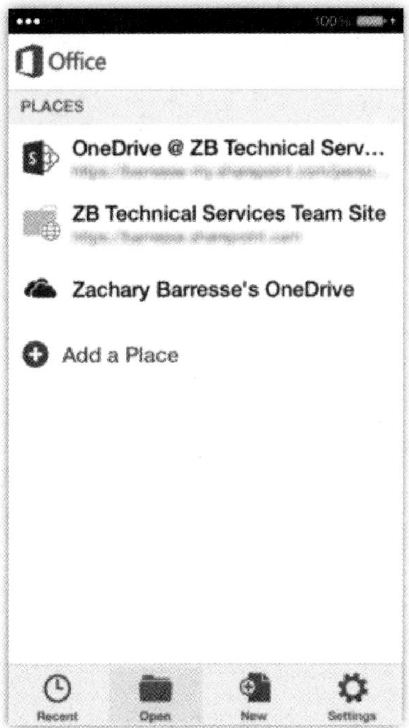

Office 365–connected places.

Unfortunately, Office Mobile severely lacks a lot of the functionality of most advanced features that are part of the Windows version. Office Mobile has Tables but without the Table style formatting because this version treats the data as a standard Excel range. Office Mobile supports basic filtering as well as an *AutoSum* feature that is similar to the status bar aggregation feature of the Windows version (see the next two figures).

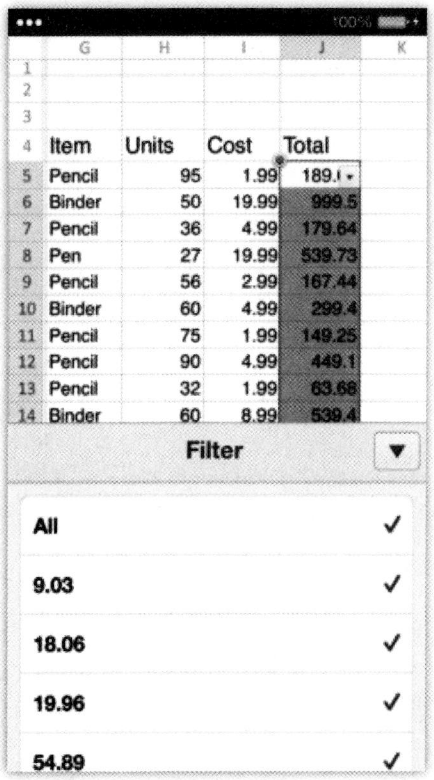

Filtering in Office Mobile.

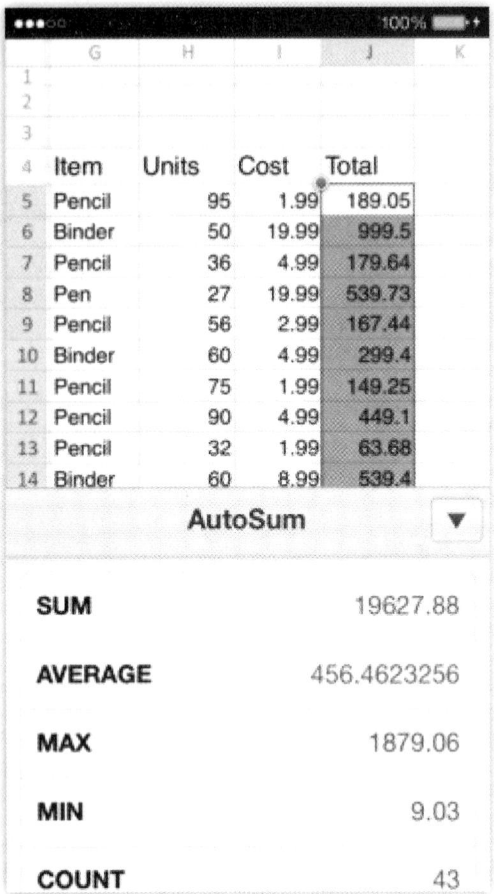

AutoSum in Office Mobile.

Tables in Excel for iPad

As with Office Mobile, the iPad version is available as a free download, and you can use the free version to view files. However, to edit files, you must have one of the following Office 365 subscriptions:

- Office 365 Home
- Office 365 Small Business Premium
- Office 365 Midsize Business
- Office 365 E3 and E4
- Office 365 Education A3 and A4
- Office 365 ProPlus
- Office 365 University
- Office 365 Personal

> ***NOTE***
>
> You must have iOS 7.0 or later to use Excel for iPad.

The iPad version is a complete rewrite of the Excel application, and therefore there isn't exact parity between the Windows version and the iPad version. Bill Jelen, aka Mr. Excel, has maintained an extensive list of the similarities and differences on his blog (www.mrexcel.com/learnexcel/); search for "Excel for iPad."

Once you're connected to an Office 365 account, click the *New* button to create a new workbook. You see a view that presents a number of templates, as shown in the next figure. You can choose one of them or choose to create a blank workbook.

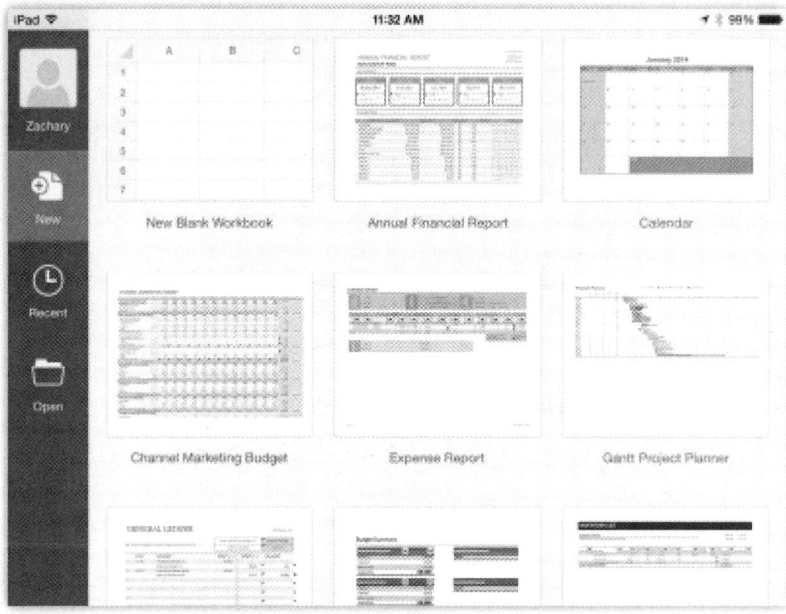

The templates view that appears when you create a new spreadsheet in the iPad version.

Unlike Office Mobile, which doesn't show Tables at all, the iPad version does have Table functionality, but not quite as much as the Windows version. The ribbon supports contextual tabs, and the *TABLE* tab appears only when a cell within a Table is selected. As shown in the next figure, the *TABLE* tab includes these options:

- ***Style Options***—Contains options to show/hide the header and total rows, band rows/columns, and apply first and last column style options.
- ***Table Styles***—Displays the same 61 built-in styles as the Windows version, along with any custom Table styles.
- ***Insert***—Inserts columns to the left or right of the selection or selects rows above or below the selection.
- ***Delete***—Deletes the selected columns or rows.
- ***Convert To Range***—Removes the Table and leaves the data in a normal range of cells.

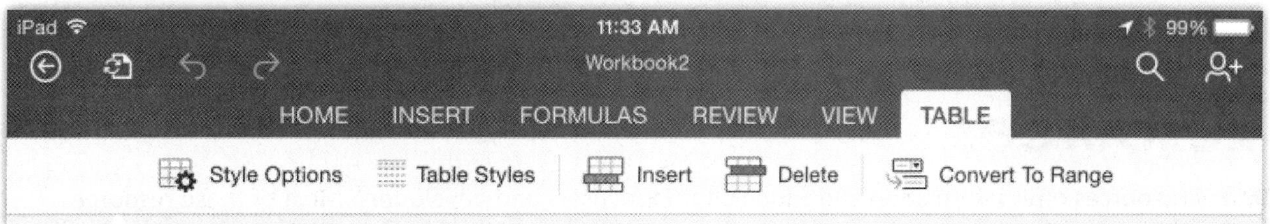

TABLE *ribbon tab in the iPad version.*

> **CAUTION**
>
> When you use *Convert To Range*, the iPad version does not display a verification prompt as the Windows version does. The easiest way to tell if your data is not in a Table is that the *TABLE* ribbon tab is not visible.

Similarities Between the iPad and Windows Versions

In terms of working with Tables, the iPad and Windows versions have some similarities and differences. Here are some of the most substantial similarities:

- **Auto expand Table**—When you enter data in the first blank column on the right of a Table, the iPad version automatically extends the Table whenever it can.
- **Total row functions**—The same lists of functions are displayed for the total row.
- **Structured referencing**—The same syntax is supported.
- **Calculated columns**—When you enter a formula into a Table cell, the formula is automatically filled into the entire column.
- **Duplicate column headers**—When you enter a duplicate column header name, the rightmost of the duplicates is automatically modified so that the names are unique.

Differences Between the iPad and Windows Versions

Here are some of the most substantial differences in working with Tables in the iPad and Windows versions:

- **IntelliSense with structured references**—The iPad version supports structured referencing when you enter formulas in a Table, but it does not support IntelliSense.
- **Insert below/right**—In the iPad version, tapping on a single cell, regardless of its location in the Table, only gives options to insert rows above the selection or insert columns to the left of the selection. To insert rows below the selection or columns to the right of the selection, use the *TABLE* ribbon's *Insert* menu.
- **Select entire row/column**—Because you use the iPad version with no mouse or keyboard, selecting entire rows or columns of a Table is slightly different. You tap and hold the first cell and then drag to the end.
- **Entering formulas in multiple cells**—When you're working with the Windows version, if a formula is entered with multiple cells selected, pressing CTRL+ENTER enters the formula into the entire selection, whereas pressing ENTER enters the formula in the active cell only. In the iPad version, entering a formula with multiple cells selected puts the formula in all the selected cells.

> ***NOTE***
>
> Microsoft makes new iPad versions available, as it does with Office Mobile and Excel Online, with greater frequency than it offers new desktop versions.

Resources

Many resources offer information and support for Excel users and developers. Most of these resources offer general Excel-related information, and some focus on specific areas. Here we have listed Excel resources in four categories: books, blogs, forums, and websites. This list is not all inclusive, but it's a great start for those desiring to learn more about how to leverage Excel.

We have no financial interest in any of these tools and sites. These recommendations are based on our own usage of Excel, help found online, and tools available.

Books

Excel 2013 In Depth, by Bill Jelen: www.amazon.com/Excel-2013-Depth-Bill-Jelen/dp/0789748576/

Excel 2013 VBA and Macros (MrExcel Library), by Bill Jelen: www.amazon.com/Excel-2013-Macros-MrExcel-Library/dp/0789748614/

Excel 2013 Bible, by John Walkenbach: www.amazon.com/Excel-2013-Bible/dp/1118490363/

DAX Formulas for PowerPivot: The Excel Pro's Guide to Mastering DAX, by Rob Collie: www.amazon.com/DAX-Formulas-PowerPivot-Excel-Mastering/dp/1615470158/

Microsoft Excel 2013 Step by Step, by Curtis Frye: www.amazon.com/Microsoft-Excel-2013-Step-By/dp/0735681015/

Ctrl + Shift + Enter, by Mike Girvin: www.amazon.com/Ctrl-Shift-Enter-Mastering-Formulas/dp/1615470077/

Excel 2013: The Missing Manual, by Matthew MacDonald: www.amazon.com/Excel-2013-The-Missing-Manual/dp/144935727X/

Don't Fear the Spreadsheet: A Beginner's Guide to Overcoming Excel's Frustrations, by Tyler Nash, Bill Jelen, Kevin Jones, and Tom Urtis: www.amazon.com/Dont-Fear-Spreadsheet-Frustrations-ebook/dp/B008CISAKO/

Blogs

Blogs are useful for tracking current events such as new releases and new features. Blog posts often provide thoughtful and focused presentations of various topics. Blogs usually offer a subscription service that delivers new posts directly to your email inbox when they are published.

colinlegg.wordpress.com

www.smittypro.com/Blog/

www.excelguru.ca/blog/

fastexcel.wordpress.com

blog.contextures.com

www.teylyn.com

dailydoseofexcel.com

exceluser.com/blog/

www.excelhero.com/blog/

chandoo.org/wp/

blogs.office.com/b/microsoft-excel/

msmvps.com/blogs/nateoliver/default.aspx

excelandaccess.wordpress.com

www.siddharthrout.com/my-blog/

Forums

Forums are great sources of help to many users. Experts support users, and uses support each other when they need assistance. If you really want to become an expert in a particular topic such as Excel, helping others on one of these forums is one of the best ways to learn by solving problems and watching other experts answer questions. Both Zack and Kevin learned much of what they know today by collaborating with other experts on forums while helping users solve Excel and other problems. Except where noted, there is no cost to sign up for a forum and ask questions once you provide a valid email address.

www.mrexcel.com/forum/forum.php

www.vbaexpress.com/forum/

www.excelguru.ca/forums/forum.php

answers.microsoft.com

forums.techguy.org

www.experts-exchange.com (This forum requires a small monthly fee to ask questions. Experts who earn a few points by answering questions each month can ask questions without paying the fee.)

www.tek-tips.com

www.thecodecage.com

www.xtremevbtalk.com

Websites

Some Microsoft Excel MVPs have their own websites where they publish articles, blogs, tools, and other interesting resources. Below is a list of some of the most popular websites for current MVPs, with brief notes on their specialty areas.

Andy Pope: www.andypope.info (charting, VBA, tips)

Bob Phillips: www.xldynamic.com/source/xld.html (formulas, VBA, dynamic ranges)

Charles Williams: www.decisionmodels.com (FastExcel, formula optimization)

Charley Kyd: www.exceluser.com (charting, dashboards, a list of past/present Excel MVP websites)

Chip Pearson: www.cpearson.com/Excel/MainPage.aspx (anything Excel, COM development)

Daniel Ferry: www.excelhero.com (coursework, formulas, VBA, development)

Dominic: www.xl-central.com (formulas, VBA, mega-formulas, videos)

Debra Dalgleish: www.contextures.com (anything Excel)

Jan Karel Pieterse: www.jkp-ads.com (VBA, defined names, troubleshooting)

Jon Acampora: www.excelcampus.com (charting, formulas, videos, formatting)

Jon Peltier: peltiertech.com (charting, add-ins, dashboards)

Ken Puls: www.excelguru.ca (customizing the ribbon, VBA, formulas, BI)

Ron de Bruin: rondebruin.nl (VBA, customizing the ribbon, Mac/AppleScript)

Tom Urtis: www.atlaspm.com (VBA, filters, formulas)

Index

T

U

V

W

X

alibris

CONOVER BOOKS
608 JEFFERSON STREET
MARTINSVILLE, VA 24112
UNITED STATES

To: ALIBRIS APEX DC 76902046-28
APEX
800 AVONDALE AVE.
GRANDVIEW HEIGHTS, OH 43212-3473

Shipping Instructions for CONOVER1

Print this Packing Slip and enclose inside the front cover of the book.

Please ship this item no later than Tue Sep 22, 2026.

Ship to:

ALIBRIS APEX DC 76902046-28
APEX
800 AVONDALE AVE.
GRANDVIEW HEIGHTS, OH 43212-3473
UNITED STATES

PN #	Item ID	Alibris ID	Media Type	Title / Author	Seller List Price	Order Date
76902046-28	053984	B084279198	BOOK	Excel Tables: a Complete Guide for Creating, Using and Automating Lists and Tables Barresse, Zack; Jones, Kevin	$20.00	Sep, 10 2026

76902046-28